Nachtjäger

PART ONE

The Early Years 1939–1943

"Germany will not be subjected to a single bomb. If an enemy bomber reaches German soil, my name is not Hermann Göring; you can call me Meier!"

Generalfeldmarschall Hermann Göring

"The Nazis entered this war under the rather childish delusion that they were going to bomb everybody else, and nobody was going to bomb them. At Rotterdam, London, Warsaw, and half a hundred other places they put that rather naive theory into operation. They sowed the wind and now they are going to reap the whirlwind!"

Air Chief Marshal Sir Arthur Harris

CLASSIC

An Imprint of
Crécy Publishing

Publisher's Note

The study of Luftwaffe camouflage and markings is a complex subject compounded by a general lack of quality colour photographs. Inevitably, therefore, most photographs appearing in this series are black and white and, while the authors and publisher have offered their own assessments of the aircraft colours in these photographs, this naturally involved a degree of guesswork. This should always be considered, even when the use of 'believed to have been' or 'thought to have been' etc, has sometimes been deleted in order to avoid tedious repetition. Recognising that readers may have contrary opinions, we have endeavoured throughout Classic Colours to include as many photographs and as much associated information as possible so that, although the photograph captions, colour profiles and badges have been produced in accordance with the publisher's, authors' and artists' best interpretations, the reader may, if he wishes, reach his own conclusions. Furthermore it should be stressed that the personal accounts contained in this series are as they have been related to the authors and are the product of the individual pilot's personal recollections.

CLASSIC

An Imprint of
Crécy Publishing

Volume One and Two first published 2005
This revised single volume edition 2021
Reprinted 2022

ISBN 978-1-90653-756-2

Produced by Chevron Publishing Limited
Project Editors: Martin Pegg / Robert Forsyth
Book design: Mark Nelson

Published by Crécy Publishing Ltd.

An imprint of Crécy Publishing Ltd.
1a Ringway Trading Estate,
Shadowmoss Road, Manchester, M22 5LH

Visit the Crécy Publishing website at: **www.crecy.co.uk**

Printed in Turkey by Pelikan Print

Acknowledgements

The author wishes to acknowledge the kind assistance of the following:

FORMER LUFTWAFFE PERSONNEL OR THEIR FAMILIES (f)
Martin Becker, Branse Burbridge, Wolfgang Falck, Georg Hermann Greiner, Thomas Harvel, Karl-Ludwig Johansenn, Constanze Johnen (f), Walter Knickmeier, Hans Krause, Erwin Leykauf, Heinz Rökker, Peter Spoden, Gerhard Wagner, Günther Wolf, Paul Zorner.

RESEARCHERS AND ENTHUSIASTS
Nick Beale, Brenda Collins, Mark S. Copeland, Eddie Creek, James V. Crow, Robert Forsyth, Norman Franks, Wim Govaerts, Peter Hinchliffe, Marcel Hogenhuis, Dave McDonald, Ken Merrick (†), Martin Pegg, Peter Petrick, Brian Press (†), J. Richard Smith, Christiaan Vanhee, John Vasco, Dave Wadman, Pam Wright.

ABOUT THE AUTHOR

In recent years David Williams has travelled extensively around Germany and Austria to interview former Luftwaffe pilots and their families in the course of his research into German fighter operations during the Second World War. He has gathered a substantial collection of documentation and photographs. He is the author of *Hunters of the Reich: Day Fighters*, for which he worked closely with five leading German fighter pilots, and a similar biographical study, *Hunters of the Reich: Night Fighters*. He is married and lives in the west of England.

Early Night Fighting and the Interwar Years

Wilhelm Frankl was born on 20 December 1893 and, at the outbreak of the First World War, joined the German Army Air Service as a reconnaissance pilot. He underwent fighter pilot training in 1915 and within a year he had shot down 15 enemy aircraft. His destruction of a BE 2b on the night of 6 April 1917 was his 16th victory, as well as being the first German night victory, but Frankl was killed two days later when his tally of kills stood at 20. In this photograph he is wearing the Pour le Mérite, awarded on 12 July 1916 after his eighth victory.

THE German Night Fighter Force or, to give the organisation its correct title, the *Nachtjagd*, was formed in June 1940 and disbanded in May 1945. Yet despite an operational period spanning less than five years, the *Nachtjagd* achieved a large number of successes and a fearsome reputation amongst the opposing crews of Bomber Command. By the war's end, Bomber Command had lost over 10,000 aircraft and some 55,500 aircrew killed by the combined German defences, of which the *Nachtjagd* formed a major part.

It is often incorrectly assumed that night fighting was a method of warfare developed during the Second World War, but its origins can be traced back to the First World War of 1914-1918, when flight itself was still in its infancy. As the First World War progressed, aeroplanes, which had at first been used in the role of aerial reconnaissance, were equipped to become fighters and bombers, and it was as a counter to the latter that the Germans began to formulate a method for attacking them at night. The obvious difficulty facing the Imperial German Air Force was how to track accurately the bombers during the hours of darkness. Such measures as ground observer units and sound detectors, used during the day against the fighters, were rendered virtually useless at night, especially if the bombers frequently changed their course or flew into clouds to avoid searchlight batteries. This usually resulted in the bombers' intended target being identified only when it was too late and the bombs were already falling. The only realistic means of defence against such attacks at that time was the anti-aircraft gun.

During 1916, in an effort to ward off raids against its own airfields, the Imperial German Air Force adopted a method of mounting patrols across the routes most frequently used by Allied bombers. This sounded straightforward in theory, but in practice the pilots found it extremely difficult. The main problem was that the aircraft types in use at that time were basic in design, as were their navigational instruments. Merely flying and navigating at night were difficult enough, let alone locating and shooting down an enemy bomber in the dark; yet despite these initial difficulties, a few successes were achieved. The first of these occurred a little after midnight on 6 April 1917, when *Leutnant* Wilhelm Frankl of *Jasta* 4 secured the first recognised German night fighter kill after pursuing British bombers that had just attacked his airfield at Douai in northern France. The unfortunate honour of being the first Allied bomber to fall to a German night fighter was a BE 2b from 100 Squadron which crashed near Quiéry le Motte. Frankl followed this with a second night victory on the 7th, bringing his overall total of victories to 20. Unfortunately for Frankl, his successes were short-lived because, on the following day, he was shot down and killed by British fighters from 48 Sqn. near Vitry-Sailly.

The first true German night fighting victory occurred soon after midnight on 6 April 1917 when Lt. Frankl of Jasta 4, who had already won the Pour le Mérite, took off from Douai airfield in this Albatros D III, W.Nr. 2158/18, and shot down a BE 2b of 100 Sqn. The British aircraft had carried out a bombing attack against Douai airfield and was shot down over Quiéry le Motte. The following night, Lt. Frankl destroyed a Nieuport of 60 Sqn.

A small number of other victories followed Frankl's, but it was not until May 1918, during Germany's last attack in Flanders, that a concerted effort was made to coordinate the German air defences. Finally, a system of close support and cooperation between the fighters, searchlight batteries, anti-aircraft units and listening posts was implemented. This system, almost identical to the one used 23 years later by Josef Kammhuber, was simple and effective.

Once the listening posts, which had been set up in front of the German positions, had identified an enemy aircraft, its position and direction of travel were passed to anti-aircraft batteries. They in turn would mark the target's position by firing tracer ammunition in its general direction. Searchlights would then attempt to illuminate it so that a fighter, already waiting and circling in a nearby 'Standby Zone' could attempt to engage the enemy aircraft and shoot it down.

On the night of 22/23 May 1918, *Leutnant* Fritz Thiede put this experimental method of night fighting into practice and succeeded in shooting down three enemy aircraft. Other German pilots followed his example and further victories followed. Unfortunately these successes were too little, too late and, with the failure of their May offensive, the Germans were steadily pushed back to their own borders. In November 1918 Germany sued for peace and the First World War came to an end.

During the 1920s and the greater part of the 1930s, what had been learnt about night fighting by the early pioneers was simply forgotten. This was not helped by the fact that one of the conditions of the Treaty of Versailles imposed on Germany by the Allies at the end of the First World War prevented Germany from possessing an air force.

This all changed in March 1935 when, just two years after Hitler had come to power, Germany announced the formation of the Luftwaffe. However, under the direction of Hermann Göring, the Luftwaffe was built as an offensive force and very little thought was given to defence. Nevertheless, some experiments were conducted in 1936 using night fighters in conjunction with searchlight units. The results of these exercises were detailed in a report and further experiments were authorised, which subsequently took place during 1937. By the end of that year, and with the findings set out in the form of a booklet, it was concluded that night fighting, particularly in the role of home defence, was possible.

As a result of these positive findings, the *Reichsluftfahrtministerium* finally authorised the formation of two experimental night fighter *Staffeln* at the beginning of 1939. By June of the same year, further units had been activated, but within just a few weeks all but two of them had been transferred to the day fighter force.

The Formation of the Nachtjagd

With the outbreak of the Second World War in September 1939, Bomber Command began to fly sorties to Germany, initially dropping nothing deadlier than propaganda leaflets. As a consequence of these nuisance raids, three fighter *Staffeln* – all of which were equipped with Bf 109s – were designated as night fighter units. The first of these, 10./(N)JG 26, was stationed at Bonn-Hangelar to provide aerial cover to the area around Cologne. The second, 10./(N)JG 72, is believed to have been stationed at Heilbronn in southern Germany, while the third, 10.(N)/ZG 26, was based in northern Germany to protect the North Sea approaches.

On the night of 20/21 April 1940, Ofw. Willi Schmale of IV./(N)JG 2 shot down a Fairey Battle reconnaissance aircraft over Germany and achieved what is believed to have been the first night victory of the Second World War. The Battle was flown by Pilot Officer H.D. Wardle of 218 Sqn., shown standing, far left, in the officers' mess at Auberive in France during April 1940.

Although they were actually designated as night fighter units, neither formation actually operated in the dark but flew at dawn and during the evening twilight when there was an increased chance of observing a bomber. However, there was no coordination or cooperation with the searchlight batteries and ground stations and, as a consequence, the chances of achieving any success were extremely slim.

Despite the fact that no intruders had been shot down and Göring himself was of the opinion that there was no need for further expansion of the night fighter establishment, in late December 1939 a night fighter *Gruppe*, IV./(N)JG 2, was formed by amalgamating 10./(N) JG 26 and 10./(N)ZG 26 with 11./LG 2. This *Gruppe* was then transferred to Jever and the East Frisian Island of Langeoog, where it was intended that it would patrol the North Sea, thus affording protection to German naval targets in and around Wilhelmshaven and the Heligoland Bight.

There has been much speculation as to which German pilot actually achieved the first night victory of the Second World War, but it would appear that this accolade, according to German claims files, falls to *Oberfeldwebel* Willi Schmale of IV.(N)/JG 2 who claimed to have shot down a Fairey Battle north of Crailsheim at 00.45 hrs on 21 April 1940. This claim is substantiated in William Chorley's book, 'Bomber Command Losses of the Second World War', which records the loss of a Fairey Battle from 218 Sqn. that failed to return from a reconnaissance mission to Mainz and Darmstadt in Germany on the night of 20/21 April 1940. The aircraft, piloted by Pilot Officer H.D. Wardle, was reported by German radio to have been shot down near Crailsheim, killing two of the three-man crew.

Following this initial success, *Oberfeldwebel* Hermann Förster, also from IV./(N)JG 2, claimed a Hampden bomber at 01.10 hrs on 26 April in the area of Hörnum, close to the island of Sylt. This aircraft is believed to have been one of three Hampdens lost by 49 Sqn. of the Advanced Air Striking Force during minelaying operations to Kiel and the Frisian Islands. The pilot, P/O A.H. Benson, and his three-man crew were all killed.

April 1940 was also the month in which the German invasion of Denmark took place and as a direct result of this, Bomber Command began to target the Luftwaffe's newly acquired Danish airfields. One of these airfields was Aalborg, situated in the far north of the country, where I./ZG 1, a Bf 110 *Zerstörer Gruppe*, was operating in support of the German Army's invasion of Norway with *Hauptmann* Wolfgang Falck in command. By a stroke of good fortune, Aalborg airfield was protected by '*Freya*', a new type of radar that had already been successfully tested against the RAF during the 'Battle of the Heligoland Bight'.[1] '*Freya*' had a range of 120 kilometres and could detect aircraft flying at altitudes of up to 10,000 feet.

This early warning system had already proved its value to the personnel at Aalborg by giving them time to take to their slit trenches before the bombers arrived. Falck envisaged using this time to scramble some of his aircraft and then, in cooperation with the radar installation, intercept and attack the enemy aircraft as they neared the airfield. He also outlined his ideas to the commanders of the searchlight and Flak batteries and divided a large-scale map of the area around Aalborg into rectangular grid squares, or *Planquadrate*. In particular he concentrated on the area north of Denmark and the western North Sea, where each *Planquadrat* was allocated its own two-letter reference.

With everything in place, Falck selected three of his best crews – *Oberleutnant* Werner Streib, *Oberleutnant* Günther Radusch and *Feldwebel* Thier – to evaluate the possibilities of night operations with the Bf 110. It was hoped, in theory at least, that once the bombers had been detected by radar, the fighters would be scrambled and vectored to the enemy's position. Unfortunately for Falck, the practical effectiveness of this system failed to yield any quick results and he was forced to rethink his ideas. The most telling change he made to the system was to arrange for fighters to fly at a pre-arranged height in holding areas where they were in continuous radio contact with the ground radar station. In spite of the modifications, no successes followed and frustrations within the unit increased.

Despite the lack of victories, the crews were, however, gaining invaluable night-flying experience and they soon discovered an important fact. By approaching other aircraft from slightly below, the targets became silhouetted against the lighter northern sky and were therefore easier to see, while the approaching fighter was much more difficult to spot against the dark backdrop of the ground. This technique would soon be adopted by the pilots of the *Nachtjagd* and used throughout the war with devastating effects.

During the night of 30 April/1 May 1940, Wellingtons from 61 Sqn. attacked Aalborg and an infuriated Falck, along with Streib, Radusch and Thier, took off after the bombers and pursued them westwards across the North Sea. It was almost dawn when three of the Wellingtons were spotted and attacked by Falck, Streib and Radusch, but as soon as they came under fire the bombers dived into the early morning fog and disappeared. No claims were made but Günther Radusch flew so close to one of the Wellingtons that he came under fire himself and returned to Aalborg with bullet holes in his fighter.

To date, this had been the closest that anyone from the *Gruppe* had come to shooting down a bomber and, with renewed vigour, Falck began to rethink his ideas. He wrote a comprehensive report detailing how, with flame-dampers on the exhausts and ammunition that did not ruin the pilot's night vision when it was fired, the Bf 110 would be better suited to its role as a night fighter. He also emphasised the importance of specialist night-flying training for the crews as well as close cooperation with the other branches responsible for defence, such as the Flak, searchlight batteries and radar.

The report was submitted by Falck to the *Reichsluftfahrtministerium* and, amazingly, within approximately one week, he was visited by the *Generalinspekteur der Luftwaffe*, Erhard Milch. In a lengthy discussion, Milch showed a genuine interest in Falck's ideas and recommendations but any further action was frustrated by the beginning of the German invasion of France and the Low Countries on 10 May 1940.

In April 1940 Hptm. Wolfgang Falck compiled a report outlining the possibilities of combating the RAF at night. The report made an immediate impression on the staff in the Reichsluftfahrtministerium, and in the same month Generaloberst Erhard Milch, the State Secretary of Aviation and Inspector General of the Luftwaffe (left), visited Falck at Aalborg in Denmark to discuss his report. In the centre is the Gruppenkommandeur of I./ZG 1, Hptm. Reinecke.

[1] The 'Battle of the Heligoland Bight' occurred on 18 December 1939 when 24 Wellingtons were sent to attack shipping off Wilhelmshaven. Two of the bombers aborted with mechanical problems, but the rest were intercepted over the North Sea, close to the island of Heligoland, by Bf 109s and Bf 110s which had scrambled after being forewarned by '*Freya*' radar installations situated on the East Frisian Islands. No match for the fast and manoeuvrable German fighters, 12 of the Wellingtons were shot down and another three were damaged and crash-landed on their return to England.

On 26 June 1940, Göring announced the formation of the Nachtjagd and the creation of the first night fighter Geschwader, Nachtjagdgeschwader 1. At the same time, he appointed Wolfgang Falck, then a Hauptmann, its Kommodore.

Meanwhile, Falck and I./ZG 1 had been transferred back to Germany in preparation for the invasion and as the *Wehrmacht* rolled westwards, the *Gruppe* flew sorties against Dutch and Belgian forces. As the campaign developed, I./ZG 1 found itself involved in protecting German troops in France, and it was whilst stationed at Le Havre in June 1940, that Falck and his *Gruppe*, minus one *Staffel*, were ordered by *Generaloberst* Kesselring to fly back to Düsseldorf. There, Falck learnt that his *Gruppe* had been recalled from the front to commence night-flying operations and to counter the growing number of RAF raids mounted against Cologne and the important industrialised Ruhr district.

Being able to attack German industrial targets was a recent and welcome change in tactics for the RAF. Many in Bomber Command had felt ever since the outbreak of the war that, being restricted to attacking shipping and certain military targets, they had been fighting with one hand tied behind their backs. However, since the bombing of Rotterdam on 13 May 1940, the British War Cabinet had authorised the RAF to operate east of the Rhine. The gloves were now off. What was to follow over the next five years was a deadly game of cat and mouse between Bomber Command and the German defences; it would result in the deaths of tens of thousands of German and Allied aircrew and hundreds of thousands of German civilians.

Within several days of being recalled from the Channel Coast, Falck was summoned to a high-level meeting at Wassenaar in Holland, where the commanding officer of *Wehrmacht* forces in the Netherlands, *General* Friedrich Christiansen, had his headquarters. This conference was attended by some of the most powerful and influential Luftwaffe personnel including *Feldmarschall* Göring, *General der Flieger* Bruno Loerzer and *Generals* Albert Kesselring, Gustav Kastner and Ernst Udet

When Falck walked into the conference hall on 26 June 1940, he noticed that as a *Hauptmann* he was the lowest ranking officer in attendance and immediately felt ill at ease. Göring opened the meeting with a long speech about the progress of the war. He then moved on to discuss the raids carried out by the RAF on the Ruhr, which were causing him some embarrassment as he had earlier issued assurances that no bombs would ever fall on the Reich. Although the raids themselves had caused little damage, he had decided to counter these attacks by creating the *Nachtjagd*, or Night Fighter Force, which would be designated *Nachtjagdgeschwader* 1 (NJG 1). In another surprise announcement, Göring appointed none other than *Hptm*. Falck as the unit's new *Geschwaderkommodore*, a remarkable decision considering that at this time these positions were usually held by officers with the rank of at least *Oberst* or *Oberstleutnant*. In addition to this, Falck's I./ZG 1 was to become the first *Gruppe* of the newly formed unit and redesignated I./NJG 1. In turn, IV./(N)JG 2,[2] which had been operating at night with Bf 109 Ds from Mönchengladbach, temporarily became II./NJG 1 before being redesignated III./NJG 1 on 1 July 1940.

For Falck, the future task of building up and organising the new *Nachtjagd* was mammoth. Among the most pressing problems was the fact that only a very small number of the men under his command were suitably trained to fly at night and their aircraft had still to be adapted for their new role. These obvious deficiencies, as well as many other technical and training issues, had to be addressed immediately. Falck also had to develop close cooperation with the other facets of the German defences, such as the Flak regiments, searchlight batteries, listening posts and, most importantly, the radar units.

The enormity of the task of building up the night fighter organisation must have been obvious even to Göring for, on 17 July 1940, he appointed *Oberst* Josef Kammhuber to command the newly created *Nachtjagddivision*, or Night Fighter Division. His choice was an inspired one as Kammhuber was known to be an exceptional organiser and he quickly set about his work with his usual zeal and enthusiasm. Kammhuber set up his headquarters at Zeist in Holland, where he ran the Division at staff level, while Falck chose to establish his command post at Deelen, situated north of Arnhem, where he assumed responsibility for running the *Nachtjagd* at an operational level.

---

[2] At the time of the formation of NJG 1, the *Gruppenkommandeur* of IV./(N)JG 2 was *Major* Blumensaat. He was, however, replaced a short time later by *Hauptmann* Philip von Bothmer who became the first official *Gruppenkommandeur* of II./NJG 1.

Walter Knickmeier, shown here as a Hauptmann in 1944, participated in the destruction of some 88 RAF bombers, making him the most successful night fighter controller of the war.

"The Luftwaffe leadership had been caught entirely unprepared!"

Hauptmann Walter Knickmeier, NJG 1

IN the spring of 1940, when the first English bombers penetrated the North German coastal area during the evening twilight and, in isolated cases, also at night, the Luftwaffe leadership was forced to acknowledge that no method of defence against these intrusions existed. There were neither aircrews specially trained for night fighting, nor a ground organisation capable of giving the night fighters the navigational assistance necessary for them to find the enemy. The Luftwaffe leadership had been caught entirely unprepared and confusion was absolute.

The urgent necessity was to establish a network of stations to control the night fighters and to assess the air situation. Therefore, priority was given to set up a ground organisation which, until then, had been completely non-existent, and *Nachtjagdgeschwader* 1 was set up at the end of July 1940.

By the end of 1940 we had succeeded in setting up an air defence line in north Germany, Holland and Belgium. '*Freya*' radars were positioned in the coastal areas to the far west and on a number of North Sea islands. The '*Freya*' equipment had a range of about 120 kilometres and made it possible to measure the bearing and range but not, however, the altitude of the target. This respectable range provided the basis for early warning and indicated the exact track that the enemy was flying.

Between the forward '*Freya*' radars and the bombers' likely targets – Hamburg, Bremen, the Ruhr, Cologne etc – a number of Flak and *Scheinwerferregiment* (Searchlight Regiments) were deployed in a so-called '*Helle Nachtjagdsriegel*' (illuminated night fighting barrier). It was their task to pick up enemy aircraft and to keep them coned until a fighter, directed by the control station, could attack. In support of the Flak and Searchlight Regiments there were '*Würzburg*' radars which measured the bearing, range and altitude of the approaching aircraft, but only to a range of about 25 kilometres. Within the chain of the ground organisation, the Fighter Control Centre was the most important link, because it was from there that the night fighter was vectored towards the enemy. The fighter control officer evaluated the data that arrived and, by means of radio transmissions, broadcast them to the night fighter crews on a transmitter that was dedicated to the Fighter Control Area.

This organisation, created as it was from very basics, understandably required several months of 'running in' before it became efficient, and it was not until after March 1941 that significantly successful results were achieved. During the period from March to December 1941, I was working as a Fighter Control Officer or '*Jägerleitoffizier*' in the area near Meyl in Holland. The night fighters that manned this area were from I./NJG 1 stationed at Venlo, and the number of bombers we shot down in this period was 24.

One unfortunate result of Falck's new position was that Kammhuber, recognising Falck's value to the organisation, immediately grounded him. At that time, NJG 1 still only consisted of I. *Gruppe* and, with Falck grounded, Günther Radusch – a friend of Falck's since their training at Lipetsk[3] in Russia – became *Kommandeur* of I./NJG 1.

In order to overcome his disappointment and frustration at being prevented from flying operationally, Falck immediately buried himself in his work. With limited resources at his disposal and after some consideration, he decided to withdraw searchlight units from other cities and proceeded to set up a belt of searchlights to the north-west of Münster. This city had been chosen with care, for due to its geographical location the night fighters could protect Berlin in the east, the important German coastal towns in the north and also the Ruhr in the south. As a temporary measure, until '*Freya*' early warning radars could be incorporated into the defensive system, sound detectors were positioned in front of the searchlight belt to warn of approaching bombers. To avoid impeding the effectiveness of these sound detectors, the fighters of I./NJG 1 were transferred to Gütersloh airfield some 40 kilometres to the east of Münster. It was hoped that once the listening posts had detected the incoming enemy bombers, the night fighters would be alerted. Once airborne, they would patrol to the east of the searchlights at an altitude slightly higher than that of the bombers, until the searchlights were able to illuminate one of them. Once this occurred, the fighter would have about three minutes to intercept and shoot down the bomber before it cleared the searchlight belt.

The most preferred and least dangerous method adopted by night fighter pilots when attacking a bomber was known as '*von hinten unten*'. This involved the night fighter pilot manoeuvring below his target from behind and then pulling up the nose of his aircraft to fire a quick burst, usually into the wings

3. In April 1925 a secret agreement was signed between the German and Soviet governments allowing German personnel to receive pilot training at Lipetsk, situated 300 miles to the south-east of Moscow, in exchange for technical data. In April 1932, Wolfgang Falck, together with nine other cadets, was chosen to attend this secret training base. Among the other trainee pilots who went there with him were Günther Radusch, Hannes Trautloft and Günther Lützow.

'Himmelbett' Night Fighting

Walter Knickmeier, *Jägerleitoffizier*

RESPONSIBILITY for all operations within a night intercept area lay in the hands of the *Jägerleitoffizier*. The functioning of the '*Himmelbett*' system can be best demonstrated by the description of a controlled night interception; however, it must be mentioned that only a single night fighter could be operated within one intercept area.

Even in 1941, as their range was so good, the most westerly '*Freya*' stations could pick up RAF aircraft shortly after they had taken off, i.e. while they were still within British airspace, and the night fighters allocated to the *Nachtjagdraum* (Night fighter area) lying on the forecasted approach route were then scrambled. On its way to the *Nachtjagdraum* the fighter had to climb as quickly as possible to operational height. Shortly after take-off the fighter crews and the fighter controllers established radio contact. At the same time, the officer in charge of the '*Würzburg*' radar that was to control the fighter, was instructed to pick up the fighter and to begin sending details of its position, etc, to the intercept station. By means of an optical device, the location of the fighter was displayed for the *Jägerleitoffizier* on the glass surface of the '*Seeburgtisch*'* as a point of green light. As soon as the information from the '*Freya*' radar showed that an enemy aircraft was about to enter the range of the '*Würzburg*', the fighter pilot was given a heading which was intended to position him ahead of the enemy. It was most important that while carrying out this manoeuvre he did not fly beyond the range of the '*Würzburg*' as he would then not be seen by the *Jägerleitoffizier*.

On the basis of data from the '*Freya*', the second '*Würzburg*' was informed of the exact direction from which the enemy bomber would approach. As soon as it came within coverage, measurements could begin and the data was sent to the fighter control post where the bomber appeared on the '*Seeburgtisch*' as a spot of red light. Details of the movements of the coloured points of light were drawn on the glass surface. Thus the *Jägerleitoffizier* was able rapidly to let the night fighter have the track and ground speed of his target, and to give him instructions on the course corrections he needed to make in order to get within visual range astern of the bomber as quickly as possible. It goes without saying that, from the very start, details of altitude were broadcast to the fighter. It was most important for a successful interception that the fighter flew at the correct ground speed. If he flew too fast there was a danger that he would fly past his target and, given the short acquisition range of the radars, such a miscalculation would mean that a second controlled approach to the bomber was impossible.

There was always a critical point during an interception when an aircraft flew directly over, or in close proximity, to the radar station. Measurement was impossible in the sector immediately above the radar so that the aircraft was invisible to the *Jägerleitoffizier* on the *Seeburgtisch*. In such a situation the practice was to keep completely silent until the points of light appeared again. In most cases, however, further alterations of course were unnecessary.

To bring a fighter into visual range of its target called for precise work on the part of all involved. Small errors in measurement at the radar posts, in the transferring of the data to the '*Seeburgtisch*', an incorrect calculation of the ground speed or course by the *Jägerleitoffizier*, or inexact execution of the flight corrections by the pilot, could easily lead to failure. Such findings applied particularly to the period following the introduction of '*Himmelbett*' night fighting, when the aircraft had not yet been equipped with airborne interception radar. After the introduction of '*Lichtenstein*', and the subsequent conversion to the considerably improved SN2 radar, which had a greater range and a wider acquisition angle, the number of successful controlled intercepts increased. Close-controlled night interception thus became perceptibly more perfect.

* See page 47 for details of '*Seeburgtisch*'

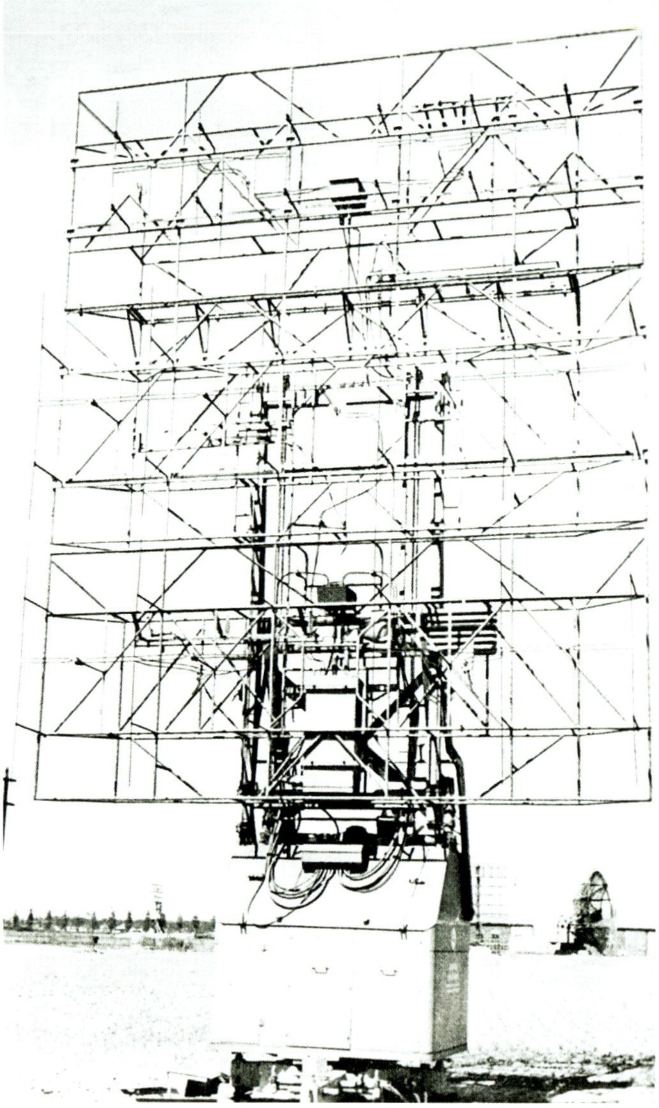

In the autumn of 1941, and as a result of improving radar technology, the 'Himmelbett' system of night fighting was gradually introduced into the German defences. A typical 'Himmelbett' radar station comprised a single 'Freya' radar, as seen here in the foreground of this photograph, and two 'Würzburg-Riese' radar installations. One such 'Würzburg-Riese' can be seen to the rear and to the right of the 'Freya'.

An early ground radar station comprising a 'Freya' (centre) and two 'Würzburg' D model radar installations. It was a station such as this that allowed Lt. Ludwig Becker to be guided into visual contact with a Wellington of 311 Sqn. on 16 October 1940. Lt. Becker succeeded in shooting down the bomber and thus achieved the first night kill using the Dunkel Nachtjagd method of night fighting. By the end of the war, 'Freya' had become the Germans' most widely-used type of radar.

of the bomber. The night fighter pilot would then quickly dive away into the darkness before the bomber's rear gunner had an opportunity to return fire. This form of interception was to become known as *Helle Nachtjagd* (Illuminated Night Fighting). *Oblt.* Werner Streib from 2./NJG 1 achieved the first recorded success using this method when he shot down a Whitley at 02.15 hrs on the morning of 20 July 1940. This aircraft was almost certainly a Whitley Mk.V from 51 Sqn. based at Dishforth and piloted by Flight Lieutenant S.E.F. Curry. It was shot down during a raid on Gelsenkirchen and is reported to have crashed 20 kilometres west of Osnabrück, killing all but one of the crew.

Streib followed up this success with another on 22 July and, by the end of the month, a total of six bombers had fallen victim to night fighter pilots using the *Helle Nachtjagd* procedure. Despite these initial successes, however, it was obvious that this method of interception was only a temporary measure until the introduction of radar and the acquisition of more searchlights and better-suited aircraft.

Werner Streib with the rank insignia of Hauptmann, and wearing the Knight's Cross, awarded on 6 October 1940. On 20 July 1940 Streib achieved the first Helle-Nachtjagd victory by shooting down a Whitley Mk.V bomber during an attack against Gelsenkirchen.

Eventually it became obvious to Bomber Command that the German defences had constructed their searchlight belt in and around Münster, so the bombers simply flew around it. With the initiative temporarily lost, Kammhuber used all his persuasiveness and organisational skills to obtain further searchlights and set about extending his illuminated belt. The task took almost a year, but when completed it was almost 900 kilometres long and 30 kilometres wide and ran from Schleswig Holstein in the north down as far as Liège in Belgium, with a second, shorter searchlight belt to the north-west of Berlin.

In the meantime, the Germans began to regain the initiative by introducing the long-awaited '*Freya*' radar into their defensive system. Since the beginning of the war, *Leutnant* Hermann Diehl, a signals officer stationed at an experimental early warning station on the island of Wangerooge, had been conducting experiments using '*Freya*'. Diehl's theory was that '*Freya*' could be used as a close-control radar to direct a fighter into visual contact with a bomber by means of communication from a ground station. Initial difficulties with its accuracy were overcome by the introduction of a newer, improved model that possessed a direction-finding capability known as 'AN-*Peilung*'.[4] The receiving aerial on this particular model was divided into two parts: left and right. An electronic switch within the unit would transmit from one to the other at a rate of 75 times a second and both aircraft would appear on a cathode ray tube divided by a central vertical line which represented the vertical time base. The bomber would appear on this line and it was the fighter controller's task to direct the night fighter until its signal was positioned symmetrically on the same line, at which point the night fighter was directly behind its intended target. The night fighter pilot was then constantly updated from the ground until visual contact was made. Despite the obvious difficulties, the most serious being that '*Freya*' had no height measuring capability, Diehl carried out a series of practice daylight interceptions and successfully directed a fighter to its target.

In June 1940, when Falck had been transferred to Düsseldorf, he had the good sense to realise the importance of radar and had taken Diehl with him. Several months later, in August, both Falck and Diehl visited Kammhuber at his headquarters and outlined the theory of radar-controlled interception. Kammhuber immediately recognised the potential of '*Freya*' and authorised operational trials to begin the following month. After some careful consideration, it was decided to build a '*Freya*' installation in Nunspeet in north-west Holland, a village often overflown by RAF bombers on their way to Germany. The problem of estimating the height of the bomber was overcome by using the second operational radar that the Germans had at their disposal. This was known as '*Würzburg*' and had originally been designed to control anti-aircraft guns. It was then adapted for use with searchlights, before finally becoming an integral part of close-controlled night fighting. 4./NJG 1 was selected to take part in the first trials using this system, which became known as *Dunkel Nachtjagd* (Dark Night Fighting).

Using this method of interception, Diehl manoeuvred *Leutnant* Ludwig Becker into visual contact with a Wellington bomber on 16 October 1940. At 21.25 hrs, Becker opened fire and with its starboard engine on fire the Wellington went into a dive and crashed near Oosterwolde, some 28 kilometres north-west of Apeldoorn, Holland.[5] Following this victory – the first *Dunkel Nachtjagd* victory of the war –

---

4. *AN-Peilung* means direction finding.

5. The crash site recorded by Becker matches that of Wellington L7844 from 311 Squadron, which is recorded in W.R. Chorley's 'Bomber Command Losses' as having crashed near Oosterwolde, Holland. The pilot, P/O B. Landa, was killed as were three other members of the six-man crew.

other similar installations were set up along the Dutch and German coastlines and by the end of 1940 the *Nachtjagd* had claimed a total of 42 victories. Compared with what was to come, this was a very small number but it was certainly a step in the right direction and 1941 would see further technological advances and a large increase in the number of bombers shot down.

In the summer of 1940, a third night fighting technique was devised that combined the principles of *Helle* and *Dunkel Nachtjagd*, and was known as *Kombinierte Nachtjagd*, or combined night fighting. It was hoped that all the facets of the German defences – Flak, searchlights, radar and the *Nachtjagd* – could be coordinated to work together. A number of combined night fighting zones were established around some of Germany's principal cities such as Berlin, Frankfurt, Cologne, Bremen and Hamburg, in an effort to afford them better protection. Unfortunately, this particular technique proved almost unworkable, principally because a system could not be satisfactorily implemented that would prevent the Flak from firing on its own fighters. At this stage of the war aircraft did not carry the appropriate electronic equipment that could identify them as friend or foe, and the only way aircrew could identify themselves to the ground defences was to fire coloured flares. The increased threat of being shot down by their own defences undoubtedly made the German night fighter pilots wary about entering these zones, hence only a small number of bombers was shot down using this technique.

Below: Although Wolfgang Falck himself never shot down a bomber at night, he was decorated with the Knight's Cross on 1 October 1940 for his seven day victories and, more importantly, for his contribution in the creation of the Nachtjagd.

Below: From his command post at Deelen, Falck began the unenviable task of organising and expanding the Nachtjagd from nothing. At that time, there was no aircraft designed as a night fighter, and ground and airborne radar were both in their infancy.

Towards the end of 1940 an airfield was constructed at Deelen where Falck set up his headquarters. Seen in these photographs is the Kommodore's new office (above) and (below) the officers' mess.

Josef Kammhuber

Oberst Josef Kammhuber shortly before taking command of the newly formed Nachtjagddivision on 17 July 1940. Several months later, on 17 October 1940, he was promoted to Generalmajor.

JOSEF KAMMHUBER was born on 19 August 1896 in the small Bavarian town of Burgkirchen, close to the German/Czechoslovakian border, where his father was a local farmer. After obtaining his *Abitur*, or Higher School Certificate, at the Ludwigs Grammar School in Munich, he joined the Army as a volunteer in 1914. In August of that year Kammhuber joined the 3rd Bavarian Pioneer Battalion in Ingolstadt, and two years later he had become an officer cadet with the 20th Bavarian Infantry Regiment. In 1917, Josef Kammhuber was commissioned as a *Leutnant* and by the end of the First World War he had been decorated with the Iron Cross First and Second Class.

Kammhuber was one of the 100,000 men who remained in the *Reichswehr* after the war, serving first with the 3rd Battalion of the 19th Bavarian Infantry Regiment until 1923, when he was transferred to Munich. He then joined the Regiment's 1st Battalion and was later promoted to Battalion Adjutant. Between 1926 and 1929 he served on the General Staff of the Army at the *Reichswehrministerium*, and at the same time began training as a pilot and an observer. In May of 1930, Kammhuber was temporarily released from his duties, becoming one of a select band of German aviators to receive specialist flying training at Lipetsk in Russia. By the end of September 1930, with his training complete, he returned to Germany and on 1 February 1931 he was promoted to *Hauptmann*.

Two years later, in August 1933, Kammhuber left the Army and joined the newly formed *Reichsluftministerium* (RLM) where he was employed as the head of its organisational department. When the Luftwaffe was formed on 1 March 1935, Kammhuber was transferred to the new organisation and, in July of the same year, he underwent fighter pilot training at Schleissheim near Munich.

On his return from Schleissheim, Kammhuber joined the General Staff at the RLM where he remained until 12 March 1936, when he was transferred to Dortmund as *Kommandeur* of I./JG 134. In 1937, Kammhuber became Operations Officer and head of the *Wehrmacht's* field training staff for *Luftkreiskommando* II in Berlin, a post that he held until returning to the organisational staff of the Luftwaffe a year later. After being promoted to *Oberst* in January 1939, Josef Kammhuber was appointed Chief of Staff for *General* Helmuth Felmy, the commanding officer of *Luftflotte* 2, and when war broke out in September 1939 he was Chief of Staff to V. *Fliegerkorps*.

In March 1940, prior to the invasion of France and the Low Countries, Kammhuber was given command of *Kampfgeschwader* 51 '*Edelweiss*', which he successfully led during the initial stages of the French campaign in May 1940. However, on 3 June 1940, while leading a bombing raid against airfields in the Paris area, Kammhuber's aircraft encountered technical difficulties that forced him to leave the main formation. During the return flight the lone German bomber was attacked and shot down by French fighters over Meaux and the entire crew was taken prisoner. Fortunately for Kammhuber, the French capitulated several weeks later and, following his repatriation, he was appointed *Kommodore* of *Kampfgeschwader* 1 '*Hindenburg*'.

Following the formation of the *Nachtjagd* in June 1940, Kammhuber was given command of 1. *Nachtjagddivision* and set up his headquarters at Zeist in Holland on 17 July 1940.

Widely regarded by others in the Luftwaffe hierarchy as an exceptional organiser, Kammhuber immediately began to organise the German air defences into a cohesive and effective force. In October 1940

Continued overleaf

With the expansion of the Nachtjagd and the formation of the Nachtjagddivision on 17 July 1940, Josef Kammhuber, shown here later in the war as a Generalleutnant, was placed in command.

The General takes advantage of some free time to play billiards with his staff.

On 10 August 1941, following the growth of the Nachtjagd, the Nachtjagddivision was renamed XII. Fliegerkorps and came under the command of Generalleutnant Kammhuber on 1 October 1941.

On 9 July 1941, a year after assuming command of the Nachtjagd, Kammhuber was awarded the Knight's Cross for his achievements in building up the organisation and for its successes against Bomber Command.

he was promoted to *Generalmajor* and on 9 July 1941 he was awarded the Knight's Cross in recognition of his development of the *Helle Nachtjagd* and *Himmelbett* night fighting procedures, which had by this time accounted for some five hundred bombers.

As the *Nachtjagddivision* continued to expand it became difficult to operate effectively, and in an effort to overcome mounting organisational problems it was redesignated XII. *Fliegerkorps*, which had overall command of a newly formed *Nachtjagddivision* under the command of *Generalmajor* von Döring. This principally amalgamated all the units of the night defences and Kammhuber became the Commanding *General* of XII. *Fliegerkorps*, as well as *General der Nachtjäger* on 1 August 1941. Several months later, in October 1941, he was promoted to the rank of *Generalleutnant* and, in January 1943, to *General der Flieger*.

Following the disastrous raids against Hamburg in July 1943, and the introduction of 'Window', which rendered the German radar systems useless, Kammhuber was replaced as Commanding *General* of XII. *Fliegerkorps* on 15 September 1943 by *Generalmajor* Josef Schmid. On 15 November 1943 he was transferred to Norway to command *Luftflotte* 5 following continual differences of opinion with the German High Command. He remained with *Luftflotte* 5 until 10 October 1944 when, after further differences with the Luftwaffe hierarchy, he was removed from his command and placed on the reserve list. After spending several months without a command, he was recalled to active duty in February 1945 and appointed special representative for jet fighters and combating four-engined bombers.

At the end of the war, Kammhuber was taken prisoner by the Americans and interrogated for almost 18 months before being released in December 1947. After more than 30 years as a soldier, Josef Kammhuber began to rebuild his life as a civilian and found work as a sales representative. When Germany began to reform its military in 1955, Kammhuber joined the *Bundesluftwaffe* in June 1956 with the rank of *Generalleutnant*. He was put in command of *Abteilung* VI within the German Ministry of Defence and on 1 June 1957 he was made the first *General Inspekteur* of the *Bundesluftwaffe*.

During the remainder of his service he oversaw the expansion of the new *Bundesluftwaffe* and the introduction of the F-104 Starfighter. By the time of his retirement in September 1962, he had been promoted to *Generaloberst* and was awarded the Grand Service Cross of the Federal Service Organisation for his work in building up the *Bundesluftwaffe*. Josef Kammhuber spent the remainder of his life in Munich, where he died on 25 January 1986.

From the left: Falck; unknown (half hidden); and Kammhuber dining with the aircraft designer Professor Ernst Heinkel at his factory in Rostock-Marienehe in January 1942. Professor Heinkel is shown fourth from left.

Josef Kammhuber delivered the eulogy at the funeral for Hauptmann Herbert Bönsch of II./NJG 2 and his crew, Feldwebel Otto Böttcher and Oberfeldwebel August Wille, who were killed in a flying accident near Gilze-Rijen. Here Kammhuber is saluting the graves of the fallen airmen.

Above and left: Between 10 and 15 August 1942, an Italian delegation led by General Biseo flew to Germany and visited various night fighter units in Holland and Germany. The delegation was accompanied on its inspection tour by Kammhuber and his staff.

Emblem of 10.(Nacht)/JG 72

In May 1939, a single-engined night fighter Staffel was created with the formation of 10.(Nacht)/JG 2 and in September, 11.(Nacht)/JG 2 was formed by redesignating 11.(Nacht)/LG 2. Also in September, a further single-engined night fighter Staffel was formed with the creation of 10.(Nacht)/JG 26, but this was redesignated 12.(Nacht)/JG 2 in December to form a full Gruppe, the IV.(Nacht)/JG 2, equipped with the Ar 68 F and the Bf 109 D-1. These early, single-engined night fighter units existed only for a short time before being disbanded or absorbed by the day fighter force. Note that the Ar 68 Fs (above right) were sometimes fitted with an early type of flame damper, shown more clearly (above left). Although the Pik As, or Ace of Spades emblem, has led to the assumption that this aircraft belonged to JG 53, it is believed that it was in fact operated by 10.(Nacht)/JG 72, which had been formed in July 1939 from personnel of II./JG 53. In February 1940, 10.(N)/JG 72 was redesignated 12.(Nacht)/JG 2 before finally becoming 6./NJG 1 in June 1940. A similar emblem but showing an owl on a branch was sometimes employed by 11.(Nacht)/JG 2.

Arado Ar 68 F-1 'Red 1+N' of 10.(Nacht)/JG 72, Oedheim/Heilbronn, September 1939

This aircraft was camouflaged in an uppersurface splinter pattern of 70/71 which extended well down the sides of the fuselage to meet a permanent black where the original 65 undersurfaces had been overpainted. Note the propeller blades are light grey on the front faces but black on the rear and that the national insignia on the uppersurface of the mainplane were either toned down or completely overpainted.

These two views of another Ar 68 F of 10.(Nacht)/JG 72 which crashed in south-west Germany in 1940 clearly show the splinter pattern on the uppersurfaces, but this time apparently in 71 and 02.

Although the Bf 109 D-1 was originally delivered in a factory finish of 70/71/65 with a low demarcation line which ran along the lower fuselage, this defensive scheme was later changed to one better suited to conceal the aircraft while in the air. The demarcation line between the upper- and undersurface colours was therefore raised so that most of the fuselage sides were in 65, and the green 70 on the uppersurfaces was replaced by grey 02. These aircraft, some clearly showing spinners finished in 70 while others are 65, belonged to 11.(Nacht)/JG 2 and were probably photographed at Oslo-Fornebu or Trondheim-Vaernes in the late spring or early summer of 1940. 'Black 10', the subject of the accompanying profile, may be seen in the background of the photographs (below and on opposite page). In June 1940, when NJG 1 was formed under Hptm. Wolfgang Falck, IV.(N)/JG 2 was redesignated II./NJG 1.

Messerschmitt Bf 109 D-1 'Black 10+N' of 11.(Nacht)/JG 2, Norway, 1940

This machine had been recently repainted in 70/02/65 and was therefore quite clean with minimal weathering and exhaust staining. Note the modified exhaust stubs and that, to prevent the pilot's night vision being affected by exhaust glare during night operations, an anti-glare shield has been fitted over the port and starboard exhaust outlets. The spinner on this aircraft was 70 overall.

This photograph of Bf 109 D-1s of 11.(Nacht)/JG 2 was taken shortly after the German invasion of Norway in April 1940, and shows sailors of the Kriegsmarine with one of the Staffel's aircraft at Oslo-Fornebu.

Bf 109 D-1s of IV.(N)/JG 2 apparently being readied for a night sortie, although the use of bright lighting to illuminate the scene suggests the photograph may have been taken for propaganda purposes.

The First Radar-Controlled Night Fighter Victory, 16 October 1940

Oberleutnant Ludwig Becker, 4./NJG 1

I flew the first sortie in fighter control area 'Zuidersee' at about 21.20 hrs. I was under the tactical control of *Leutnant* Diehl using the systems known as '*Freya mit Zusatz*' and '*Würzburg*'. We were using Morse wireless transmissions.

I was controlled very well by *Leutnant* Diehl to the correct height of 3,300 metres in a curve-of-pursuit approach to the enemy machine from starboard and astern with frequent course corrections until, in the moonlight and about 100 metres to port and above, I saw an aircraft. As I came closer, I recognised it as a Wellington.

I gradually positioned myself astern of it and manoeuvred in very close. Aiming at the fuselage and wing roots I gave it a burst of about five or six seconds. The starboard motor caught fire at once; I pulled my machine above the bomber and away. For a short period the British machine flew on, losing height; then the fire went out and I saw the enemy aircraft dive to earth in a typical spinning motion. There was a fire where he hit the ground. I did not see any parachutes. I went back to my holding area.

Note: This aircraft was almost certainly Wellington L7844 from 331 Squadron based at East Wretham. The aircraft had been on a mission to Kiel and its pilot, P/O Officer Landa, and three of the crew were killed. This account was translated from Becker's own combat report submitted after the encounter.

In the centre of this photograph is Karl Bolle, a pilot who shot down 36 enemy aircraft in the First World War and who was awarded the Pour le Mérite in August 1918. During the Second World War, Bolle was given the role of special advisor to the Luftwaffe and is seen here at Arnhem with Wolfgang Falck, celebrating the second anniversary of the formation of the Nachtjagd.

Another photograph of Obstlt. Karl Bolle shown in conversation with members of NJG 1. From the bottom left corner of the photograph and working clockwise around the table, the personalities are: Hptm. Walter Ehle (Kommandeur of II./NJG 1); unknown; Major Edler, with his hand raised to his face; Hptm. Wolfgang Thimmig; Hptm. Werner Streib, the Kommandeur of I./NJG 1; Obstlt. Bolle; and in the centre foreground with his back towards the camera, Hptm. Adolf Edler von Graeve, the Kommandeur of III./NJG 1.

The level of daytime British radio traffic intercepted by the Luftwaffe monitoring service as RAF crews flight-tested their machines frequently provided advance warning of bomber raids and activity on Luftwaffe night fighter flight lines increased accordingly as units were brought to readiness.

Below: A similar scene showing aircraft of Lehrgeschwader 1. Although these aircraft carry the Staffel letter 'K' of 3(Jagd)./LG 1, this Staffel was redesignated 15./LG 1 in August 1939 but retained its Staffel letter. When the unit was again redesignated and became 3./NJG 3 in October 1940 , the original letter 'L' was again appropriate although the 'L1' code was retained for some time afterwards.

Wolfgang Falck

Early Career

GENERALLY regarded as the creator and father of the *Nachtjagd*, Wolfgang Falck remained with the organisation from the time of its formation in June 1940 to its eventual demise in May 1945. Under his leadership and guidance he saw it expand from humble beginnings to an effective and deadly force feared and respected by its adversaries in Bomber Command.

Wolfgang Falck was born in Berlin on 19 August 1910, the son of a priest and the youngest of three children. He spent his entire childhood in the German capital where he witnessed Germany's defeat in 1918, the Kaiser's abdication, life under the Weimar Republic and experienced all the political changes of that period. After finishing his schooling in 1931 he applied to join the Army, which at that time was still restricted in size to 100,000 men under the provisions of the Treaty of Versailles. Falck's application was successful, but before he could join his Regiment he was selected by the *Reichswehrministerium* (Air Ministry) as one of 30 officer cadets most suitable to receive pilot training.

In the autumn of 1932, Wolfgang Falck joined 15th Company of Infantry Regiment No.7 and then underwent 14 weeks of basic army training at Schweidnitz, where this picture was taken.

In April of that year Falck was posted to the *Deutsche Verkehrsfliegerschule* (German Commercial Flying School) at Schleissheim near Munich where he underwent basic flight training. Although the school trained commercial pilots for *Lufthansa*, there were also men like Falck who, it was intended, would become fighter pilots. At the conclusion of the training, ten of the 30 students were selected to go to Lipetsk in Russia for fighter pilot training. Falck was one of the lucky ten and he departed for Russia in April 1932 together with the future Luftwaffe aces Günther Lützow and Hannes Trautloft.

Returning to Germany six months later, he resumed his army training with the training battalion of the 7th Infantry Regiment at Schweidnitz where he underwent 14 weeks of basic infantry training. Between February 1933 and September 1934 he attended the Infantry School at Dresden, and on 1 October 1934 he was promoted to *Leutnant*. On receiving his commission, he was advised to resign from the Army so that he could join the Luftwaffe. At that time, however, the Luftwaffe did not officially exist as far as the rest of the world was concerned and to keep its existence secret, the pilots and personnel operated under the guise of the *Luftsportverband* (Air Sports Association).

With his resignation accepted, Falck returned to the *Deutsche Verkehrsfliegerschule* at Schleissheim as a pilot instructor and for the next eighteen months he was responsible for assessing student pilots, deciding which were suitable to become fighter pilots and which were not. On 1 April 1936 he was promoted to *Oberleutnant* and transferred to *Jagdgeschwader* 132 '*Richthofen*' which was based at Jüterbog-Damm near Berlin. As one of the most accomplished and capable fliers in the *Geschwader*, Falck was automatically chosen to instruct any new pilots joining the unit and to pass on his valuable expertise.

In early 1937 he was transferred to the staff of *Jagdgeschwader* '*Richthofen*' and appointed *Geschwader Adjutant*. The monotony of the paperwork, combined with its numerous administrative duties, however, soon took its toll on Falck who began looking for a way to return to flying duties. An opportunity to do so presented itself in July 1938 when it was decided to add a third *Gruppe* to the *Geschwader's* establishment and Falck, on hearing the news, immediately applied to become a *Staffelkapitän* in the new unit. The *Geschwaderkommodore, Major* Gerd von Massow, accepted his application and Falck became the *Staffelkapitän* of 8. *Staffel*, stationed at Fürstenwalde.

After the German occupation of Czechoslovakia, Falck's *Gruppe* was transferred to Olmütz in Bohemia-Moravia, where it received familiarisation training on the new, twin-engined Messerschmitt Bf 110. As it became available, this heavy fighter gradually replaced the *Gruppe's* Bf 109s and, once conversion was complete, the III. *Gruppe* was redesignated I./*Zerstörergeschwader* 76 (I./ZG 76), one of the first such Destroyer *Gruppen* to be formed.

The Outbreak of War

Towards the end of August 1939, as war loomed ever closer in Europe, I./ZG 76 was transferred to a small airfield at Ohlau, Silesia, close to the Polish border. When war finally broke out on 1 September 1939, Falck and his men flew a bomber escort mission to Krakow but, disappointingly, failed to engage the Polish Air Force. On 5 September, however, I./ZG 76 attacked Dalikow airfield and Falck achieved his first confirmed victory of the war when he shot down a PZL P-23 bomber. Less than a week later, on 11 September, he increased his tally to three victories when he shot down a Fokker F IX and a single-engined reconnaissance aircraft. Two days later, as the highest-scoring pilot of his *Gruppe*, Falck was decorated by Göring himself with the Iron Cross, Second Class.

When the Polish campaign came to an end, I./ZG 76 moved to Nellingen, near Stuttgart. On 16 December, after several months of flying border patrols, Falck was promoted to *Hauptmann*, and the *Gruppe* was transferred to Jever. The following day, 24 Wellington bombers were dispatched from England to attack the docks at Wilhelmshaven. However, as they crossed the North Sea, they were intercepted over the Heligoland Bight by a large number of German fighters. In the ensuing air battle, Falck claimed two of the 12 Wellingtons shot down but the RLM credited him with only one. The German press immediately took advantage of this propaganda opportunity, and Falck, together with other successful pilots, soon became well known to the German public.

As a direct result of the RAF losses experienced over the Heligoland Bight, Bomber Command changed its strategy and began operating mainly at night. It did, however, carry out a number of raids against German shipping in the North Sea, and it was against raids on 10 January and 17 February 1940 that Falck shot down two Blenheims, increasing his personal tally of victories to six. Both bombers were from 110 Sqn. and were shot down whilst carrying out reconnaissance flights over the North Sea.

Two days later, on 19 February, Falck was transferred from ZG 76 and appointed *Kommandeur* of I./ZG 1. This *Gruppe* was based at Barth on the Baltic Coast and on 9 April it took part in the invasion of Denmark. During the first day of the operation, codenamed '*Weserübung*', Falck

Following the Luftwaffe's successful interception of RAF Wellington bombers over the Heligoland Bight on 18 December 1939, a few days later a press conference was called to announce the news to the German public. Seated second from the right in this photograph is Obstlt. Carl Schumacher, the Kommodore of JG 1, responsible for protecting the German naval bases at Wilhelmshaven. Two places to his right is Oblt. Johannes Steinhoff of 10./(N)JG 26, soon to be redesignated to form part of IV.(N)/JG 2.

After the press conference, the Reich's Press Officer, Dr. Otto Dietrich (centre), speaks with Obstlt. Carl Schumacher and Hptm. Wolfgang Falck (right).

claimed his seventh and what proved to be his last victory when he shot down a Fokker D-21 over Copenhagen-Vaerlöse. When the Danes capitulated, I./ZG 1 flew sorties against Norway from its new airfield at Aalborg in Northern Denmark. Whilst operating from Aalborg, the airfield was often attacked by British bombers returning from operations against Germany and, as a consequence of these nuisance raids, Falck began to formulate plans to counter the bombers. He reported his theories to the Luftwaffe's High Command and, within a week, Falck was visited by *Generaloberst* Erhard Milch. The possibilities of night fighting were discussed at the meeting, but before any plans could be put into effect Germany invaded France and the Low Countries on 10 May 1940.

The Creation of the Nachtjagd

Thoughts of night fighting were soon forgotten as the *Wehrmacht* rapidly advanced to the English Channel. Falck's own *Gruppe* flew countless sorties in support of the ground forces and losses began to rise accordingly. Then, just as the French capitulated, Falck's own *Gruppe*, minus one *Staffel*, was ordered back to Düsseldorf. Since the German bombing of Rotterdam, Bomber Command had been flying nocturnal operations to attack industrial targets in the Ruhr and Falck was tasked with defending them. On 26 June 1940, Falck was summoned to a meeting at Wassenaar where Göring appointed him the *Kommodore* of NJG 1. However, with this appointment came the task of organising, expanding and developing Germany's night defences, a role in which Falck would prove instrumental.

Falck returned to Düsseldorf and began the mammoth task that lay ahead of him and, together with *Oberst* Josef Kammhuber, German night defences were transformed into an effective and formidable obstacle against Bomber Command. On 1 October 1940, in recognition of this pioneering night defence work and his previous operational service, he was awarded the Knight's Cross.

At the same time, however, Kammhuber banned Falck from all operational flying, although he remained *Kommodore* of NJG 1 until the end of June 1943. Thus, in addition to the day-to-day running of his *Geschwader*, Falck spent the next three years visiting all theatres of operations to improve existing night fighter defences or to establish them where they were most needed.

After the catastrophic raids against Hamburg in July 1943, during which some 40,000 civilians were killed in a single night, Kammhuber was replaced by *Generalmajor* Josef Schmid and transferred to Norway to take charge of *Luftflotte* 5. Falck, who had been promoted to *Oberst* on 1 July 1943, was transferred to the General Staff and had to hand over command of NJG 1 to his friend and fellow pioneer of night fighting, Werner Streib. In September 1943, Falck was assigned to Berlin where he became head of operations for the *Reich's* night fighter defences. Coincidentally, just a few short weeks before Falck arrived in Berlin, Air Chief Marshal Harris had begun an offensive against the German capital. The 'Battle of Berlin', as it was known, was destined to last almost seven months and from the time of the first raid on 23 August 1943 until the last raid on 24 March 1944, Bomber Command mounted 19 raids against the city, killing over 10,000 of its inhabitants. From his bunker at Berlin-Wannsee, Falck was able to oversee the *Reich's* defences in response to the strength and direction of any incoming bomber stream. By the time of the last raid, the combined efforts of the German defences had accounted for more than 600 bombers. Apart from representing a huge loss in men and machines, the loss rate was one that Bomber Command could not sustain indefinitely.

On 20 July 1944, *Oberst* Claus von Stauffenberg attempted to assassinate Hitler during a military conference at Rastenburg in East Prussia. This came as a shock for Falck as he was related by marriage to the Stauffenberg family and had met Claus von Stauffenberg a week before the attempt. Fearing arrest because of his close association with the family, he approached his friend, the *General der Jagdflieger*, Adolf Galland. After a brief discussion, Galland agreed to transfer him to Pancevo near Belgrade as *Jagdführer* (Fighter Leader) Balkans. Falck arrived in Yugoslavia in August and remained there until the

Continued on page 26

Falck photographed while he was at Rom in Northern Denmark coordinating protection flights for the battle cruisers Admiral Scheer and Prinz Eugen which, in February 1942, left their berths at Wilhelmshaven for the safety of the Norwegian Fjords.

The heavy cruiser Prinz Eugen with two of its escorts.

Temporarily setting aside the initial difficulties of establishing and building up the Nachtjagd, Falck relaxes at a garden party in the grounds of his headquarters at Deelen.

This photograph was taken on 24 February 1942 at Trondheim in Norway, and shows members of 5./NJG 1 who took part in 'Donnerkeil'. Fourth from the left is Lt. Georg Greiner. Sixth from left is Lt. Heinz Schnaufer and third from the right is Schnaufer's Bordfunker, Fritz Rumpelhardt.

Right and far right: Falck at Velno showing his unit's aircraft and command post to visiting Italian officers of the Regia Aeronautica. The two parties also exchanged relevant technical data.

This Bf 110 C-1 coded G9+AA was flown by Major Wolfgang Falck, the Kommodore of NJG 1, shown (left) as an Oberleutnant. Major Falck led this Geschwader from 26 June 1940 to 30 June 1943, during which period the unit was based entirely at Deelen-Arnhem in Holland. Falck having been prevented from flying combat missions by Kammhuber in 1940, this machine was used purely for non-operational flying.

Messerschmitt Bf 110 C-1 'G9+AA' flown by Major Wolfgang Falck, Kommodore of NJG 1, Deelen-Arnhem, 1942

As explained previously, when Major Falck became Kommodore of NJG 1, he was forbidden to fly operational missions but retained a Bf 110 C bearing the markings G9+AA in grey 77 with the aircraft letter in the bright blue of the Geschwaderstab. The camouflage consisted of a green 70/71 splinter pattern on the uppersurfaces which had evidently been lightly polished and showed a slight sheen, with 65 on the undersurfaces. Note that although this was a non-operational machine, the white areas of the fuselage Balkenkreuz have been oversprayed grey while the Balkenkreuz under the wings have been removed entirely.

Left and below: During a fact-finding tour of the Eastern Front in August and September 1942, Major Falck visited numerous Luftwaffe units to evaluate their ability to protect themselves at night against Russian bombers. In the course of this tour he met up with Hannes Trautloft, a close friend and Kommodore of Jagdgeschwader 54. These photographs were taken at Siverskaya where Trautloft had his headquarters.

Above: Photographed at the Luftwaffe testing facility at Werneuchen in the spring of 1943 are, from left to right: Falck; General Wolfgang Martini (Chief of Communications); Generaloberst Hans-Jürgen Stumpf (Chief of Luftflotte 5); and with his back to the camera, Generalmajor Andreas Nielsen.

In early 1943, Kammhuber ordered Falck to Rumania where he was to set up Jagdfliegerführer Balkan, a command post for the protection of the Ploesti oilfields. This photograph shows Falck with his operations officer, Major Douglas Pitcairn (standing) and, at the head of the table, Ritterkreuzträger Obstlt. Bernard Woldenga, the officer responsible for fighter units in the Balkans.

In September 1943 Falck was transferred to Berlin-Wansee where he became operations officer of Luftflotte Reich and was responsible for all ground defences and day and night fighters operating throughout the Reich. On the right in this photograph is Generalmajor Andreas Nielsen, and on the left, Oberleutnant Wever, the son of General Wever.

On 11 May 1944, Oberst Walter Oesau was shot down and killed south-west of St. Vith in Belgium. His subsequent funeral was attended by a large number of high ranking Luftwaffe officers including Wolfgang Falck (left); Generaloberst Hans-Jürgen Stumpff (foreground); and Generalmajor Walter Grabmann (behind and to Stumpff's left).

Wolfgang Falck in conversation with the commander of 2. Jagddivision, Generalmajor Walter Schwabedissen (left), whose divisional headquarters were located at Stade. Schwabedissen was responsible for all the night fighter units based in north-west Germany.

On 2 May 1945, Wolfgang Falck, on the right, was taken prisoner by American troops at Schloss Schönau in Bavaria, where he was briefly interrogated before being released several weeks later.

beginning of October. During this time the Soviets invaded Rumania and Bulgaria and when they were advancing into Yugoslavia, Falck was obliged to transfer his headquarters to Vienna. However, within a short time of his arrival in Austria he was again transferred, this time to Potsdam where he became Chief of Staff to *Generalmajor* von Massow who was responsible for flying training at Potsdam-Werder near Berlin.

In March 1945, Falck was seconded to Army Group B, commanded by *Feldmarschall* Model at Bensberg, near Cologne. With the Allies expected to cross the Rhine at any time, his task was to identify landing areas that could be used by enemy gliders and parachutists and to advise preventative measures, but it was immediately obvious to him that the situation for Germany was grave and that the war was as good as lost. By the end of April 1945, Falck was at Bad Aibling in Bavaria, awaiting the inevitable German capitulation. On 2 May he was captured by American troops but spent just five weeks in captivity before being released.

Post-War Life

In July 1950, following a variety of jobs which included working for the British Army in Germany, Wolfgang Falck secured a job as a sales representative with a company manufacturing playing cards.
He remained with this company until 1961, by which time he had risen to the position of Chief Executive Officer, but then left. He was then approached by North American Aviation and offered a position as a consultant, which he accepted, and in 1966 he was offered a similar position with McDonnell Douglas, remaining with this company until his retirement in March 1986. Wolfgang Falck died in March 2007 aged 96 in the Austrian Tyrol.

Although possibly accentuated by the bright light which enabled this night photograph to be taken, this view of a Bf 110 shows the uneven finish sometimes seen on Luftwaffe night fighters. Such an appearance could result from an overspray in varying densities on the aircraft's original camouflage colours, although normal weathering would also be an additional factor. The pilot seen here entering the cockpit of his machine is believed to be Ofw. Paul Gildner of NJG 1.

Fernnachtjagd – Intruder operations over England

From the moment he took command of the *Nachtjagd*, Josef Kammhuber was determined to engage his night fighters not only in the defence of the Fatherland, but to take the fight to the enemy and engage him in an offensive role. With this in mind, he chose II./NJG 1 to become the *Nachtjagd's* first long-range night fighters, or *Fernnachtjäger*. The *Gruppe*, which had first been formed from IV./(N)JG 2, was re-formed on 1 July 1940 from the *Zerstörer Staffel* of KG 30,[6] which was equipped with Ju 88 C-2s and Do 17 Z-10s. The pilots and crews were transferred to Düsseldorf where, together with crews from other units, they received their night fighter training.

Within a matter of weeks the *Gruppe* found itself on the move again, this time to Schiphol near Amsterdam. On 1 September 1940 the *Gruppe*, under the command of *Major* Karl-Heinrich Heyse, was redesignated I./NJG 2 and transferred to Gilze-Rijen. This airfield was better suited to night fighting operations and previously had been used by the Dutch as a military landing ground. Prior to the German invasion, the Dutch had begun to extend the airfield and the Germans themselves finally completed this work when they took it over so that when finished the airfield had three concrete runways, each 1,700 metres long, and an abundance of workshops, hangars and dispersal shelters.

Ofw. Paul Gildner of 3./NJG 1 shot down a Hampden bomber on the night of 2/3 September 1940 and achieved one of the first recorded night victories of the war. He was one of the early innovators in the organisation and his loss on 24 February 1943 was keenly felt.

Now that the unit had its own identity, aircraft and trained personnel, it began to concentrate on establishing procedures and tactics for the role ahead. One of the most important elements introduced was that of the German wireless telegraphy interception service, whose job it was to monitor the transmissions between the British bombers and their ground control units as they prepared for a forthcoming operation. Any information that was received via the transmissions was passed directly to the control centre at Gilze-Rijen by 15.00 hrs each day.

When the idea of taking the offensive to Bomber Command was first conceived it was initially envisaged that the night fighters would be sent out in three waves. The first of these would attack the bombers as they took off from their airfields. The second would then patrol along the known routes flown by the bombers over the North Sea, while the third wave would fly to selected Bomber Command airfields and wait for the bombers to return, shooting them down as they attempted to land.

Unfortunately, putting the first two proposals into practice was a far more complicated proposition than the theory had first suggested. Neither the information received from the interception service, nor the standard of navigation, was sufficient at that time for the night fighters easily to attack the bombers on take-off. In addition, it was virtually impossible without airborne interception radar to locate the bombers as they flew in over the North Sea. What therefore proved to be the most effective way of attacking the bombers was the third proposal, which involved night fighters being filtered into the bomber stream as it headed back to England. As the bombers neared their illuminated airfields with landing and navigation lights switched on, and with many of the crews fatigued and preoccupied, the German fighters chose this vulnerable moment to make their attacks against the bombers.

6. This *Staffel* had formerly been stationed at Trondheim in Norway.

As the vast majority of Bomber Command airfields were situated in the east of England this area was divided into three patrol zones, designated A, B and C. A covered the Yorkshire region of the country, whilst B covered the Midlands and Lincolnshire, and C incorporated East Anglia and London. While preparations were being made to begin operations against the British, Kammhuber was busy trying to enlarge the *Gruppe* and had received authority from Göring to establish two entire *Geschwader*. Later, in December 1940, he received further authorisation to establish a third. Unfortunately for Kammhuber, due to shortages in equipment, most noticeably in aircraft, the force remained at *Gruppe* strength, and at most I./NJG 2 rarely had more than 20 aircraft at its disposal.

Despite its organisational and logistical difficulties, I./NJG 2 achieved its first confirmed victory over England on the evening of 24 October 1940 when, at 21.30hrs, *Oblt*. Kurt Hermann attacked a Blenheim from No. 17 Operational Training Unit making a cross-country flight over Norfolk. The attack set the bomber's port fuel tank on fire and damaged its hydraulic system, but despite this the pilot was able to land his aircraft at Docking airfield. Five minutes later, Herrmann attacked and damaged a Beaufort, but this aircraft too was able to land without further incident. Later that night, at 22.10 hrs, *Fw*. Hans Hahn met with greater success when he shot down a Whitley from No. 102 Sqn. which was taking off from Linton-on-Ouse. The aircraft crashed in flames killing two of the crew and injuring the other three.

Two further victories followed in the early hours of 28 October when *Lt*. Heinz Völker attacked two Hampden bombers from No. 49 Sqn., which were returning from a raid on Hamburg. The first was slightly damaged in the attack but was able to land safely at Lindholm, whereas a less fortunate machine from the same squadron was so severely damaged that it crashed into the North Sea half a mile off the coast of Skegness, killing the four-man crew.

In addition to its main role of shooting down bombers, I./NJG 2 also attacked targets of opportunity when they presented themselves. It was not uncommon for the *Gruppe* to drop fragmentation bombs on the airfields or to strafe parked aircraft and their ground crews, causing considerable damage to equipment and buildings, as well as the inevitable disruption to night-flying operations.

By the end of 1940, claims from I./NJG 2 amounted to a total of 18 aircraft destroyed although, according to official RAF records, only two bombers were actually lost and three others damaged. This was certainly not by any means an auspicious start for the *Gruppe*, especially in view of the high price it paid for these few successes. From the time of its formation in July 1940, the unit lost a total of 12 aircraft plus 32 aircrew killed, one of whom was the *Kommandeur*, Major Heyse. He was lost on 23 November 1940 during a sortie to England and is believed to have been shot down into the North Sea, possibly by the gunners of a Hampden bomber from No. 83 Sqn. The death of its commanding officer was a harsh blow for the *Gruppe* and to minimise the effect on morale, *Hptm*. Karl Hülshoff, formerly the *Staffelkapitän* of 3./NJG 2, replaced Heyse the following day.

Despite the losses and difficulties experienced by I./NJG 2 in 1940, the New Year started well with four claims being made in the first three days of 1941. In the early hours of 16 January, *Oblt*. Albert Schulz from the 2. *Staffel* opened his account with a 'double', reporting the destruction of two Blenheims over Church Fenton, Yorkshire. In fact, these aircraft were Boulton Paul Defiants from No. 54 Operational Training Unit, which were taking part in a night-flying exercise. Both crash-landed as a result of being attacked by Schulz and their respective pilots escaped serious injury.

Oblt. Albert Schulz of I./NJG 2 with other members of the Gruppe (below left) and in the cockpit of his Do 17 Z at Gilze-Rijen (below right). Clearly seen on the fuselage of the aircraft is the night fighter emblem which was designed in 1940 by Viktor Mölders and which subsequently adorned many of the Nachtjagd's aircraft. By the time long-range intruder missions against Britain were cancelled in October 1941, Schulz had six kills to his credit. He would increase this total to 17 by the time of his death on 31 January 1944.

Combat Report submitted by *Oberleutnant* Egmont *Prinz* zur Lippe-Weissenfeld, 4./NJG 1

On 15 January 1941 I was briefed to fly a *Dunkel Nachtjagd* in the area of Den Helda. After several unsuccessful attempts at interception I was given a heading of 320 degrees at an altitude of 3,200 metres. After two alterations of course to port, I saw a dark shadow at a distance of about 150 metres. I altered course towards it and approached with a high speed advantage.

In order not to overtake, I pulled up and recognised the target with certainty as a Whitley-Armstrong (sic)*. I positioned myself some 30 metres away in order to make my attack, but from this distance I could no longer see my target because my bulletproof windscreen was almost completely obscured by frost.

At this moment the enemy saw me. He made a number of evasive manoeuvres and the rear gunner gave several long bursts of fire without actually hitting me. I now approached closely and, through the armoured windscreen, was able to see the two exhaust flames from the twin engines at a distance of about 10 metres. I gave a short burst and as I pulled away I could see that the bomber was on fire. After about two minutes the wing came off and the aircraft went down.

* It would appear that this aircraft was almost certainly Armstrong Whitworth Whitley N1521 GE-J from No. 58 Squadron, flown by Pilot Officer W.E. Peers. This aircraft had taken off from Linton-on-Ouse at 17.55 hours as one of 96 aircraft taking part in a raid on Wilhelmshaven. According to W.R. Chorley's 'Bomber Command Losses', the aircraft crashed at 22.46 hrs between the Zwanenwater Lake and Callantsoog, just south of Den Helder in North Holland.

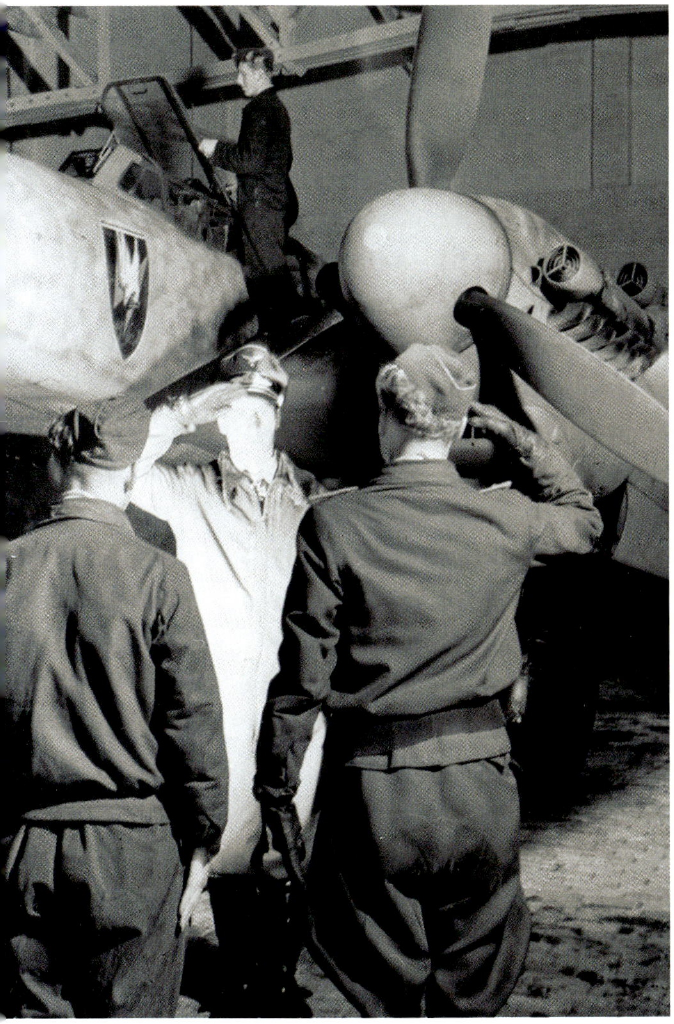

Left and above: Oblt. Paul Semrau, seen here facing the camera (left) saluting his two aircrew before a night sortie later in the war. In the photograph (above) he has donned his flying helmet and is preparing for the flight with one of these aircrew (on his left). The ground crew (seen standing on the wing in the photo at left) is now in the cockpit and has started the starboard engine. Paul Semrau first made a name for himself as a night fighter with I./NJG 2. With this unit he participated in long-range intruder operations to the British mainland in 1941, during which time he claimed to have destroyed a total of nine enemy aircraft. Of particular note on this aircraft is the gondola mounted under the fuselage which normally housed a pair of 20 mm MG FF cannon and the underside of the starboard wing and engine nacelle, areas of which have been painted black. Although these images are essentially realistic in their depiction, it is possible they were staged for propaganda purposes.

Hptm. Karl Hülshoff (left) in conversation with the Kommandeur of I./NJG 1, Werner Streib. Hülshoff led I./NJG 2 during its long-range intruder missions over the British mainland and shot down four RAF bombers.

The following month the *Gruppe* claimed another 12 victories, six of which were achieved in a single sortie on the night of 10/11 February. *Oblt.* Paul Semrau, eventually credited with 46 confirmed night victories, claimed to have shot down two Blenheims returning from a raid against Hannover. One of these aircraft was Blenheim Z5877, which was attacked by Semrau as it made its final approach. The aircraft caught fire as it came to a stop and only the gunner, Sgt. Birch, survived the attack. On his return to Gilze-Rijen, *Oblt.* Kurt Hermann also claimed to have destroyed two bombers which he identified as Hampdens. Indeed, according to W.R. Chorley's 'Bomber Command Losses of the Second World War', two Hampdens were lost that night, but the first of these was credited to *Lt.* Leopold Fellerer of 5./NJG 1, whose victim crashed in Northern Holland. The second Hampden, AD719 piloted by Sgt. G. Bates from 49 Sqn., is listed as having been shot down by Herrmann and crashed three miles north-east of Lincoln, killing two of the four-man crew. Another Hampden from 144 Sqn.[7] was reportedly attacked and sustained damage to its hydraulic system and undercarriage, but was able to land safely at its airfield at Hemswell.

This marked increase in the number of claims obviously buoyed the confidence of the crews and despite making only six further claims during March, I./NJG 2 followed this in April by having the most successful month in its operational history. *Lt.* Heinz Völker submitted the first of the month's 25 claims on 4 April when he shot down a Wellington of No. 115 Sqn. as his first victory. The Wellington was on the return leg of an operation, having just participated in an attack against German battle cruisers harboured at Brest, and crash-landed on mud flats close to King's Lynn. Only one of the three-man crew survived. According to German records, Völker went on to claim four Bristol Blenheims on 25 April, all of which were shot down in the space of 15 minutes.

In the meantime other pilots such as *Fw.* Hans Hahn were also steadily increasing their personal scores. At the beginning of April, Hahn had already been credited with four victories, and after shooting down a Hampden and a Wellington on the 8th, he increased his tally to eight with a further Hampden on the 17th and another on 21 April. Other pilots who also contributed to the successes of the unit were the *Gruppenkommandeur*, *Hptm.* Hülshoff, and *Lt.* Johannes Feuerbaum from 2. *Staffel*, both of whom claimed two bombers each on 8 April.

Oberfeldwebel Hermann Sommer completed this outstanding month for the *Gruppe*, claiming the destruction of three Blenheims and a Beaufort in the air, whilst destroying five further aircraft on the ground during the early hours of 30 April. Taking off from Gilze-Rijen late on the night of the 29th, Sommer entered the region of The Wash. At about 00.15 hrs he reported seeing aircraft firing recognition

[7] See 'Intruders Over Britain' by Simon Parry.

Below: Lt. Hans Hahn (right) pictured with his Bordfunker, Ofw. Meissler. Between 24 October 1940 and 11 October 1941, Hahn flew numerous sorties to Britain and was credited with 12 victories until his death on 11 October 1941 when his aircraft collided with his twelfth and final victim.

Generalmajor Josef Kammhuber (centre), the commander of 1. Nachtjagddivision, with Lt. Hans Hahn of I./NJG 2 (left) and Ofw. Paul Gildner of 5./NJG 1. This photograph was almost certainly taken on or soon after 9 July 1941, on which date all three men were awarded the Knight's Cross.

Taken shortly before his death, this photograph shows Hans Hahn wearing the Knight's Cross awarded on 9 July 1941 for destroying ten bombers.

Above: A Bf 110 E of 7./NJG 1 coded G9+ER. Note the entire spinners appear to be white, which corresponds to the Staffel colour, whereas G9+DR (left) has only the spinner tips painted white. The individual aircraft letter on both machines has also been outlined in white.

flares and, having flown towards them, located an illuminated airfield that he later identified as Tollerton, south-east of Nottingham. After discreetly infiltrating the airfield's circuit he was able to close within two to three hundred metres of an aircraft before opening fire. In his post-mission report, Sommer claimed that the aircraft simply exploded before crashing to the ground. Five minutes later he attacked a second aircraft which had its landing lights switched on. At a range of just 80 metres he dispatched this bomber in the same way as its unfortunate predecessor. Before leaving the airfield, Sommer dropped his bombs on the runway and reported the destruction of three parked aircraft and two preparing to take off. Approximately 20 minutes later, whilst circling over Hucknall, he attacked a Blenheim that was in the process of landing and shot it down from behind at 00.50 hrs. His last claim that night was for a Bristol Beaufort, which he reportedly intercepted near to the Norfolk town of Bircham Newton during his flight back to Gilze-Rijen.

During May and June, I./NJG 2 reported the destruction of a further 36 bombers, taking its overall number of claims, since its formation, to over 100. However, while the number of victories had increased dramatically, the British defences – particularly the RAF's night fighters – had become so formidable that the *Gruppe* was obliged to revise its tactics. Henceforth, an increasing number of interceptions were carried out over the North Sea, and of the 22 bombers claimed in June, 18 were shot down over the sea.

Operations by I./NJG 2 were then carried out almost on a daily basis. Throughout July the *Gruppe* completed in the region of 270 sorties and claimed to have attacked 58 airfields resulting in the destruction of 19 aircraft, of which almost half were over the North Sea. The most successful pilot that month was *Ofw*. Wilhelm Beier, who claimed a total of five bombers and so increased his personal tally of victories to 11. Another event in July that undoubtedly boosted flagging morale was the award of the Knight's Cross to *Ofw*. Hans Hahn, the first of only two *Fernnachtjäger* pilots to win this much sought-after decoration, after his tenth victory.

The second *Fernnachtjäger* pilot to win the Knight's Cross was *Oberfeldwebel* Wilhelm Beier, who was personally decorated with the award by *General* Kammhuber on 10 October 1941 for his 14 victories. Beier's last three victories had actually been achieved two months previously on

Two views of G9+BR, also with its individual aircraft letter outlined in white and with white spinner tips.

8 August when he claimed to have shot down a Blenheim, a Halifax and a Wellington, all during the same operation to the east coast of England. These were three of five claims submitted that night and were destined to make Beier the highest scoring of all the *Fernnachtjagd* pilots. Further multiple claims were made during the same month: *Ofw*. Robert Lüddeke was credited with two Wellingtons on 15 August and *Ofw*. Heinz Strüning with two Blenheims four days later.

By the end of August 1941, I./NJG 2 had claimed a total of 135 victories, more than any *Nachtjagd* unit, although during the following month the *Gruppe's* pilots only managed to add a further four victories to this number. In October, however, the *Gruppe* was dealt a series of devastating blows. On the evening of 11 October, Hans Hahn was patrolling over the town of Grantham in Lincolnshire, when he intercepted an Airspeed Oxford of No. 12 FTS on a training flight. In the pilot's seat was Cpl. Edwards with his instructor, Sgt. Tom Graham, next to him. Hahn opened fire on the advanced trainer, but in his eagerness to ensure the victory he collided with his victim and both aircraft plummeted to the ground. After having survived so many daring intruder missions, Hahn's luck had finally run out.

Then, only hours after the *Gruppe* received the news that Hahn was missing, Kammhuber called the personnel of I./NJG 2 together and informed them that the *Gruppe* was being transferred to Sicily. The news was received with absolute incredulity and a sense of betrayal. After more than a year of a hard-fought and costly campaign in which they had taken the fight to the very heart of Bomber Command, the aircrew of I./NJG 2 felt that they were the elite of the night fighter force. But despite the effect of its raids on operational as well as training units, it was decided that the missions to England were to terminate immediately and that the *Gruppe* would be better employed in the Mediterranean where it was to protect Axis convoys carrying reinforcements and supplies to Rommel's forces in North Africa. It would be almost two years before German intruders would reappear in English skies.

An overall black Bf 110 of 6./NJG 1 with the fuselage markings G9+CP. Note, however, that the Staffel letter 'P' has been repeated on the upper wingtip instead of the individual aircraft letter 'C'.

Bf 110 night fighters of 9./NJG 1, apparently at Schleswig in early 1941. Note the unusual presentation of the fuselage Balkenkreuz on G9+BT in the foreground and also on G9+HT behind it.

Luftwaffe technical ground staff refuelling a Bf 110 of II./NJG 1 at Deelen-Arnhem in the autumn of 1940. The aircraft is camouflaged black overall and the machine's individual aircraft letter has been applied to the nose. Note also the Roman II adjacent to the Englandblitz emblem.

This Ju 88 C of NJG 2 appears to be camouflaged overall in a single dark grey, probably RLM 75, with the fuselage code in RLM 74. This supposition is based on the contrast between these colours compared with the known black of the fuselage Balkenkreuz where the original white segments have been overpainted.

Another Bf 110 which served with Nachtjagdschule at Schleissheim, shown with the Stammkennzeichen DK+ZL. Note that the aircraft retains a day fighter scheme and that the individual aircraft identification is now a numeral, in this case '17'.

One of the units raised to train night fighter pilots was Nachtjagdschule 1 where the emphasis was on blind and bad weather flying. This formation was created at Schleissheim in the summer of 1941 by redesignating the former Zerstörerschule 1 and eventually comprised three Gruppen. In March 1943 the unit was again redesignated and became NJG 101. The unit operated a wide variety of such single and twin-engined aircraft types as the Ar 96, Bf 108, Bf 109, Do 215, Do 217, Fw 58, Go 145, Ju 86 and, as shown here, the Bf 110. Shown in the centre of this flight is a Bf 110 C-4 with the Stammkennzeichen DE+MA and an additional letter 'L' on the fuselage.

Messerschmitt Bf 110 C-4 'White L' of Nachtjagdschule 1, Schleissheim

This machine was camouflaged in an overall black night finish which had faded on the spine and is believed to have carried the Nachtjagd emblem on the nose as shown. Although the aircraft's four-letter Stammkennzeichen had been retained and overpainted in grey 77, a white letter 'L' was added for unit identification purposes. The spinners and propeller blades were green 70 and the W.Nr. 3259 was painted in white on the fin.

This page and opposite: This sequence of photographs showing L1+DH having its weapons harmonised illustrates that the Staffel badge was applied to both sides of the nose.

Above and below: A particular feature of V.(Z)/LG 1, the destroyer Gruppe of the instructional and demonstration unit Lehrgeschwader 1, was that throughout its existence it used Staffel letters corresponding to I. Gruppe. Similarly, when V.(Z)/LG 1 was redesignated in October 1940 to form I./NJG 3, the Gruppe continued to use its old 'L1' code at least until June 1941. These photographs of L1+CH of 1. Staffel were taken sometime between February and May 1941 when I./NJG 3 was based in Sicily. The aircraft, a Bf 110 C, is finished black overall but with the tips of the spinners and the individual aircraft letter 'C' painted in white, the Staffel colour, which was repeated above and below each wingtip. The emblem on the nose only came into existence with the formation of I./NJG 3 and shows an owl perched on a quarter moon. It was normal for German aircraft operating in the Mediterranean area to have a white theatre band around the rear fuselage as a recognition marking, but on this machine it has been applied only to the upper part of the fuselage to avoid compromising its night finish when viewed from below.

Emblem of 1./NJG 3

Right: The practice of repeating the aircraft letter under the wing of some machines is seen more clearly in this photograph of L1+DH, another Bf 110 C-4 of 1./NJG 3. This photograph, however, is thought to have been taken a little later than the one of L1+CH (shown opposite), probably after the Staffel had moved from Sicily to Benghazi where it operated under Fliegerführer Afrika from May to August 1941 and from Derna until October. As the aircraft shown here still carries the unit code 'L1', which was not changed to 'D5' until June 1941, this photograph was almost certainly taken at Benghazi. In this scene, the aircraft is being repaired and although already fitted with replacement undercarriage doors and tail components, these have yet to be camouflaged in black.

Messerschmitt Bf 110 C-4 'L1+DH' of 1./NJG 3, North Africa, Summer 1941

This aircraft was finished black overall but with its replacement undercarriage door and tail components still in the day fighter finish of blue 65 with a light mottle of 71 on the tail. The propeller blades were green 70, as were the spinners, which had white tips. The fuselage code was grey 77, and the individual aircraft letter 'D' was outlined in white. The badge of 1./NJG 3 appeared on both sides of the forward fuselage and only the upper half of a wide white band appeared on the rear fuselage.

Right: In July 1940, II./NJG 1 specialised in mounting night intruder operations to British bomber aerodromes which had been located by radio intercepts. On 11 September 1940, the Gruppe was redesignated I./NJG 2 but the number of intruder aircraft available was inadequate and the perceived lack of results resulted in the end of such operations on 12 October 1941. In mid-November 1941, I./NJG 2 was ordered to the Mediterranean theatre and was based at Catania in Sicily. On its arrival at Catania, the Gruppe flew daylight missions to escort convoys of vital supplies destined for German troops in North Africa as well as night intruder sorties over Malta, Crete and North Africa. This Ju 88 C-6 was flown by Lt. Heinz Rökker of 1. Staffel and although the person on the right is unknown, the NCO on the left is Rökker's Bordmechaniker, Uffz. Georg Frieben. The absence of flame-dampers over the exhausts suggests the aircraft was used predominantly for daylight operations although it is clearly equipped with Lichtenstein radar. As the C-6 was originally intended as a day Zerstörer, it is finished in a 70/71/76 scheme but with a tan wave-mirror overspray on the uppersurfaces and spinners.

Right: Lt. Heinz Rökker of 1./NJG 2 also flew this Ju 88 C, W.Nr. 5664, shown at Catania after a landing accident in which the port undercarriage collapsed. The aircraft, coded R4+CK, was evidently on loan from 2. Staffel.

Another Ju 88 C, believed to have been flown by 2. or 3./NJG 2 in the Mediterranean, showing a partial white band around the rear fuselage. Note also the weathered area at the base of the tail where the action of sand, thrown up by the propellers, has abraded the finish.

In addition to its Ju 88 C-6 night fighters, I./NJG 2 used a number of Ju 88 A-4s for bombing operations. One such aircraft, R4+DK operated by 2./NJG 1, is shown here with the glazed nose area just visible. Note the white band around the rear fuselage, applied to almost all Luftwaffe aircraft operating in the Mediterranean area, and the yellow undersurfaces on the engine cowlings which were to assist Axis ground forces in identifying friendly aircraft.

This Ju 88 C, also of NJG 2 but probably seen in Holland or Belgium, has again retained its 70/71 uppersurfaces but has had the undersurfaces, including the national markings and most of the code letters, overpainted in matt black. Only the individual aircraft letter 'C' remains, and the sooty appearance of the black suggests this may have been a temporary distemper. This machine carried only a single gun in the rear canopy.

Emblem of the Nachtjagd

Above and above right: The yellow identification markings under the engines are also shown in these views of two otherwise overall black Ju 88 Cs, also of I./NJG 2, but with the white fuselage band positioned further forward. The aircraft coded R4+HH with the damaged wingtip (above) is believed to have been flown by Oblt. Gerhard Böhme of 1./NJG 2, and although the forward part of the fuselage is covered to protect the cockpit from the sun, the Englandblitz emblem was almost certainly carried on the nose in the same position as shown in the detail (above left).

Junkers Ju 88 C-6 'R4+HH' of 1./NJG 2, Catania, early 1942

Although camouflaged in a dull, overall matt black scheme, the overall appearance of this aircraft was relieved by the white of the national markings, the grey 77 code, the white fuselage band and the yellow identification panels under the engines. The tail was marked with three victory bars and although this aircraft is believed to have been flown by Oblt. Gerhard Böhme in early 1942, he had only two confirmed victories at that time: a Blenheim, destroyed on 17 April 1940 when he was flying with 1./ZG 76, and a Whitley on 3 January 1941. Note that although the whole nose is covered in the accompanying photograph (ABOVE LEFT), what appears to be a Nachtjagd badge shows faintly though the material and has therefore been shown in the profile.

The first examples of the Bf 110 G-4 were delivered to III./NJG 3 at Stade in early 1943 and this photograph showing two aircraft of 9./NJG 3 in daylight over northern Germany was probably taken soon afterwards, by which time the earlier all-black night fighter finish began to give way to the standard 74/75/76 day fighter scheme. These machines are coded D5+DT and D5+LT and, for security reasons, have the first two characters of the code about one-fifth of the size of the remaining letters. Both aircraft are fitted with FuG 212 airborne radar, but note that the machine nearest the camera also has bomb racks under the wings and the fuselage centre section.

Messerschmitt Bf 110 G-4 'D5+LT' of 9./NJG 3, Stade, early 1943

This aircraft was finished in the standard 1943 day fighter scheme of grey 76 on the undersurfaces with 74 and 75 on the uppersurfaces, these two colours breaking up into mottles on the fuselage sides. The fuselage Balkenkreuz was the white outline type and the fuselage code was in black. Note that this aircraft retained the bomb racks under the wings and fuselage and has the same tail fins as on earlier Bf 110 variants.

This aircraft belonged to 4./NJG 1 and is reported to have taken part in Operation 'Donnerkeil', for which purpose the uppersurfaces were re-camouflaged in a green finish more appropriate for operations over the sea. Note again the white rear fuselage band, possibly applied for the operation to identify the aircraft as friendly to the German warships.

Right: A number of photographs depicting night fighters belonging to units known only to have been based in the West show the application of theatre markings normally associated with the Eastern Front or the Mediterranean. The white band around the rear fuselage and the white under the wingtips of G9+BS, a Bf 110 of 8./NJG 1, are therefore unusual but may have been applied as a recognition aid during Operation 'Donnerkeil' when the battleships Scharnhorst and Gneisenau and the heavy cruiser Prinz Eugen sailed from France to Germany via the English Channel.

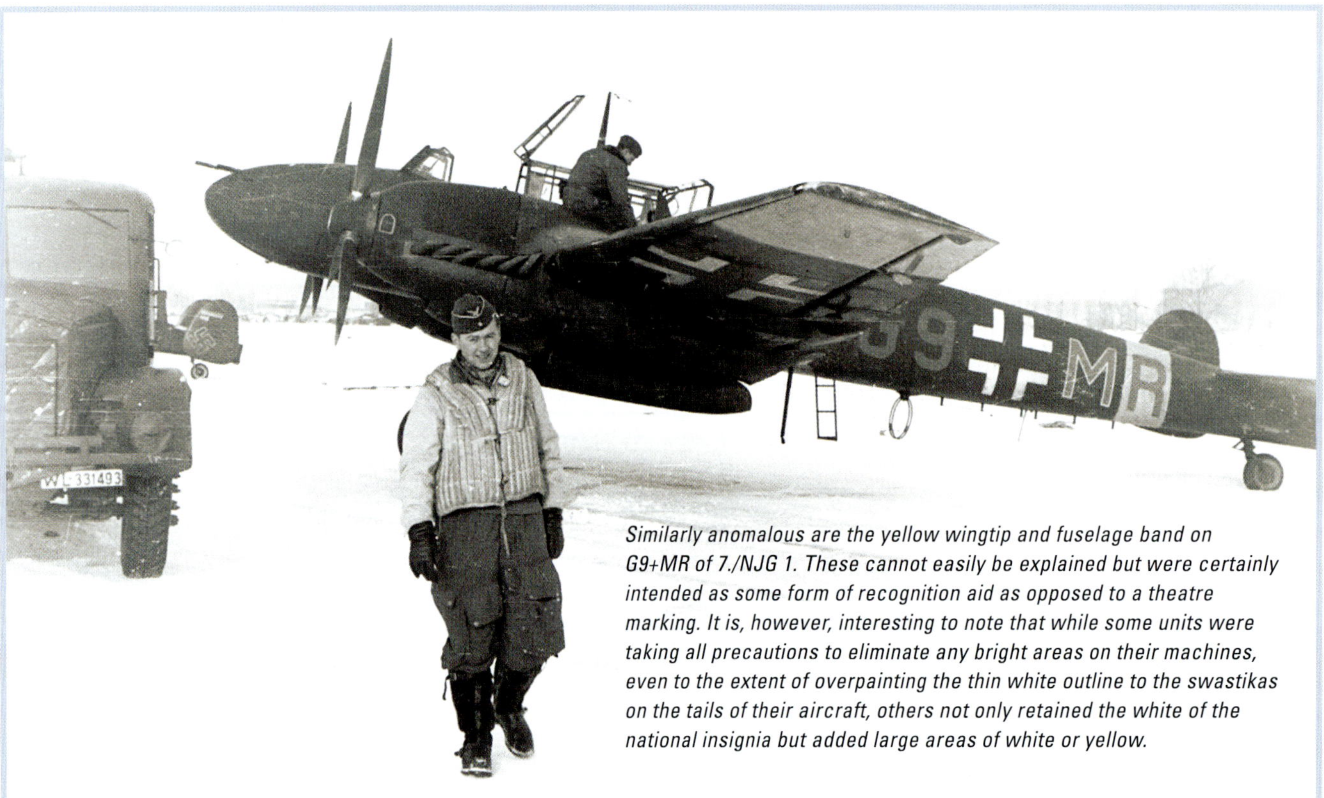

Similarly anomalous are the yellow wingtip and fuselage band on G9+MR of 7./NJG 1. These cannot easily be explained but were certainly intended as some form of recognition aid as opposed to a theatre marking. It is, however, interesting to note that while some units were taking all precautions to eliminate any bright areas on their machines, even to the extent of overpainting the thin white outline to the swastikas on the tails of their aircraft, others not only retained the white of the national insignia but added large areas of white or yellow.

"I saw ahead of me the shadow of a Wellington"

Lt. Heinz Rökker, I./NJG 2

In November 1941, just a month after the cessation of its long-range intruder missions to England, I./NJG 2 was transferred to Catania in Sicily. From here it was deployed on long-range night fighter missions to Malta, Sicily, Crete and to North Africa where, in June 1942, Lt. Heinz Rökker of I./NJG 2 achieved his first night victories.

MY first night fighter victory came on 25 June 1942 in North Africa. With Carlos Nugent as my radio operator and Georg Frieben as mechanic, we had taken off from Derna at 22.00 hrs with the task of finding and shooting down in freelance action, enemy aircraft that were bombing German supply traffic.

It was a bright, moonlit night. Visibility was good, as one would expect in a desert climate. In order to better locate their targets, the British were using flares, but by doing so they made our job easier because, logically, they must have been close to and above the flares. Finding the bombers' altitude, however, was a matter of luck. We discovered that the height from which they carried out their attack was mostly in the region of 500 to 1,000 metres, because at this altitude they were just out of the range of the light Flak, and the 8.8 cm guns of the German anti-aircraft units could only rarely be brought into action because it was more important to deploy them in the front line.

At 23.45 hrs, in the vicinity of Mersa Matruh, at an altitude of about 500 metres and a range of about 400 metres, I saw ahead of me the shadow of a Wellington. At once I switched on my guns and the reflector sight (*Revi*) and opened my throttles in order not to let the enemy out of my sight. I had not, however, allowed for the slow speed of the Wellington, so that I approached the aircraft so rapidly that I only had time to throttle back and give a short burst. I scored hits in the fuselage and the tail unit without coming under fire from the rear gunner, who had been taken completely by surprise by our rapid appearance. I had approached the bomber so quickly that it was only with difficulty that I avoided a collision. I managed to dive away when I was only a few metres below the burning enemy aircraft. I flew a full circle and then, through a thin layer of cloud, we saw the enemy machine hit the ground in flames.

During the same night, at about 00.09 hrs, we located another Wellington at about the same altitude. I adjusted my speed to that of the bomber and then shot its port engine into flames with a single burst. Without any defensive fire from the rear gunner, the aircraft went into a dive, but when it was near the ground it pulled out and made a belly landing. As it did so, the fabric covering the fuselage caught fire, and we could clearly see the lattice construction in the light of the flames. We landed at Derna without any problem at 02.10 hrs.

I had a very negative experience when I shot down my next Wellington on 28 June 1942, again near to Mersa Matruh, which I picked up at a height of 600 metres. We had taken off from Derna at 21.40 hrs and saw the Wellington at approximately 23.58 hrs. After matching its speed I moved into firing position and pressed the firing buttons. Unfortunately, only one machine gun and one cannon fired. We saw that we had scored hits, but the Wellington did not catch fire and immediately went into a dive. I was faster, however, and by reason of the good visibility it was unable to escape. In pursuing it we came close to the ground. Although we were flying close to the Wellington we did not receive any defensive fire from the rear gunner. It is probable that he was hit in the first burst of fire. Finally, we were flying so low that I could clearly see a group of lorries below me. I opened fire again, and set its port engine on fire. As I did so the Wellington lost speed so suddenly that despite throttling back I was unable to stay behind the enemy but overtook him on his port side. Suddenly there was a metallic noise in our cabin that I recognised from the first time I was shot down. We had come under fire from the nose gunner of the Wellington flying alongside, who was bravely defending his machine despite the burning engine. Again we saw the Wellington make a belly landing.

As we had been hit in the crew cabin and my radio operator and I both had slight splinter wounds, I began to climb in order to return to base. Suddenly we noticed that the water temperature indicator and the oil temperature on the starboard engine had risen to 'maximum'. I immediately feathered the airscrew and switched the engine off. As we did this, we were no higher than about 200 metres. Suddenly Carlos Nugent shouted out, "The port engine's on fire!" Because I was concentrating on switching off the starboard engine I hadn't been looking at the port instruments. Red flames were coming from the port engine.

The pilot of a Ju 88 had only a remote chance of survival if he tried to bale out through the ventral gondola at so low an altitude, and if he tried to get out through the cabin roof he was in great danger of hitting the tail fin, so I decided to make a belly landing in the desert. To make matters worse, as happened almost every night, a sheet of fog had formed on the ground. We had to rely on fliers' luck to find a suitable spot on the desert floor. The landing flaps were lowered successfully, and in that way we came down towards the ground in a state of tense awareness.

With my good night vision I could soon see the desert floor and started my first belly landing. In doing so, however, I stalled the aircraft very early in order not to hit the ground at high speed and so increase the danger of fire. The result was a 'passenger lift landing'. Our tail wheel touched the ground first. There was a heavy bump and the aircraft came to a halt after skidding no more than about 50 metres. There was a great cloud of dust, and then an eerie silence. My radio operator jettisoned the cabin roof as we touched down.

We left the aircraft by the rear exit as quickly as possible. The port engine was no longer burning as it had probably been extinguished by the desert sand. The belly gondola had been ripped off and was lying about 50 metres behind us. Fortunately, however, the ground thereabouts was relatively flat. After our first shock we were able to inspect the damage to the engines at our leisure. We could only find two shell holes in each engine and one in the cabin. It was a puzzle to us how we had come to be forced to make an emergency landing by only three hits. Probably the same hits had penetrated the water pipes in each motor. As we were getting our parachutes out of the aircraft, German soldiers approached out of the darkness with their machine pistols at the ready. They thought they were going to be able to take a British crew prisoner. We identified ourselves as a German crew and told them of our success and our bad luck. The Wellington was probably lying in the desert several kilometres away and further from the road. We never heard what became of the crew.

Continued on page 46

It was with heavy hearts that we took our leave from our fine Ju 88. It felt to me as if I was having to leave a badly wounded comrade behind. The German soldiers took us in a lorry to their camp. They belonged to a reinforcement unit. We were supplied with blankets and offered one-man foxholes to sleep in and as protection against bomb splinters, because there were several hours to go before sunrise. When I woke up the following morning, there was a scorpion on my blanket. He was carefully shaken off and quickly disappeared beneath some stones. Because of the distance involved and the remoteness, there was no question of informing our unit. Naturally, we wanted to be back at Derna as soon as possible. We left our parachutes behind and were able to travel in the back of an empty lorry in the direction of Tobruk, where the two drivers were going to recover food from a British supply depot which had fallen undamaged into German hands following the fall of Tobruk. Following an adventurous ride in the open lorry we reached Tobruk that evening.

The next day we began by going for a swim in the bay of Tobruk. Suddenly, Carlos gave a loud cry, waving his hands about and thrashing with his feet. We didn't know what was happening at first, but when he got back on land we saw that he had been bitten by a shark. On the lower part of his back could be seen the bleeding row of wounds of a shark's teeth. When we had recovered from the shock we went to the British supply depot. We each stuffed a British rucksack with preserved foods from all over the world. The contents of a pineapple tin had never tasted so good to me as they did on that day. Then we reported to our unit, which had already posted us missing. The same day we were picked up by car and greeted enthusiastically by our unit.

Luftwaffe aircraft participating in Operation 'Anton', the German occupation of Vichy France which followed the Allied 'Torch' landings in North Africa in November 1942, were marked with narrow white bands on each wing. This marking is clearly visible on these Ju 88 Cs of 2./NJG 2, apparently on a flight to Bordeaux which, prior to Operation 'Anton', was just outside the unoccupied area of France.

'*Himmelbett*' and the 'Kammhuber Line'

Towards the end of 1940, Kammhuber, impressed by the first successes using radar, began to integrate this technology into his air defence plan. His first step was to introduce a number of radar night interception areas, or *Dunkelnachtjagdräume*, in front of the searchlight belt which ran along the Dutch and North German coastlines. Initially there were six *Raume*, each with a code name that, in these specific cases, related to an animal or a fish, i.e. 'Lobster' or 'Tiger'. Each *Raum* was equipped with a radio beacon and allocated its own '*Freya*' and '*Würzburg*' radars. The information and readings obtained from these was then evaluated by a fighter control officer, known to the Germans as a *Jägerleitoffizier*, whose task was to direct the fighter towards a potential target.

The year 1941 saw several important technological advances that would eventually allow the German night fighters to intercept and ultimately shoot down greater numbers of bombers. The first of these was the continued improvement of the '*Würzburg*' radar and the subsequent introduction of the '*Würzburg-Riese*' ('*Würzburg* Giant') in the autumn, the effective range of which was increased from 18.6 to 49.7 miles. Furthermore, the '*Würzburg-Riese*' benefited from being able to rotate through 360 degrees and was fitted with a height-finding capability, an important advance for the controllers and the night fighters alike.

With these improvements, a new system of tracking and plotting the course of the bombers was devised. The '*Freya*', with its greater operational range of up to 120 kilometres, was used primarily to detect the approach of an enemy aircraft, and would track it until it entered one of the *Dunkelnachtjagdräume* (radar-control areas). Once inside the *Raum*, one of the '*Würzburg*' radars, known as the '*Rote Würzburg*' ('Red *Würzburg*'), would take over the tracking. In the meantime, a night fighter would have been scrambled to the relevant *Raum* and would be standing by, orbiting a radio beacon until the *Jägerleitoffizier* could vector it towards the bomber. The second '*Würzburg*', known as the '*Blaue Würzburg*' ('Blue *Würzburg*'), would then track and follow the course of the fighter. The position of each aircraft was then reported by telephone to the fighter control centre and their positions marked on a plotting table in appropriately coloured chinagraph pencils. This plotting table was known as the '*Seeburgtisch*' and was basically a ground glass table upon which was etched a map of the area covered by the radar. As the system became more refined, the chinagraph pencils were replaced with appropriately coloured lights projected onto the '*Seeburgtisch*' from below. Although there was a small delay between the times the target and the night fighter were reported and their positions plotted on the '*Seeburgtisch*', the *Jägerleitoffizier* was still presented with a fairly accurate picture of the aerial situation. The information was constantly updated and, with practice and experience, the *Jägerleitoffizier* was able to increase the number of occasions he guided accurately the night fighter into visual contact with the target.

Although not always possible, the intention was to bring the night fighter at least to within several hundred metres of the target. However, once this occurred, visual acquisition depended very largely on the weather and visibility. Therefore, in a further attempt to improve detection at night, the Germans produced a device codenamed '*Spanner*', an infrared system fitted in the nose of the night fighter. The device emitted an infrared light in order to illuminate any aircraft ahead of it, while a receiver detected the reflected energy from the target. Despite positive expectations, the Germans soon discovered that the range of '*Spanner*' was poor and that, usually, by the time the presence of an aircraft had been detected, the pilot could already see the target with his own eyes. Consequently, a new model, known as '*Spanner* II' was introduced. This model consisted only of a sight which resembled a telescope and was fitted in the cabin of the aircraft so that it protruded through the front of the canopy. It had been designed principally to detect the heat emissions from an aircraft's engine exhausts, the theory being that once the pilot had been guided to the vicinity of an aircraft, he was to use the device to pinpoint its exact location. Again, test results did not live up to expectations. It was found that in order to detect the heat emissions, the night fighter had to be directly behind and at the same altitude as its target. In further tests, its performance was so poor that it could not even differentiate between exhaust emissions and stars, and once flame-dampers were introduced, '*Spanner* II' was rendered completely useless. The failure of these systems, and the knowledge that the British were ahead of them in the field of radar, led directly to the second German technological advance in 1941 – the development of an airborne interception radar.

Prior to the outbreak of the war, the British had already developed their own airborne interception radar, and after overcoming what seemed like myriad technical problems with its effective range and reliability, the AI Mark III was fitted to Blenheim night fighters in the autumn of 1939. Nearly a year went by without any operational successes but, on the night of 22 July 1940, the honour of achieving the first radar intercepted victory fell to F/O Glyn Ashfield flying a Blenheim from the Fighter Interception Unit, who intercepted and shot down a Do 17Z[8] at 23.37 hrs,

[8] This aircraft was from 2./KG 3 and piloted by *Lt.* Kahlfuss. Both he and his three-man crew were rescued from the sea.

Bottom left and below: This Dornier Do 17 Z-10 was one of a small number of aircraft fitted with 'Spanner I', an experimental infrared device that had been designed to help pilots see in the dark. It consisted of an infrared searchlight mounted in the nose of the aircraft and a sight mechanism that protruded through the windscreen. Once the aircraft was airborne, the device would be switched on and the searchlight emitted an infrared light. The sight was then used by the pilot to detect any reflected energy, principally from the exhausts of a bomber's engines. However, in practice, the device proved to be rather ineffective and its operational life was short. 'Spanner II' was different in that the searchlight was deleted and the sight had a wider acquisition angle.

By the time of his transfer to the Nachtjagd in 1941, Wilhelm Herget had already shot down 14 enemy aircraft by day, nine of which were destroyed over England in 1940. He was one of a number of established Zerstörer pilots who made a successful transition to night fighting and finished the war with 58 night victories and 15 day victories.

off the Sussex Coast between Bognor Regis and Selsey Bill. By the end of 1940, several enemy bombers had been shot down using the new system but it was still far from perfect.

Despite this, Kammhuber became increasingly concerned by the British successes against German bombers which made him starkly aware of the deficiencies in his own defences and he therefore immediately invited the German radio industry to submit tenders for an airborne interception radar. One of the first companies to reply was Telefunken, which proposed adapting an existing radio altimeter, known as '*Lichtenstein A*', into an airborne interception radar. Subsequent testing of the device confirmed that such a conversion was possible, despite its operating wavelength being much longer than that of its British counterpart. This meant that *Lichtenstein*, unlike the British model, would require the fitting of large external aerials onto whichever aircraft it was installed. This did not sit comfortably with the Luftwaffe's High Command who at first rejected the idea because it was feared that the aerials would reduce the fighter's speed and operational ceiling, as well as its rate of climb. After some delay resulting from this rejection, the aerials were fitted and operational testing of the prototype, '*Lichtenstein BC* (FuG 202), began at Leeuwarden in Holland.

Once again it fell to pilots from 4./NJG 1 to be Kammhuber's guinea pigs in the testing of this new equipment, just as it had fallen to them in 1940 when they had proved the operational effectiveness of *Dunkel Nachtjagd* close-controlled night fighting. At first, many of the pilots and their *Bordfunkers* (radio operators), were opposed to the idea of having '*Lichtenstein*' fitted to their aircraft because of its detrimental effect on the fighter's performance. Despite these reservations, testing continued at Leeuwarden and the potential of '*Lichtenstein*' gradually became apparent to even the most cynical of the aircrew.

After entering the Luftwaffe in October 1939 and qualifying as a pilot, Heinz Rökker underwent night fighter training at Neubiberg near Munich. On joining the Nachtjagd he was posted to I./NJG 2 on 6 May 1942 and remained with this Gruppe until the end of the war.

The role of the Bordfunker was extremely important in night fighter operations. Carlos Nugent was posted to I./NJG 2 in May 1942 and became Heinz Rökker's Bordfunker. Nugent flew almost 150 missions with Rökker, participating in 62 of his 64 victories, and on 28 April 1945 became one of only a very few Bordfunkers decorated with the Knight's Cross. In this portrait, Fw. Nugent is shown wearing the German Cross in Gold which he received on 1 January 1945.

The importance of the role that the *Bordfunker* was to play in future night fighting operations should not be underestimated. Previously, it had been his responsibility to man the radio, provide navigational assistance to the pilot, and help defend the aircraft in case of attack by operating the rear-facing 7.92 mm MG 15 machine gun, but with the advent of airborne intercept radar it became his responsibility also to operate the '*Lichtenstein*' set. The device itself consisted of three circular cathode-ray tubes. The first provided the target's range, the second indicated whether it was above or below the night fighter and the third indicated whether the target was to its port or starboard side. It was able to detect another aircraft's presence up to two to three kilometres away and, with a capable operator, the pilot could be directed to within about 200 hundred metres of it. This was a tremendous step forward for the *Nachtjagd* crews who hoped that it would increase their chances of success against the growing number of bombers now flying almost nightly to Germany, and also boost their confidence in this new technology as their victories grew. Much, however, depended on the ability of the *Bordfunker* to interpret the information displayed to him and then direct the pilot towards a target. All the most highly decorated night fighter pilots in the history of the *Nachtjagd* benefited greatly from having a competent and reliable *Bordfunker* to whom they owed much of their personal success.

The first success using '*Lichtenstein*' was not long in coming. At 00.25 hrs on the morning of 9 August 1941 *Oblt*. Ludwig Becker, the same pilot who had claimed the first *Dunkel Nachtjagd* victory, shot down a Wellington[9] which subsequently crashed near the town of Nieuweschans on the Dutch-German border. This first victory

9. This aircraft was from 301 Squadron based at Hemswell and was one of 44 Wellingtons tasked with bombing railway and shipyard targets in Hamburg. The Wellington was flown by F/O M. Liniewski who was killed, together with his entire crew. It was the only aircraft lost that night.

The introduction of airborne radar in August 1941 was intended to simplify the last phase of a night interception. However, the 'Himmelbett' defensive system, in which ground controllers directed night fighters to within visual range of their target, was now well established and early technical difficulties with 'Lichtenstein' resulted in the use of airborne radar being rejected by aircrews more experienced in the use of the purely radar-assisted ground control system. Only perseverance by the likes of Hptm. Ludwig Becker and his crew – whose aircraft was equipped with the only operational set until it became defective in October 1941 – proved the value of the airborne equipment and demonstrated that successes could be achieved, particularly on very dark nights. By 1 July 1942, Oblt. Ludwig Becker, second from right, had accounted for 25 enemy bombers and was rewarded with the Knight's Cross. The decoration was presented by Generalleutnant Kammhuber, on the far left, and the award ceremony was also attended by Hptm. Helmut Lent (third from left) and Oblt. Paul Gildner (fourth from left). The officer to the right of Becker is Obstlt. Walter Grabmann.

Originally a pilot with I./ZG 1, Ofw. Paul Gildner, seen here standing on the far left, claimed four day victories before becoming a night fighter pilot and when awarded the Knight's Cross on 9 July 1941, had been credited with 14 night victories, raising his total to 18. In this photograph showing aircrew of 5./NJG 1 at Leeuwarden in Holland in July 1942, the tail of Gildner's Do 17 Z-10 may be seen in the background. The scoreboard records 33 night victories, the latest being a Lancaster which he destroyed in the early hours of 9 July 1942. With a final tally of 44 night victories, he was killed on 24 February 1943 when his aircraft crashed following an engine fire. Gildner was posthumously awarded the Oak Leaves two days later.

using airborne intercept radar against Bomber Command was soon followed by five others, all achieved by Becker. This system of close-controlled night fighting, which had slowly developed over the previous year using ground radar units, *Jägerleitoffiziere* and airborne intercept radar, was to become known to the Germans as the '*Himmelbett*' procedure.

The full impact of this procedure was delayed due to the limited number of sets available for testing, and the *Nachtjagd* was unable to exploit this advance in technology. It would take further months of frustration before replacement sets from Telefunken began to arrive at the front-line units. In fact, it was not until February 1942 that the first four were actually delivered to II./NJG 1. There then followed several more weeks of delay before they were finally installed and declared operational. These few '*Lichtenstein*'-equipped night fighters were then eagerly distributed between the *Gruppenkommandeur* of II./NJG 1, *Hptm.* Walter Ehle, and the *Gruppe's* other leading crews. It then took until the end of the year before sufficient sets were available to supply most of the *Nachtjagd's* front-line units.

By the end of 1941, however, the German defences, nicknamed 'The Kammhuber Line' by Bomber Command crews, provided a formidable barrier. In the centre lay the '*Helle Gürtel*' or 'Illuminated Belt', approximately 20 kilometres wide and equipped with radar assisted searchlights and anti-aircraft guns. To the west were the *Dunkelnachtjagdräume*, each containing up to three roving night fighters that circled a radio beacon until they could be vectored onto a target, either by a ground controller or, when within range of '*Lichtenstein*', by airborne intercept radar. To the east of the Illuminated Belt were other night fighters waiting in the darkness for a bomber to be lit up by the searchlights before they moved in to attack.

The effectiveness of the *Nachtjagd*, using the various techniques available to it, can be measured by the number of victories claimed during these early formative years. By the end of 1940, just 42 bombers had fallen to the guns of the night fighters. With improvements in technology this figure increased dramatically during the next 12 months to 421 – a ten-fold increase by the end of 1941.[10]

---

10. Figures taken from the 'History of the German Night Fighter Force' by Gebhard Aders and published by Jane's Publishing Company.

Right: Walter Ehle (right) originally flew with 3./ZG 1 and was credited with three daylight kills before the unit was redesignated 3./NJG 1 and Ehle became a night fighter pilot. He is seen here as a Hauptmann with an NCO member of his crew and the tail of his Bf 110, G9+AC, showing nine victory bars. Following the first three bars representing day victories are six more bars, each with a black diagonal line to denote night victories. At the time of this photograph, Hptm. Ehle was the Kommandeur of II./NJG 1 and his sixth night victory was a Blenheim which he shot down in the early hours of 2 June 1942. Ehle was one of the longest serving Kommandeure and led II./NJG 1 from October 1940 until 17 November 1943 when he and his crew were killed near St. Trond. Since promoted to Major, he was landing when the airfield lights were extinguished; his aircraft crashed and he and his crew perished. Major Ehle was awarded the Knight's Cross on 29 August after 31 victories and at the time of his death he was credited with 39.

Right: Another photograph of Walter Ehle (left) who became the Kommandeur of II./NJG 1 in October 1940. In the centre is Hptm. Wolfgang Thimmig and on the right is Major Werner Streib.

Below left: The Nachtjagd's 100th victory was scored on 10 April 1941 when Oblt. Egmont Prinz zur Lippe-Weissenfeld of 4./NJG 1 shot down a Wellington south of Den Helder in Holland. Lippe-Weissenfeld was of Austrian descent and a former member of the Austrian Air Force. At the outbreak of the war he was operating with II./ZG 76 but transferred to the Nachtjagd shortly after its formation and scored his first victory on 17 November 1940. At the time of his death on 12 March 1944, he had been awarded the Oak Leaves and had 51 victories.

Right: Wolfgang Falck addressing members of NJG 1 gathered at the Hotel Amstel in Amsterdam on 26 April 1941 to celebrate the Geschwader's 100th victory.

The First 100 Victories Achieved by the *Nachtjagd*

	Rank & Name	Unit	Type Claimed	Time	Date	Location
1.	*Feldw.* Fritz Förster	8./NJG 1	Whitley	02.50	09.07.40	Heligoland
2.	*Oblt.* Werner Streib	2./NJG 1	Wellington	02.00	20.07.40	Münster
3.	*Oblt.* Walter Ehle	3./NJG 1	Wellington	01.40	21.07.40	Münster
4.	*Oblt.* Siegfried Wandam	*Stab* NJG 1	Wellington	07.40	21.07.40	Borken
5.	*Oblt.* Werner Streib	2./NJG 1	Whitley	07.40	22.07.40	Münster
6.	*Feldw.* Otto Wiese	5./NJG 1	Wellington	22.30	23.07.40	North Sea
7.	*Feldw.* Georg Schramm	5./NJG 1	Wellington	22.30	23.07.40	North Sea
8.	*Lt.* Pack	3./NJG 1	Wellington	01.14	26.07.40	Coesfeld
9.	*Ofw.* Peter Lauffs	4./NJG 1	Hurricane	23.00	17.08.40	England
10.	*Ofw.* Merbach	*Stab* NJG 1	Hurricane	21.30	27.08.40	England
11.	*Oblt.* Werner Streib	2./NJG 1	Wellington	23.24	30.08.40	Emmerich
12.	*Oblt.* Werner Streib	2./NJG 1	Whitley	00.30	31.08.40	Arnhem
13.	*Feldw.* Paul Gildner	3./NJG 1	Whitley	00.45	03.09.40	Sittard
14.	*Lt.* Kurt Hermann	4./NJG 1	Wellington	23.00	08.09.40	England
15.	*Feldw.* Hermann Sommer	5./NJG 1	Blenheim	23.15	10.09.40	England
16.	*Feldw.* Paul Gildner	3./NJG 1	Hampden	22.30	18.09.40	Groenlo
17.	*Feldw.* Paul Gildner	3./NJG 1	Hampden	00.28	19.09.40	Ziuwent
18.	*Oblt.* Heinrich Griese	1./NJG 1	Wellington	00.34	30.09.40	Bramsche
19.	*Oblt.* Werner Streib	2./NJG 1	Wellington	22.49	30.09.40	Bersenbrück
20.	*Oblt.* Werner Streib	2./NJG 1	Handley Page	23.19	30.09.40	Badberge
21.	*Oblt.* Werner Streib	2./NJG 1	Wellington	23.21	30.09.40	Menslage
22.	*Oblt.* Heinrich Griese	1./NJG 1	Wellington	00.38	01.10.40	Lonsingen
23.	*Lt.* Hans-Georg Mangelsdorf	2./NJG 1	Whitley	24.00	02.10.40	Arnhem
24.	*Ofw.* Gerhard Herzog	3./NJG 1	Wellington	00.55	15.10.40	Gardeleben
25.	*Lt.* Hans-Georg Mangelsdorf	2./NJG 1	Handley Page	03.02	15.10.40	Röwitz
26.	*Hptm.* Werner Streib	*Stab* NJG 1	Handley Page	03.05	15.10.40	Kalbe
27.	*Lt.* Ludwig Becker	4./NJG 1	Wellington	21.25	16.10.40	Zuidersee
28.	*Hptm.* Karl Hülshoff	3./NJG 2	Hampden	21.30	20.10.40	England
29.	*Lt.* Kurt Hermann	1./NJG 2	Blenheim	22.05	24.10.40	England
30.	*Lt.* Kurt Hermann	1./NJG 2	Blenheim	22.10	24.10.40	England
31.	*Oblt.* Walter Fenske	1./NJG 1	Wellington	22.40	24.10.40	Bremervoerde
32.	*Feldw.* Hans Hahn	3./NJG 2	Wellington	23.03	24.10.40	England
33.	*Lt.* Heinz Völker	2./NJG 2	Hampden	00.30	28.10.40	England
34.	*Oblt.* Lippe-Weissenfeld	4./NJG 2	Wellington	02.05	17.11.40	Medemblik
35.	*Hptm.* Karl Hülshoff	3./NJG 2	Wellington	18.30	23.11.40	England
36.	*Lt.* Kurt Hermann	1./NJG 2	Hampden	18.45	23.11.40	England
37.	*Feldw.* Heinz Strüning	1./NJG 2	Wellington	18.40	23.11.40	England
38.	*Feldw.* Hans Rasper	4./NJG 1	Wellington	23.23	15.12.40	In sea
39.	*Oblt.* Paul Böhn	3./NJG 2	Hampden	04.00	17.12.40	England
40.	*Feldw.* Wilhelm Beier	3./NJG 2	Hurricane	06.36	17.12.40	England
41.	*Uffz.* Gerhard Blum	1./NJG 2	Blenheim	09.00	21.12.40	England
42.	*Lt.* Heinz Völker	2./NJG 2	Blenheim	21.15	22.12.40	England
43.	*Lt.* Rudolf Stradner	1./NJG 2	Wellington	18.40	01.01.41	England
44.	*Uffz.* Helmut Arnold	1./NJG 2	Wellington	18.45	02.01.41	England
45.	*Feldw.* Hans Hahn	3./NJG 2	Whitley	19.02	02.01.41	England
46.	*Lt.* Gerhard Bohme	3./NJG 2	Whitley	18.50	03.01.41	England
47.	*Oblt.* Reinhold Eckardt	6./NJG 1	Whitley	23.18	09.01.41	Erlekom
48.	*Oblt.* Lippe-Weissenfeld	4./NJG 1	Whitley	22.46	15.01.41	Petten
49.	*Oblt.* Albert Schulz	2./NJG 2	Blenheim	02.30	16.01.41	England
50.	*Oblt.* Albert Schulz	2./NJG 2	Blenheim	02.45	16.01.41	England

Rank & Name		Unit	Type Claimed	Time	Date	Location
51.	*Hptm.* Walter Ehle	*Stab* NJG 1	Wellington	23.28	10.02.41	Nunspeet
52.	*Lt.* Leopold Fellerer	5./NJG 1	Handley Page	03.56	11.02.41	Alkmaar
53.	*Oblt.* Albert Schulz	2./NJG 2	Blenheim	01.10	11.02.41	England
54.	*Hptm.* Rudolf Jung	2./NJG 2	Wellington	02.30	11.02.41	England
55.	*Oblt.* Paul Semrau	3./NJG 2	Blenheim	04.15	11.02.41	England
56.	*Oblt.* Paul Semrau	3./NJG 2	Blenheim	04.20	11.02.41	England
57.	*Oblt.* Kurt Hermann	1./NJG 2	Hampden	06.49	11.02.41	England
58.	*Oblt.* Kurt Hermann	1./NJG 2	Hampden	06.58	11.02.41	England
59.	*Oblt.* Jusgen	*Stab* NJG 3	Whitley	23.19	14.02.41	Nijmegen
60.	*Feldw.* Heinz Strüning	1./NJG 2	Hudson	09.15	15.02.41	England
61.	*Feldw.* Heinz Strüning	1./NJG 2	Wellington	19.58	15.02.41	England
62.	*Feldw.* Ernst Kalinowski	6./NJG 1	Wellington	23.05	15.02.41	Zutphen
63.	*Oblt.* Herbert Bönsch	1./NJG 2	Blenheim	01.25	16.02.41	England
64.	*Feldw.* Ernst Ziebarth	2./NJG 2	Blenheim	23.40	25.02.41	England
65.	*Oblt.* Herbert Bönsch	1./NJG 2	Blenheim	00.10	27.02.41	Scampton
66.	*Oblt.* Kurt Hermann	1./NJG 2	Blenheim	01.40	27.02.41	Waddington
67.	*Ofw.* Paul Gildner	4./NJG 1	Wellington	02.58	01.03.41	Groningen
68.	*Oblt.* Herbert Bönsch	1./NJG 2	Blenheim	02.55	02.03.41	Scampton
69.	*Hptm.* Werner Streib	*Stab* NJG 1	Hampden	22.18	10.03.41	Venlo
70.	*Feldw.* Hans Rasper	4./NJG 1	Wellington	21.46	12.03.41	Medemblik
71.	*Feldw.* Heinz Mittelstadt	2./NJG 2	Blenheim	22.10	12.03.41	England
72.	*Oblt.* Heinrich Wohlers	8./NJG 1	Hampden	00.05	13.03.41	Nordhorn
73.	*Uffz.* Karl Kupfer	3./NJG 3	Wellington	00.55	13.03.41	Gr. Fullen
74.	*Feldw.* Hans Hahn	3./NJG 2	Blenheim	01.15	13.03.41	Leeming
75.	*Feldw.* Hans Hahn	3./NJG 2	Hudson	22.00	13.03.41	Waddington
76.	*Ofw.* Paul Gildner	4./NJG 1	Blenheim	22.48	13.03.41	Tolbert
77.	*Ofw.* Paul Gildner	4./NJG 1	Wellington	23.10	13.03.41	Burlanger
78.	*Lt.* Ernst Schmidt	3./NJG 3	Wellington	00.54	14.03.41	Cloppenburg
79.	*Feldw.* Hans Rasper	4./NJG 1	Wellington	03.20	14.03.41	Petten
80.	*Hptm.* Werner Streib	*Stab* NJG 1	Wellington	22.32	14.03.41	Helenaveen
81.	*Feldw.* Peter Lauffs	1./NJG 2	Wellington	06.53	18.03.41	Cromer
82.	*Lt.* Rudolf Pfeiffer	1./NJG 2	Wellington	07.20	18.03.41	Mildenhall
83.	*Ofw.* Gerhard Herzog	3./NJG 1	Wellington	23.05	27.03.41	Helenaveen
84.	*Ofw.* Gerhard Herzog	3./NJG 1	Manchester	23.30	27.03.41	Bakel
85.	*Oblt.* Walter Fenske	3./NJG 1	Wellington	23.50	27.03.41	Heuschen
86.	*Feldw.* Karl-Heinz Scherfling	7./NJG 1	Wellington	22.36	31.03.41	Harn
87.	*Lt.* Heinz Völker	3./NJG 2	Wellington	01.20	04.04.41	Raynham
88.	*Ofw.* Paul Gildner	4./NJG 1	Whitley	00.27	08.04.41	Groningen
89.	*Lt.* Hans Leickhardt	2./NJG 3	Whitley	00.29	08.04.41	Papenburg
90.	*Lt.* Hans Feuerbaum	2./NJG 2	Hudson	01.20	08.04.41	Wells
91.	*Lt.* Hans Feuerbaum	2./NJG 2	Hampden	01.23	08.04.41	Wells
92.	*Feldw.* Hans Hahn	3./NJG 2	Handley Page	01.40	08.04.41	Upwood
93.	*Hptm.* Karl Hülshoff	*Stab* NJG 1	Wellington	22.50	08.04.41	England
94.	*Hptm.* Karl Hülshoff	*Stab* NJG 1	Hampden	23.00	08.04.41	England
95.	*Feldw.* Hans Hahn	3./NJG 2	Wellington	23.45	08.04.41	England
96.	*Uffz.* Hans Berschwinger	4./NJG 2	Wellington	23.15	09.04.41	England
97.	*Oblt.* Fritz Gutezeit	*Stab* NJG 1	Whitley	23.27	09.04.41	Nordhorn
98.	*Feldw.* Karl-Heinz Scherfling	7./NJG 1	Short Stirling	23.37	09.04.41	Lingen
99.	*Uffz.* Karl Kupfer	3./NJG 3	Wellington	00.14	10.04.41	Rhauderfehn
100.	*Oblt.* Lippe-Weissenfeld	4./NJG 1	Whitley	00.59	10.04.41	Insel Burk

Bomber Command and the Thousand Bomber Raids

During 1941, many more Bomber Command aircraft than in 1940 had participated in raids on Germany and in particular in operations against ports, railway installations and industrial sites in the Ruhr. However, while the sortie rate had increased from some 17,000 mounted between mid-May and the end of December 1940 to 27,000 in the following 12 months, the bombers were operating with only the most basic navigational aids and the damage caused was very little. In fact, the Butt Report, first commissioned by Winston Churchill and published on 18 August 1941, concluded that on a moonlit night only two in five of the bombers were releasing their bombs within five miles of the target area. The report therefore caused a great deal of consternation within the British War Cabinet, as well as in the corridors of power at Bomber Command itself, for while the claims made for bombing accuracy were clearly flawed, the German defences were also beginning to enjoy greater success. This was particularly true of the night fighters, especially when the *Dunkel Nachtjagd* method was employed.

To further add to the RAF's problems during 1941 and early 1942, navigational aids required to increase the accuracy of the bombing were still being developed and tested. However, 1942 was to prove a turning point for Bomber Command. Two significant changes occurred at this time that provided the direction and impetus needed to put the bombing campaign back on course: one concerned policy, and the other leadership.

The shortcomings in the bombing campaign outlined by the Butt Report had convinced the Air Staff that a significant change in policy was urgently required. It was realised at a very early stage that accurate, blind bombing of specific targets was not a realistic proposition until navigational aids could be introduced operationally. It was therefore decided that instead of attempting to bomb only important industrial targets, future policy would be one of area bombing, in which the specific target was the morale of the German civil population, as well as that of industrial workers.

The second significant change came on 22 February 1942 when Air Marshal Sir Arthur Harris was appointed Commander-in-Chief of Bomber Command. Like his predecessor,

Prior to the installation of airborne radar, the German defence system relied on ground controllers directing night fighters to within visual range of their targets, hence the lack of any antennae on this Bf 110 of NJG 1, seen in Holland in 1942, with the then standard night fighter finish of overall black with code letters in grey.

"I gave a short burst of fire from my cannon and the Wellington caught fire…"

Leutnant Wilhelm Johnen, I./NJG 1

After qualifying as a pilot, Wilhelm Johnen joined I./NJG 1 and flew his first night operation on 26 February 1942, during which time he achieved his first aerial victory but was also shot down and badly wounded. Despite this somewhat erratic start, Johnen went on to complete over 200 missions and achieved 34 victories.

After I finished my course of studies at the Grammar School in Homberg in the Lower Rhine region, war broke out and I volunteered for service in the Luftwaffe on the basis of the qualifications I already had as a glider pilot. My training as a pilot in the Luftwaffe until my qualification as a night fighter pilot took place in Zeltweg, Vienna, Munich and Stuttgart. I trained on all types of aircraft up to blind-flying on multi-engined machines.

I flew my first operation on night fighters with the famous *Gruppe* I./NJG 1 which was based at Venlo in Holland, only about 32 kilometres away from my home town. This first operational flight, which took place on 26 February 1942, turned out to be nothing short of a catastrophe. British bombers were heading for the Ruhr area, which was defended by heavy Flak and searchlight units. My brief was to shoot down any bombers caught in the searchlights above 5,000 metres.

As I flew towards the target, I felt as if I was flying into Hell itself. Anti-aircraft shells were exploding at all heights. Searchlights were sweeping the area looking for bombers and bombs were exploding in the whole Ruhr area. Then I saw a Wellington coned by searchlights very near to us and on my heading. I gave a short burst from my cannon, and the Wellington caught fire and dived down into the inferno. After the attack on the Ruhr area was over, I turned on a north-westerly heading in the direction of Holland. Suddenly my radio operator, Risop, came up on the intercom – "*Herr Leutnant, there's a four-engined aircraft right above us*!" Unbelievingly I looked up against the starlit sky, because I had never seen a four-engined aeroplane before. It must have been a Short Stirling. My radio man's last words were, "*Have a go, Herr Leutnant, and God be with us*!" I made my attack obliquely from the port side and below. The bomber met our attack with all guns blazing, ripping open the cabin and fatally wounding my radio operator. A bullet wounded me across the surface of my left leg, while further bullets hit my Verey cartridges and the aircraft's fuel tanks.

The Me 110 was burning furiously. It went into a flat spin, losing height rapidly. I jettisoned the cabin roof and tried in vain to abandon the machine. The immense centrifugal force was pressing me back against the side of the cabin. I was sure that my end had come. Then there was an explosion, and I was hurled from the aircraft. I knew that I was on fire. I pulled my parachute ripcord immediately. The parachute opened – and then came the next shock: the parachute had been torn by bullets and one of the panels was fluttering in the wind. With all the strength I could muster I pulled the lines on the sound side of the parachute towards myself to try and stop the panels from turning inside out. In this way I came to earth with a bang – or, rather, a splash – in a lake in the vicinity of Südlohne. Fortunately, I still had my signal pistol, so I fired a cartridge into the air and hoped for salvation. Two men rowed out to me in a small boat and rescued me from my miserable plight. Two hours later I was in bed in a hospital in Duisburg with one leg badly shot-up and severe burns. It was about four months before my recovery was complete. Risop, my radio operator, found his last resting place in Südlohne.

Air Vice-Marshal Baldwin, Harris was given a clear and precise brief on how the campaign should be directed, i.e. with the primary objective of future operations being the morale of the enemy's population. This new bombing directive had been issued by the Air Staff a week earlier on 14 February and much of its faith in the success of future air operations was being placed in the development of a navigational aid known as 'Gee'.

'Gee', or TR 1335 as it was initially known, had been developed by the Telecommunications Research Establishment in 1940 from an idea originally conceived in 1938. It then underwent a series of service tests and operational trials in 1941 and was finally introduced into general service in March 1942. At this time, however, only some 30 per cent of the bomber force could be equipped with it as the number of available sets was limited.

To function, 'Gee' required three ground transmitters located about 100 miles apart but operating together and emitting a series of pulses in a set order. Each 'Gee'-equipped aircraft was fitted with a receiver that enabled the navigator in the bomber to measure the interval between receiving each of the three signal pulses. The navigator was also issued with a 'Gee' map on which he could plot the readings and thus work out the aircraft's position. The effective range of the device was about 400 miles from the transmitter and, at this range, it was expected that the navigator could plot the aircraft's position to within about six miles. If the range from the transmitter was shorter, the accuracy of the device was significantly improved.

The Gruppenkommandeur of II./NJG 1, Hauptmann Walter Ehle (left), wearing a prized RAF Irvin jacket, with his Bordfunker, Hans Weng, photographed on the airfield at St. Trond, Belgium. Behind them is their Bf 110 coded G9+AC with a white Roman II next to the Nachtjagd emblem to indicate the Gruppe to which this machine belonged.

The work of Luftwaffe ground crews, known as 'Black Men' because of the usual colour of their overalls, was essential in ensuring aircraft remained operational. Here, a night fighter Gruppe's armourers are seen checking and servicing the four 7.92 mm MG 17 machine guns in the nose of a Bf 110 F-4. Clearly visible in both photographs is the crest of the Nachtjagd.

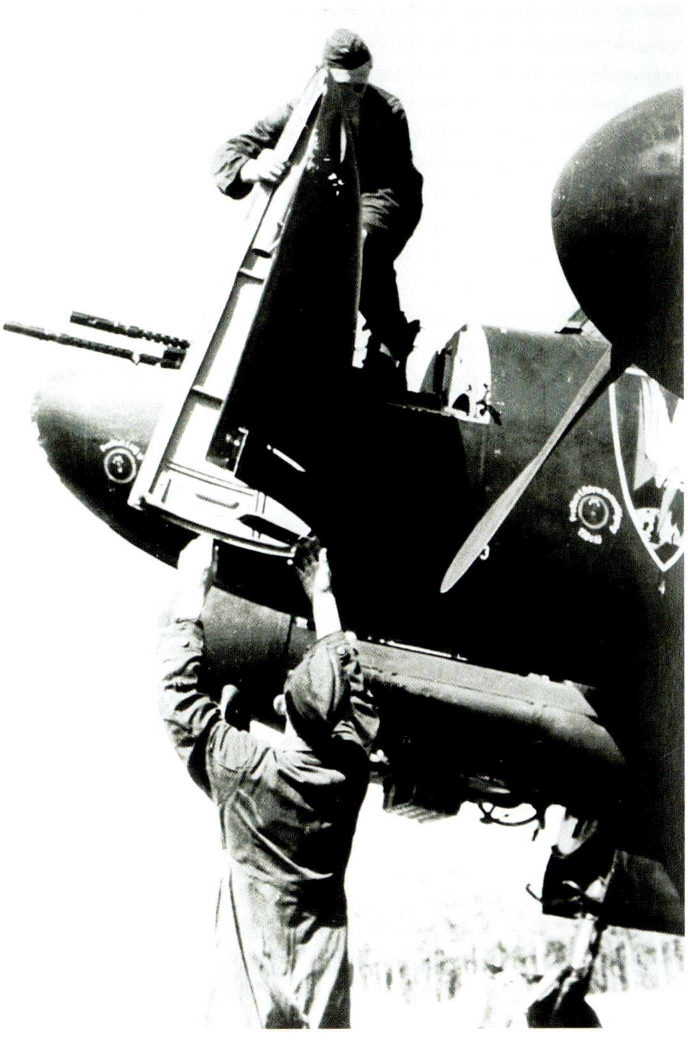

The Nachtjagd badge proved extremely popular and was applied to the mudguard of Major Falck's car (right) as well as other vehicles (below) and all types of aircraft including non-operational types. Examples are Werner Streib's glider, seen here at Venlo in Holland (middle left), and (bottom) this Fi 156 C-2 with the Stammkennzeichen CK+KF which served with the Verbindungsstaffel, or communications squadron, of NJG 1 at Quakenbrück.

The Englandblitz badge also appears on this Bu 131 which probably belonged to one of the flying schools that specialised in training night fighter aircrew.

When Harris took over Bomber Command, it was expected that the Germans would take only some six months to jam 'Gee' and he was therefore urged to make effective use of the device as quickly as possible. Initial attacks on Essen in the first half of March 1942 proved to be rather disappointing and highlighted the inaccuracy of 'Gee' at extreme ranges. Harris, however, was determined to mount a successful raid that would boost morale and show critics of the new policy what could be achieved with accurate area bombing.

After careful consideration, Harris chose the Baltic town of Lübeck, principally because it was situated on a distinctive and recognisable coastline which therefore made it easier to locate. Lübeck was also an old, Hanseatic city with narrow streets and buildings predominantly constructed of wood, which would burn well. Another important consideration for Harris was that the city was not classed as a major industrial target and the Flak defences would only be light. On the night of 28 March 1942, Harris therefore dispatched 234 bombers to Lübeck in three waves. The first wave comprised ten 'Gee'-equipped Wellingtons whose primary role was to mark the target with flares, a relatively new method of target marking first used earlier that month in an attack against the Renault works at Billancourt, near Paris. Aircraft of the second and third waves then released incendiaries and high explosives over the illuminated city. A total of some 400 tons of bombs were dropped which destroyed 190 acres of the town and killed over 300 inhabitants for the loss of just 12 bombers.

This raid was Bomber Command's most successful to date and proved that, if the target was appropriately marked and the necessary concentration of bombing was attained, similar results could be achieved against other targets. This point was again emphasised almost a month later when, on four consecutive nights commencing 23 April, Bomber Command attacked the Baltic town of Rostock, destroying a large part of the town centre and killing several hundred civilians. For the first time the German populace and press began to refer to these attacks as 'Terror Raids'.

The results of these two attacks made Harris even more determined to mount a large-scale raid that would restore confidence in Bomber Command's abilities. When he became Commander-in-Chief, Harris had some 469 bombers at his disposal, only a very small number of which were modern, four-engined types such as the Lancaster and Halifax. Opposing him was a growing German night fighter force that consisted of about 265 fighters, the majority of which were Bf 110s. By the end of 1942 the *Nachtjagd* had expanded to five *Geschwader*[11] with 15 *Gruppen*. Moreover, new technology, improved interception techniques and a growing core of experienced pilots had resulted in the *Nachtjagd* significantly increasing its number of victories. In 1940 it accounted for 15.5 per cent of the bombers shot down, whereas the remaining 84.5% was claimed by the Flak. By the end of 1941, however, German night fighters had shot down over half of all bombers lost over occupied Europe.

11. These were *Nachtjagdgeschwader* 1, 2, 3, 4 and 5.

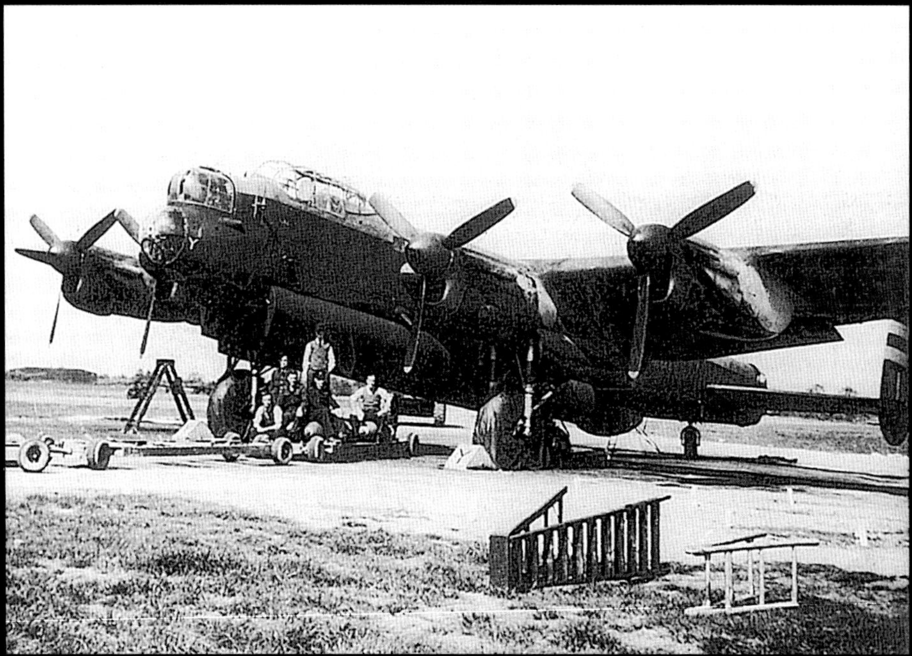

This page: At the outbreak of war in September 1939, Bomber Command possessed only a small number of twin-engined bombers that were wholly inadequate to the task of maintaining a prolonged or effective bombing campaign against Germany. One such aircraft was the Vickers Wellington (top left) which, although possessing the operational range to reach Berlin, could carry a payload which barely exceeded 5,000 lbs. The first four-engined operational type was the Short Stirling (top right) which, although capable of carrying a significantly higher payload than the Wellington, was restricted by its relatively short wingspan to a disappointing operational ceiling of only 17,000 ft. The Halifax was introduced to front-line squadrons in February 1942, early examples being fitted with Rolls Royce Merlin engines (above). Later, with the Hercules-powered Halifax Mk III, the maximum operating ceiling was increased to 24,000 ft. Also in early 1942, the first examples of the Avro Lancaster (left) were delivered to operational units and by war's end had been modified to carry a maximum bomb load of 22,000 lbs. The Lancaster proved to be the outstanding bomber of the war and over 7,300 were manufactured.

"We made a wide curve and again positioned ourselves behind our victim."

Leutnant Helmut Niklas claimed his first two victories during Bomber Command's thousand bomber raid against Cologne on the night of 30/31 May 1942. The following report was submitted by his *Bordfunker, Uffz.* Wenning.

FROM the ground we had already seen seven bombers shot down – would there be anything left for us? The waiting was agony but at last we got the order to scramble. Once we had reached our *Raum* we didn't have long to wait. We saw the first one at 1,000 metres and at a distance of 500 metres we recognised it as a Wellington. The enemy saw us almost simultaneously. He suddenly made a tight turn and we gained so much overtaking speed that we were unable to bring our guns to bear and passed the Wellington at close range. It fired at us, but much too tentatively; the threads of tracer didn't touch us. *Leutnant* Niklas pulled our aircraft round in a tight curve and we were back behind our target once more. From very close range we fired a burst into the bomber's port wing. It caught fire and we could see a faint glow.

We made a wide curve and again positioned ourselves behind our victim. We fired another burst into the fuselage and wing, which now began to burn brightly. The Wellington flew on for a short time with bigger and bigger flames shooting out of it. It then tipped over and went down like a comet, trailing a banner of fire behind it. There was an explosion just above the ground which lit up the surroundings. We were beside ourselves with joy. I slapped my pilot on the shoulders with both hands – our first kill!

We checked our position with a bearing from base, and then we were ready for the next. He was soon there. I was still bemused by the efforts of changing the ammunition drums at 4,000 metres without an oxygen mask when I saw a Tommy just ahead of us, another Wellington, about 700 metres away. He seemed to be flying rather uncertainly, but he wasn't firing. Had he seen us? We went straight into the attack.
The target grew larger, then it was suddenly vast. I held my breath and from point-blank range our guns fired into him, sawing into the fuselage and wing. I immediately saw flames coming from the stern. I was just going to shout out "He's on fire!" when *Lt.* Niklas yelled, "I'm wounded, I'll have to break off!" What I had thought were flames was return fire from the bomber's rear turret.

The engines droned on smoothly so the hits on our aircraft couldn't have been too serious. More serious, however, were my pilot's wounds. His left arm was hanging down, lifeless. *Lt.* Niklas could feel the blood pouring down and asked me to bind his arm. In the meantime ground control had told us to fly a heading of 060 degrees. But how? The instrument panel had been hit and the compass was shot to pieces. *Lt.* Niklas saw that there was a two-figure degree-scale, which would give us approximate bearings. "Tell the airfield control that we must have the lights on at once!" But the lights couldn't be switched on as there were bombers above the airfield. *Lt.* Niklas had sunk forward again but repeatedly managed to pull himself together until, finally, he said, "I think we'd better bale out – I can't go on!" He realised almost immediately, however, that to bale out in his condition would be madness. Then, to our left, the airfield lights came on.

"I can't see anything – it's all white in front of my eyes."
"A bit to the left, *Herr Leutnant* – not too much!"

Now we were flying straight for the airfield. We were almost above the lights before *Leutnant* Niklas saw them. There was not enough room to make a slow approach. He tried to get to the field by means of a side-slip. There were trees close beneath us.

"We're too low!"
"It's OK, we've got enough speed!"

I couldn't think what that had to do with it. A pond of some sort flashed past our wing tip. The airspeed indicator was still showing 300 kph.

"Don't forget the ignition and the intercom!"
"I can't go on!"

Leutnant Niklas fell forward again. Then there was a cracking noise, but quite soft. Soil was flung up against the cabin. We swept on just above the ground – it seemed endless. I sat there fascinated – was this what a belly landing was like? The cracking and banging got louder, then there was a jerk. I was flung to one side – all was then quiet. "Get out!" It was *Leutnant* Niklas – his head had been flung forward and he had regained consciousness. He sprang out of his seat, trying to loosen his parachute as he ran. Then he couldn't do any more. I let him slide down onto the ground, where I opened his blood-soaked clothing. The doctor then arrived and took him away. Only then, when I was surrounded by other men and they began asking me questions, did I realise how lucky we had been.

This Bf 110 E-1of 6./NJG 1 is the aircraft which the wounded Lt. Helmut Niklas crash-landed after shooting down two Wellington bombers on the night of 30/31 May 1942. As the Wellingtons were the pilot's first two victories, the existence of a single white victory bar on the vertical tail unit of this machine would therefore suggest that G9+GP was not his regular aircraft. The fuselage code letters are grey 77 and the aircraft's individual letter 'G' has been narrowly edged in yellow, the Staffel colour. Note that the abrasive action of the grass has worn away the black finish on the nose to reveal the 65 or 76 of the original factory finish.

From his increasing losses and the growing strength and efficiency of the 'Kammhuber Line', Harris realised that the key to any large and successful raid would be to saturate the German defences by concentrating the bomber stream. He knew that the main weakness of the '*Himmelbett*' system was that each German night fighter, operating in its own *Raum*, could only be directed against a single bomber. Therefore, by concentrating the bomber stream as it flew through the radar-controlled area, the German defences would be overwhelmed and the risk of his bombers being intercepted would be dramatically reduced.

Harris was also well aware of the propaganda value that a prestigious attack would bring him and his command, and with that in mind he decided to raid a German city with a force of a thousand bombers. After receiving official authorisation from the very highest levels he set the date of the raid, codenamed 'Millennium', for the end of May – a period of full moon. His first choice of a target was Hamburg, with Cologne as an alternative in the event of unfavourable weather over northern Germany. Harris was then faced with the arduous task of assembling the bomber force, ably assisted by his Senior Air Staff Officer, Air Vice-Marshal Robert Saundby. By drawing upon aircraft and personnel from various training and conversion units, within two weeks he had assembled a total of 1,047 bombers for the raid. On the evening of 30 May 1942, after three cancellations, the bombers finally took off on the first thousand-bomber raid. The target, due to inclement weather over northern Germany, was Cologne.

Bombers from the first wave were equipped with 'Gee' and long-burning flares so that the target would remain visible for the bombers that were to follow. Almost 900 of the aircraft involved claimed to have bombed the city and the raid was successfully concentrated into just 90 minutes, destroying some 600 acres of the city and 13,000 homes. But although the raid is generally regarded as having been a success, and provided Harris with the positive propaganda he had sought, Bomber Command had not totally overwhelmed the defences as planned. Forty-one bombers were lost, 22 of which were shot down over, or close to, Cologne. Of the 22, 16 were claimed by Flak and the other four by night fighters. Two more aircraft collided during the operation, a remarkably low number considering how many aircraft were in the air at the time. Of the remaining 19 bombers lost, most were shot down by night fighters in the radar-controlled intercept areas that lay between the Dutch-Belgian coast and Cologne.

Not wishing to lose the impetus created by this attack, and to make the best possible use of this large bomber force while he could, Harris mounted two further thousand-bomber raids, one against Essen on 1 June 1942 and the other against Bremen on 25 June. The attack on Essen proved to be a costly failure as poor visibility over the target obscured aiming points resulting in only 11 houses being destroyed – a pitiful number considering the size of the force involved. Indeed, the bombing proved so inaccurate that more property was destroyed and more casualties were inflicted in the neighbouring towns and villages of Duisburg, Oberhausen and Mülheim, than on the target itself. The third and final thousand-bomber raid on Bremen was considerably more successful. Despite heavy cloud over the town, the first wave of 'Gee'-equipped bombers started fires that were visible to the following aircraft and the destruction of property was widespread.

By the end of the three raids, Bomber Command had lost a total of 127 aircraft, over half of which had fallen victim to night fighters, an impressive performance by the *Nachtjagd* considering that Harris's policy of concentrating his bomber stream had succeeded in limiting the number of radar-controlled areas that the bombers had to pass through en route to Germany. This had significantly reduced the chances of being intercepted and shot down by roving fighters and had highlighted the inflexibility of Kammhuber's defensive system. The result was that only a few night fighter units could operate at any one time, while a greater proportion of the force remained on the ground, hoping that some of the bombers would inadvertently stray into their areas. Nevertheless, where radar-controlled night fighters did penetrate the bomber stream, they were becoming highly effective. This was demonstrated by II./NJG 2, which by the time of the raid against Bremen on the night of 25/26 June, had equipped virtually all of its aircraft with '*Lichtenstein*' airborne radar. Led by *Hptm.* Helmut Lent, this one *Gruppe* alone shot down 15 of the 48 bombers lost.

It will be recalled that Kammhuber's 'Illuminated Belt' had been created by appropriating searchlights from cities and towns. However, as many of these places were now increasingly being targeted by Bomber Command, the *Gauleiter* began to complain that the searchlights should be returned. When these increasing complaints reached Hitler, he issued the necessary order and, by

These two photographs dramatically convey the concentration and intensity of the ground defences faced nightly by the crews of Bomber Command. Clearly shown is the tracer ammunition from the anti-aircraft batteries interspersed with searchlight beams.

The morning after: a poignant photograph showing a downed Wellington bomber, behind which can be seen several 88 mm anti-aircraft emplacements with the muzzles of the guns raised skyward.

Above and above right: By the end of March 1942, RAF bomber losses over Germany averaged four per cent, one third of which were attributable to anti-aircraft guns, as the scattered remains of this Wellington bear testament, and two-thirds to Luftwaffe night fighters. The squadron to which this particular aircraft belonged is not known, but it was brought down in the southern suburbs of Hamburg in early 1943.

Below right: Because of Bomber Command's growing number of attacks and its ever-improving bombing accuracy, many German cities were forced to increase their local defences. Some of the larger cities, such as Hamburg, built large concrete Flak towers similar to the one shown here which has three double-barrelled 12.8 cm anti-aircraft guns mounted on its roof.

Right: The air war over Germany was not only successful in drawing away personnel and supplies from other fronts, but it also required German industry to produce defensive equipment rather than offensive armament. Searchlights were much sought after by local defence units and were produced in great numbers. The example shown here is a 150 cm Scheinwerfer 37.

late July, the 'Illuminated Belt' had been totally disbanded. In fact, although at first considered a retrograde step by many in the Luftwaffe, the return of the searchlights had little effect as the '*Himmelbett*' system had already resulted in an increase in *Nachtjagd* victories.

Nevertheless, at the time of its construction each of the 27 *Raume*, or areas that made up the searchlight belt, had its own control centre and two '*Würzburg-Riese*' radars. When the searchlights were withdrawn from 31 July 1942, these areas were converted from *Hellenachtjagdräume* into *Dunkelnachtjagdräume* and the radars were implemented into the *Himmelbett* system and designated either '*Rote*' or '*Blaue Würzburg*'. Now, almost by accident rather than by design, the German defences had become even more formidable as a consequence of removing the searchlights. Throughout the summer of 1942, aided by the longer summer evenings and with increasing numbers of aircraft fitted with '*Lichtenstein*' airborne radar, the night fighters continued to account for an increasing proportion of the bombers which failed to return from operations over German-controlled territory.

In spite of its losses and the growing opposition, Bomber Command continued its offensive while at the same time developing the technical and practical expertise required to improve the accuracy of its bombing and thus disrupt and destroy Germany's ability to continue the war. When 'Gee' had

Continued on page 66

Helmut Lent

HELMUT JOHANNES SIEGFRIED LENT was born in the small village of Pyrehne, close to Landsberg in the state of Brandenburg on 13 June 1918. His family was deeply religious and it was expected that Helmut would follow in his father's footsteps and become a pastor. However, from an early age Helmut showed an interest in all things military, particularly in soldiering and flying. He excelled academically and, after obtaining his Abitur, the German equivalent of the public university entrance examination, he left school in December 1935, just prior to his 18th birthday.

Lent was then obliged to serve the compulsory eight weeks of duty with the *Reichsarbeitsdienst* (Reichs Labour Service) which was necessary for any person wishing to enter the armed forces. Lent's preference was to join the Luftwaffe and he did so on 1 April 1936 with the rank of *Fahnenjunker*, or officer-cadet. He attended the *Luftkriegsschule* (Air Warfare School) at Gatow, near Berlin where he qualified for his pilot's licence on 15 November 1937 and was commissioned *Leutnant* on 1 March 1938. After completing basic flight training in July he was transferred to the fighter unit III./JG 132.

During the Sudetenland crisis in September 1938, Lent and his *Gruppe* flew a number of armed patrols over the area as a show of strength and as a deterrent against any possible uprisings by the Czech population. Following the successful annexation of the Sudetenland, III./JG 132 was transferred to Fürstenwalde and redesignated II./JG 141 on 1 November 1938. Lent subsequently became a member of the 6th *Staffel* and spent the next six months qualifying on various types of aircraft and generally improving his flying skills.

By 1 May 1939, the *Gruppe* had been redesignated I./ZG 76 and was based at Olmütz in Czechoslovakia, where it was re-equipped with the twin-engined Bf 110 C-1. Several months later, while Lent was still converting to the Bf 110, he was joined by *Gefreiter* Walter Kubisch, who had been allocated as his *Bordfunker* (Wireless Operator). Both men immediately formed a strong, professional working relationship that would endure for the next four-and-a-half years.

When war broke out with Poland on 1 September 1939, Lent flew several missions that day as part of a bomber escort to Krakow, but much to his disappointment he failed to have any contact with the Polish Air Force. The following day his luck improved and during a freelance flight over the town of Lodz he encountered and shot down a PZL 24 as the first confirmed victory of his career. He then participated in a number of further flights and, although he failed to add to his score of aerial victories, he did succeed in destroying three Polish aircraft on the ground. On 21 September he was awarded the Iron Cross Second Class.

When the Polish campaign came to an end, I./ZG 76 was redeployed and stationed at several airfields in the Ruhr area, where it carried out defensive flights over the Franco-German border. On 16 December, I./ZG 76 was transferred to Jever on the German north coast, and when Bomber Command attacked German shipping at Wilhelmshaven on the 18th, Lent submitted a claim for three bombers destroyed, although he was later only credited with two.

Following his success during this well publicised encounter, Lent spent the next three months flying uneventful patrols and training exercises. However, with the German invasion of Norway on 9 April 1940 he was again in action, this time flying as escort for Ju 52 transport aircraft detailed to drop paratroops on the airfield at Oslo-Fornebu. During this operation he encountered a number of Gloster Gladiator aircraft and, in the ensuing dogfight, shot down one of them as his fourth victory. Low on fuel and damaged by ground fire, he was then forced to land at the airfield. Within a short time of his landing the airfield was secured and troops and supplies were flown in. A few hours later the Norwegian capital was in German hands. By the end of the Norwegian Campaign Lent had shot down two further Gloster Gladiators and a Bristol Blenheim, taking his number of victories to seven. In recognition of this he was awarded the Iron Cross, First Class, and promoted to *Oberleutnant* on 1 July 1940.

Lent left Norway at the end of August, by which time France and the Low Countries had been invaded and occupied. The Battle of Britain was at its height, but Lent flew only one sortie to England and that was on 15 August from Stavanger on the western coast of Norway. During this bomber escort mission to the north-east of England, he was attacked by six Spitfires and his aircraft was slightly damaged in the ensuing air battle. Seven of his fellow pilots were less fortunate and they were shot down. Following his departure from Norway, his *Gruppe* was transferred to Bavaria where he spent three weeks practising night-flying. Then, on 1 October 1940, Lent joined *Nachtjagdgeschwader* 1, becoming *Staffelkapitän* of 6./NJG 1 stationed at Deelen in Holland.

After a frustrating period of almost seven months without achieving any success, Lent finally opened his account as a night fighter by shooting down two Wellington bombers of 40 Sqn. during an attack on Hamburg in the early hours of 12 May 1941. He then went on to score steadily throughout 1941 and by the end of the year he had raised his overall number of victories to 27 – 20 of which he had claimed at night. However, the most memorable day of 1941 was 30 August when, after having shot down a Hampden bomber the day before as his 21st victory, Helmut Lent was awarded the Knight's Cross.

On 2 September 1939, Helmut Lent of I./ZG 76 scored his first aerial victory in Poland. Soon afterwards, the Gruppe was visited by Adolf Hitler who was making an inspection tour of several operational Luftwaffe units. Here, Lent shakes hands with the Führer while in the background, fourth from right, is Leutnant Gordon Gollob, later to become the Luftwaffe's last General der Jagdflieger.

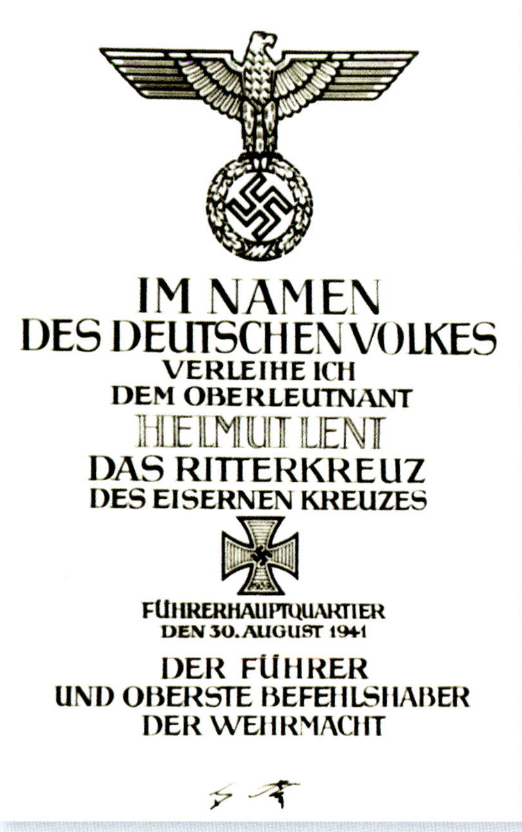

IM NAMEN
DES DEUTSCHEN VOLKES
VERLEIHE ICH
DEM OBERLEUTNANT
HELMUT LENT
DAS RITTERKREUZ
DES EISERNEN KREUZES

FÜHRERHAUPTQUARTIER
DEN 30. AUGUST 1941

DER FÜHRER
UND OBERSTE BEFEHLSHABER
DER WEHRMACHT

The award certificate that accompanied the presentation of the Knight's Cross to Helmut Lent on 30 August 1941.

Helmut Lent became Kommodore of NJG 3 on 1 August 1943, taking over from Oberst Johann Schalk, shown on the left, who had led the Geschwader since its formation on 29 September 1941.

The first day of 1942 saw Lent promoted to the rank of *Hauptmann*, and the following month he was made *Kommandeur* of II./NJG 2. Despite his extra responsibilities, he continued to fly operationally and accrue further victories. His first success of 1942 came on 17 January when he intercepted a Whitley of 51 Sqn. returning from a raid against Emden and shot it down into the North Sea close to the island of Terschelling. He continued to score slowly throughout the next four months and on 4 June he claimed a Halifax as his 40th victory. Two days later he shot down two Wellingtons and, on 8 June 1942, he was awarded the Oak Leaves to the Knight's Cross – the 98th member of the *Wehrmacht* to receive this decoration.

By the end of June, a month that proved to be the most successful of his career, Lent had claimed nine more bombers. It is interesting to note that unlike some of the other night fighter pilots who were to follow him, Lent only ever shot down one or two bombers a night. The most he ever achieved in one night was three victories and he did this only on four occasions. Nevertheless, Lent's score increased steadily and by the end of 1942 his number of victories stood at 56 making him the highest scoring night fighter pilot.

The New Year started well for Lent, who was promoted to *Major* on 1 January 1943 and, just a week later, he claimed his 57th victory by shooting down a minelaying Lancaster off the north-west coast of Holland. On 21 January 1943, a significant date in his career, Lent destroyed a Wellington bomber and became the first night fighter pilot to achieve 60 night victories.

Between March and July 1943 the number of raids against the Ruhr increased, but so did the number of Lent's successes, and by the end of Harris's campaign against the industrial heartland of Germany, Helmut Lent's total stood at 73. His courage and fortitude were rewarded on 1 August when he was appointed *Kommodore* of *Nachtjagdgeschwader* 3 and, a day later, was awarded the Swords to his Knight's Cross.

Between August 1943 and the end of February 1944, Bomber Command carried out a sustained bombing campaign against Berlin, during which time Lent added a further twelve bombers to his tally and, on 1 March, he was promoted to *Oberstleutnant* in recognition of his own continued personal success as well as that of his *Geschwader*.

During an RAF attack against railway yards at Lens and Valenciennes in France on 15/16 June 1944, Lent recorded his 100th victory by shooting down three of the raiding Lancasters. Two weeks later, during a raid against Hamburg on 29 July, he shot down two further Lancasters taking his total victories to 108 and his nocturnal score to exactly 100. As the first night fighter pilot to achieve this milestone he was awarded the Diamonds on 31 July 1944, at that time the highest decoration a member of the *Wehrmacht* could receive. His final victory came during an attack on Darmstadt on 11 September 1944 when a Lancaster bomber became his 110th confirmed victim.

On 5 October 1944 Lent flew to Paderborn airfield to visit his friend and fellow night fighter pilot, *Obstlt.* Hans-Joachim Jabs, the *Kommodore* of *Nachtjagdgeschwader* 1. Shortly prior to Lent's arrival, American bombers had attacked the airfield at Paderborn and the main concrete runway had been damaged. A temporary grass runway had been prepared for his visit and it was while he was attempting to land on this that his Ju 88 struck an overhead electricity cable, crashed into the ground and caught fire, seriously injuring the four men aboard. Walter Kubisch, the *Bordfunker*, died shortly afterwards, as did *Oblt.* Hermann Kloss, the second *Bordfunker* on board, and *Lt.* Werner Kark, a war correspondent who had accompanied Lent on several operational sorties. Lent himself suffered two very badly broken legs and died two days after the crash during an operation to amputate one of his legs, which had turned gangrenous.

Helmut Lent, posthumously promoted to *Oberst*, was subsequently buried with his crew with full military honours in the military cemetery at Stade. At the time of his death, Lent had 110 victories to his credit, 102 of which he had shot down at night – a figure that was only surpassed by one other night fighter pilot during the war.

Helmut Lent (nearest the camera), after being presented with the Swords by Adolf Hitler. Other pilots who received their Oak Leaves at the same ceremony were, from left to right : Egmont Prinz zur Lippe-Weissenfeld; Manfred Meurer; Joachim Kirschner; Heinrich Ehrler; Werner Schröer; and Theodor Weissenberger.

Following the award ceremonies at Hitler's headquarters at Rastenburg on 10 and 11 August 1943, the recipients line up for an official photograph. From left to right: Schröer, Ehrler, Lippe-Weissenfeld, Lent, Meurer, Kirschner and Weissenberger, all wearing their new decorations.

Lent with his Bordfunker, Ofw. Walter Kubisch, who received the Knight's Cross on 31 December 1943.

On 31 July 1944, Lent became the 15th recipient of the Diamonds, which he received personally from Adolf Hitler. By the end of the war only one other night fighter pilot, Heinz Schnaufer, would be presented with this rare and prestigious award.

Shortly after 13.20 hrs on 5 October 1944, Lent was approaching a temporary landing strip at Paderborn to visit his friend Obstlt. Hans-Joachim Jabs when his Ju 88 struck an overhead power cable and crashed. The three other members of the crew all died within hours of the accident and Lent himself died two days later. The four airmen were buried together in a communal grave at Stade.

Amongst the senior Luftwaffe officers who attended the funeral of Lent and his crew was Generalleutnant Josef Schmid, seen here at the graveside.

The Bf 110 D-0 was developed as a specialised long-range heavy fighter in the spring of 1940. It featured a 1,050 litre auxiliary fuel tank in a large plywood and fabric fairing under the forward fuselage which resulted in the nickname 'Dackelbauch', or 'Dachshund's Belly' and required the two MG FF cannon in the lower forward fuselage to be removed. The type first saw service with the Zerstörer units but was not popular due to the explosive fumes which remained in the tank when empty. Nevertheless, and despite the reduced forward-firing armament, II./NJG 1 operated the Bf 110 D-0, D-1, D-2 and D-3 sub-types throughout 1942 until it largely disappeared from the Gruppe's inventory at the end of the year. This particular example, which is believed to have flown with 6./NJG 1 at Deelen in 1941 or 1942, is camouflaged in a black night finish although the fuselage fuel tank is clearly still blue 65.

become operational in March 1942, it had been anticipated that the Germans would develop countermeasures within six months, so even before it entered service another type of navigational aid was already being developed. Codenamed 'Oboe', it operated using radar rather than radio waves and, unlike its predecessor, could not therefore be jammed.

In addition to the introduction of 'Oboe', a specialist unit was formed from selected bomber crews which was to find and mark targets for the main bomber force using coloured pyrotechnic flares as target indicators. This unit, originally known as the Target Finding Force, was eventually renamed the Pathfinder Force and was first employed on the night of 18/19 August 1942 against Flensburg. The results of this raid were less successful than anticipated, however, as the weather over the target was poor and the Pathfinder aircraft had yet to be equipped with sophisticated navigational aids. The long-awaited breakthrough came in December 1942 when the first Pathfinder aircraft were fitted with 'Oboe'. Initially its range was restricted due to the operational ceiling of the bomber carrying it and the curvature of the earth but 'Oboe' later became especially effective when fitted to the de Havilland Mosquito, which had a much greater ceiling of 10,000 metres. In a number of attacks made against targets in the Ruhr, the 'Oboe'-Pathfinder combination resulted in greatly improved bombing accuracy.

An unusual variation of the night fighter badge in which the diving eagle and lightning bolt has been replaced by a white Ace of Spades with stylised red wings. The central motif on this badge may be associated with that used in 1939 by 10.(Nacht)/JG 72 (see page 14) and the pilot seen here is Ofw. Paul Gildner.

Encouraged by the results of the Ruhr attacks, Harris decided to concentrate his bomber force against the industrial heartland of Germany, and between 5 March and 5 July 1943 a series of 29 major raids was carried out in which a prime objective was Essen. Although targeted on a large number of earlier occasions, inaccurate bombing had allowed this industrial town to remain relatively unscathed but, with the advent of 'Oboe', this changed. After attacks on 5/6 March and again on 12/13 March 1943, some 160 acres of the town and a substantial part of the important Krupp steelmaking works were destroyed and similar raids were repeated against such other towns and cities as Düsseldorf, Cologne and Dortmund. However, despite Bomber Command's improved accuracy and the introduction of the Lancaster bomber in greater numbers during 1942 and 1943, the German night fighters had also been making technological and tactical advances and making their presence felt in ever growing numbers.

An interesting photograph, probably taken in 1942, of a Bf 110 E-2 of II./NJG 3 at Schleswig, the main base of this Gruppe from September 1941 to March 1944. Just visible on the fuselage is the Geschwader code D5 in light grey and what appears to be a single victory bar on the starboard tail unit. Note also the Roman numeral indicating II. Gruppe positioned near the Englandblitz emblem on the forward fuselage and that only the undersurfaces and the sides of the fuselage and engine nacelles have been camouflaged in black, the uppersurfaces remaining in the day fighter colours of 74 and 75. The aircraft from which the Bf 110 was photographed is a Ju 86.

Above: A Ju 88 C-6 of NJG 2, probably in the summer of 1942. All white areas in the national markings have been blacked out, even in the Balkenkreuz under each wing, although the bright blue undersurfaces have been retained.

Right, below and opposite: This crash-landed Ju 88 C-4 was coded R4+MT and belonged to 9./NJG 2. The aircraft was photographed in the summer of 1942, and although the unit was at that time stationed at Gilze-Rijen in Holland, it is believed that these photographs were taken after the machine made a forced landing in an orchard or farm in Belgium. Note the straw spread over the wings and the camouflage netting placed over the rear fuselage to conceal the white of the Balkenkreuz.

Junkers Ju 88 C-4 'R4+MT' of 9./NJG 2, Summer 1942

This machine was somewhat unusual for a night fighter in that it retained a 70/71 splinter camouflage on the uppersurfaces with 65 on all undersurfaces. The fuselage code was in black with the individual aircraft letter 'M' outlined in white and the emblem of the Nachtjagd appeared on the nose.

Two views of 3C+AR, a Bf 110 E night fighter of 7./NJG 4 in flight, almost certainly over Holland, in 1942. The overall camouflage finish is black with the unit code in grey, the individual aircraft letter being outlined in white and repeated on the nose. This particular aircraft, shown equipped with two external fuel tanks, was flown by the Staffelkapitän of the 7. Staffel, Oblt. Karl-Heinz Kamp who, by the end of 1942, had seven or eight night victories and was awarded the German Cross in Gold on 1 October 1944.

These two photographs showing a Bf 110 C-4 of 9./NJG 3 were clearly posed for the benefit of the camera and were apparently taken at Trondheim-Vaernes in Norway in 1942 when the aircraft, coded D5+DT, was on detachment from its permanent station at Stade in northern Germany. The 9./NJG 3 was formed in November 1941 from 6./ZG 76 – part of II./ZG 76, the 'Haifisch' Gruppe – hence the shark's mouth design on the nose which has evidently been retained as a reminder of the earlier association.

Messerschmitt Bf 110 C-4 'D5+DT' of 9./NJG 3, Trondheim-Vaernes, 1942

The camouflage on this machine was a semi-matt black overall but the engine cowlings show signs of fading. The propeller blades and spinners were green 70, and the fuselage code was in grey 77 but with the individual aircraft letter 'D' in yellow, the Staffel colour, which was also applied to the tips of the spinners. Note the presentation of the shark's mouth which has retained the red outline and white teeth whereas the area inside the teeth has been overpainted with black.

Another shark's mouth aircraft was this Bf 110 C coded D5+ER of 7./NJG 3 which was detached from the rest of III. Gruppe at Stade and throughout 1942 was based at Lüneburg. This Staffel was formed in November 1941 by redesignating 4./ZG 76 which, for a short while in May 1941, had operated in Iraq.
The association with II./ZG 76 and Iraq has been maintained on this machine which has retained the shark's mouth decoration which originated with II./ZG 76 and includes the flag of Iraq in the row of flags painted beneath the canopy. Other points of interest on this machine include the white individual aircraft letter 'E' in the Staffel colour on the leading edge of both wings inboard of the engine nacelles, and the white teeth of the shark's mouth which have been overpainted with black night camouflage.

Messerschmitt Bf 110 C 'D5+ER' of 7./NJG 3, 1942

On this overall black aircraft, the red areas of the shark's mouth and its outline remained in red but, curiously, the teeth had been overpainted with matt black, although no such attention had been given to the national insignia which retained their bright white areas. The row of flags beneath the cockpit are those of the countries against which the pilot fought or in which he was stationed and represent, from the front, Belgium, France, UK, Holland, Greece, Iraq, Yugoslavia, Norway and Denmark. Note, however, that the flag of the United Kingdom is inaccurate in detail and also that the red and the blue have been reversed.

A late production Do 215 B-5 night fighter showing the aerials in the nose for the FuG 202 Lichtenstein BC radar. Also visible under the forward fuselage is a weapons tray which increased the machine's total forward-firing armament to three MG 17s and three MG/FF cannon. This machine was photographed at Leeuwarden in the spring of 1942 and was operated by Stab II./NJG 2.

Dornier Do 215 B-5 'R4+DC' of Stab II./NJG 2, Leeuwarden, Spring 1942

The upper and lower camouflage colours on this machine were divided by an undulating demarcation line which came well down the sides of the fuselage and continued to the nose in the same plane so that much of the front fuselage was in the undersurface colour. The camouflage was probably a locally applied scheme of 74 and 75 on the uppersurfaces while the undersurfaces were 76. The code letters were in grey 77 but with the individual aircraft letter 'D' in Stab green 25 with a white outline. Note that the white areas of the fuselage Balkenkreuz have been toned down and that the swastika on the tail has therefore been shown accordingly.

An air-to-air view of a Do 217 N-2 night fighter. The Do 217 N-2 entered service in late 1942 with examples reaching II./NJG 3 in February 1943. This particular aircraft belonged to 5./NJG 3 and, although the picture is of poor quality, the Lichtenstein aerials in the nose and the last two letters of the fuselage code, D5+SM, are clearly visible.

This view of another Do 217 night fighter in overall black night fighter finish provides a good indication of the size of the aircraft. In the air it was heavy and unwieldy and not particularly popular with its pilots.

Two Bf 110 C night fighters of 7./NJG 4 in the summer of 1942. The pilot of 3C+GR, the aircraft nearest the camera, is not known but 3C+LR in the background was flown by Ofw. Reinhard Kollak and is shown here with ten victory bars on the tail. Kollak claimed his first night victory while flying as a Feldwebel with 1./NJG 1 when he destroyed a Whitley in the early hours of 17 June 1941. He remained with 1./NJG 1 when it was redesignated 7./NJG 4 in May 1942 and on the night of 24/25 August 1942, he shot down a Stirling as his tenth victory. This photograph must, therefore, have been taken soon afterwards as Ofw. Kollak's eleventh victory was achieved shortly after midnight on 16 September. In the photograph (above right) Kollak may be seen wearing the German Cross in Gold, awarded on 12 April 1943, and the Knight's Cross which he received on 29 August 1943 when his tally had increased to 29 victories. Kollak was the most successful pilot of III./NJG 4 and finished the war with a total of 49 night victories.

A Do 217 belonging to the 4. Staffel of II./NJG 3. While this Gruppe's permanent base from September 1941 to March 1944 was Schleswig, the 4. Staffel was detached for most of this time to Westerland, although this photograph is reported to have been taken at Haguenau in France. For a night fighter, the Do 217 was a large machine with a wingspan of more than 19 metres and a length, including the FuG 202 aerial array and tail extension, of 19 metres.

Dornier Do 217 N-2 'D5+HM' of 4./NJG 3, Haguenau, France, 1943

Following the realisation that black camouflage was unsuitable for night operations, this Do 217 coded D5+HM was finished blue-grey 76 overall. Note the small Geschwader code 'D5' ahead of the Balkenkreuz which appears to be black, whereas the individual aircraft letter and Staffel letter are in Grey 75. The spinners and propeller blades were green 70 and the machine carried the 'Englandblitz' badge on the forward fuselage. Note the vertical tail units which were heavily discoloured by carbon deposits from the engine exhausts.

Two views of a Ju 88 C-4 coded R4+GM of 4./NJG 2, probably at Gilze-Rijen, shown after a taxiing mishap in which the machine lost its radar antennae and suffered other damage to its nose and propellers. This machine was flown by Ofw. Wilhelm Beier of 4./NJG 2, shown (opposite bottom) after being presented with the Knight's Cross by General Josef Kammhuber on 11 October 1941. Lt. Beier was at that time the highest-scoring pilot of I./NJG 2, claiming the destruction of 14 bombers. Note, however, that when the photograph (right) was taken, no victory markings are visible on the tail unit indicating that, if carried at all, Beier's tally was carried only on the port side. Note also that at this time the aircraft was clearly camouflaged in the standard 70/71/65 bomber scheme.

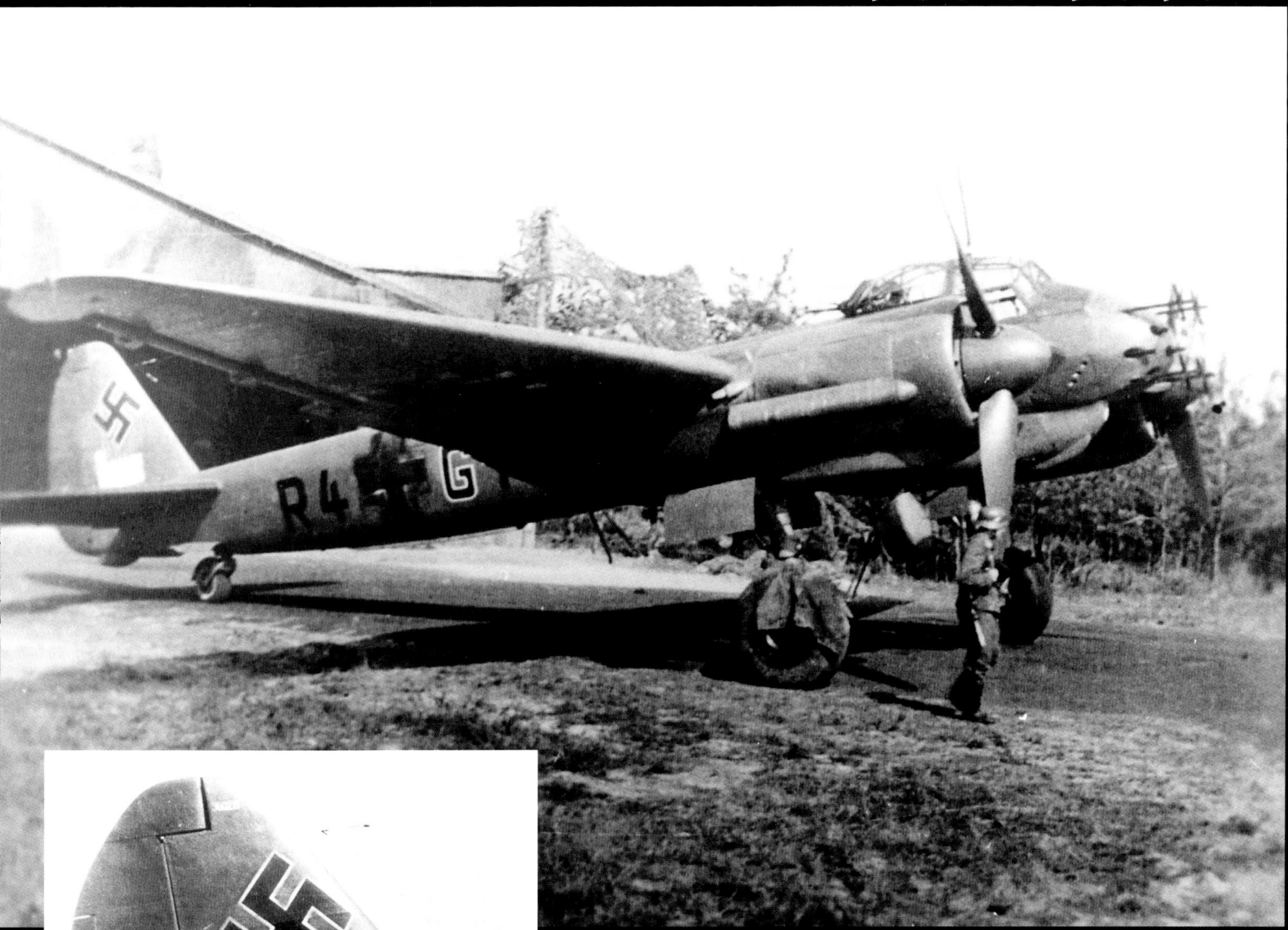

Above: This view of the same aircraft, again almost certainly photographed at Gilze-Rijen in Holland, shows that the machine has now been almost entirely repainted with grey 74. Also visible are the victory bars on the tail which have been left in a prominent white although the white segments of the Balkenkreuz on the fuselage and under the wings have been overpainted with temporary black distemper.

Above: The starboard side of the tail of the same machine showing the W.Nr. 360219 and 22 victory bars. Ofw. Beier's 22nd victory was an Avro Manchester which he shot down north-east of Moerbeke at 03.16 hrs on 29 August 1942.

Unidentified Do 217 N-2 crews with their aircraft showing (above) the aerials for the FuG 202 Lichtenstein mounted in the nose, the standard armament of four 20 mm MG 151 cannon and four 7.9 mm MG 17 machine guns and (below) the flame-dampers fitted over the exhausts of an aircraft which is believed to have belonged to NJG 4. Note that these aircraft again appear to be finished blue-grey 76 overall.

September 1942, Ofw. Wilhelm Beier was promoted to Leutnant and the following month transferred from NJG 2 to the newly formed 10./NJG 1 at Leeuwarden, apparently taking his aircraft with him. On the night of 15/16 October, Lt. Beier claimed a B-24, two Stirlings and a Manchester, raising his tally to 36 victories. These photographs were taken shortly afterwards and, although this is the same aircraft, W.Nr 360219, as shown on pages 76 and 77, the individual aircraft letter has now been changed to an 'F', but neither the Geschwader code nor the Staffel letter have yet been amended to 'G9' and 'U' respectively. In addition to the 36 victory bars, the tail has also been marked with a small representation of the Ritterkreuz awarded to Ofw. Beier in October 1941. Note also that the victory markings now appear on both sides of the tail and that the Englandblitz emblem, probably obscured by the spinner in the photograph at top of page 77, appears on the forward fuselage. Wilhelm Beier was later commissioned and was credited with 38 victories up to the end of May 1943 when he became an instructor. Although he was retraining on the Me 262 night fighter in May 1945, Beier, then an Oberleutnant, flew no more combat missions and survived the war.

Junkers Ju 88 C-4 'R4+FM' flown by Lt. Wilhelm Beier of 10./NJG 1, Leeuwarden, October 1942

This profile represents Lt. Beier's R4+FM after he achieved his 36th victory and shows the tail marked with a small representation of the Ritterkreuz and the appropriate number of white victory bars. Each bar contains a black diagonal line to denote a night victory and the date of the respective claim. Although camouflaged in a worn and apparently hastily applied grey 74, traces of the original bomber scheme of 70/71/65 remain, particularly on the tail and where the grey has weathered away from the engine cowling. Note that whereas the repainting around the fuselage code letters on the starboard side is quite crude, that on the port side is much neater. Traces of temporary black remain on the white segments of the Balkenkreuz and a variation of the diving falcon badge of the Nachtjagd probably appeared on both sides of the nose. As explained above, although operating with NJG 1 (code 'G9'), the machine still carries the 'R4' code of NJG 2, Beier's previous unit.

A Bf 110 E of Stab III./NJG 1 equipped with FuG 202 Lichtenstein BC. This aircraft is unusual in that, although of no advantage in the night fighting role, the four ETC 50 underwing bomb racks introduced with the Bf 110 E-1 have been retained. Experiments with a light grey camouflage finish had shown that shades of this colour proved superior in many respects to the earlier, widely-used overall black. From about the autumn of 1942 the black began to be phased out, although examples could still be seen some months later. This aircraft was coded G9+BD and is thought to have been finished with 76 undersurfaces and fairly large, widely spaced mottles of 74 on 75 uppersurfaces.

Below: An unusually camouflaged Bf 110 F of I./NJG 1, probably in the spring of 1943, showing the aerials for the Lichtenstein airborne radar. Note also the dark uppersurface colouring which extended down the fuselage side to terminate in an undulating demarcation line. Also of interest is the outer undersurface of the starboard wing which appears to have been painted white, the fresh paint accentuating the grime which has accumulated on the white of the Balkenkreuz.

August Geiger became a night fighter pilot in early 1941 and just a few months later, on 9 July, shot down his first bomber over the Dutch mainland. The aircraft, a Halifax, crashed some 10 km south of Nijmegen shortly before midnight. After being awarded the Knight's Cross on 22 May 1943 following his 26th victory, Oblt. Geiger destroyed a further 28 bombers before he himself was shot down and killed by a British night fighter over the Zuider Zee on 29 September 1943. He was posthumously awarded the Oak Leaves and promoted to Hauptmann.

This page: On 9 May 1943, a Ju 88 R-1 of 10./NJG 3 flown by Oblt. Heinrich Schmitt was ordered to intercept a British civil courier aircraft flying from Scotland to Sweden. The German crew, however, decided to defect and after signalling their base that they had engine failure, lost height to avoid German radar and headed for Scotland. As the Ju 88 approached the coast north of Aberdeen, it was detected by British radar and two Spitfires were scrambled to intercept it. The aircraft, W.Nr. 360043 and coded D5+EV, was then escorted to Aberdeen and landed at Dyce airfield at 16.00 hrs where Oblt. Schmitt and the two members of his crew – Ofw. Paul Rosenberger and Ofw. Erich Kantwill – were taken prisoner. The arrival of this aircraft, complete with working Lichtenstein radar equipment, was a valuable gift to British Intelligence and the machine was soon flown to Farnborough where the radar and the aircraft were thoroughly examined and evaluated. The photograph (above left) was taken when the 'Matratzen' aerials for the FuG 202 Lichtenstein BC radar were still in place, but these were later removed (above) and RAF markings applied. Note, however, that only the German national insignia were overpainted and the fuselage code replaced by a yellow 'P' in a circle. Otherwise, the original Luftwaffe 70/71/65 camouflage and the Englandblitz emblem were retained.

Night Fighting on the Eastern Front

In the summer of 1941, following Hitler's invasion of Russia, Soviet twin-engined and four-engined bombers began attacking targets in East Prussia and, on occasion, even Berlin itself. Fortunately for the Germans, these raids were carried out by only a few aircraft and the damage caused was minimal, but the Luftwaffe's High Command was forced to take action. Determined that Soviet aircraft should not be allowed to continue flying over *Reich* territory unchallenged, in June 1942 a small contingent from *Nachtjagdgeschwader* 5 was transferred to Labiau and Dammgarten in East Prussia.

Under the command of *Oblt*. Alois Lechner,[12] this contingent was supplied with a ground radar station which was mounted on a railway wagon for mobility and codenamed 'Sumatra I'. Responsibility for operating the '*Freya*' and the two '*Würzburg*' sets installed aboard the train was given to the Luftwaffe Signals Service Special Air Reporting Detachment. Carriages on the train were used to house a communications and evaluation centre, accommodation for the personnel and a generator to power the entire system.

One of the most successful day fighter pilots to engage the Soviet bombers at night was the Kommandeur of III./JG 54, Hptm. Reinhard Seiler, who claimed a total of 16 bombers destroyed during June 1942. Seiler finished the war as a Major with 109 victories and the Knight's Cross with Oak Leaves.

The only recorded success using these mobile radar stations in 1942 came on the night of 18 August when *Oblt*. Lechner himself shot down two DB-3 bombers over the East Prussian towns of Schaustenhof and Labiau. These were, however, not the first night victories claimed on the Eastern Front. In the early hours of 26 July 1941, several German bomber crews from KG 1 and KG 28 claimed to have shot down three enemy fighters. A fourth was claimed that same night by *Obergefreiter* Josef Kociok of 4./SKG 210, who reported having shot down an SB-2 bomber as his first victory of the war.

Almost a year was to pass before the next recorded successes at night were achieved and these came in June 1942 when the Luftwaffe was supporting German ground forces on the Leningrad Front. Since January 1942 the German Army had been desperately fighting to counter a Soviet offensive launched on a wide front along the Volkhov River to break the German siege of Leningrad. Here, pilots of III./JG 54, the famous '*Grünherz Geschwader*', began operating at night with their Bf 109s to counter the Soviet Air Force, which was attempting to support and resupply its own hard-pressed ground forces.

The *Gruppe's* first success was achieved by *Oblt*. Günther Fink of 8./JG 54, based at Siverskaya, on the night of 7/8 June 1942. With no form of airborne radar but taking advantage of the bright summer night, he proceeded to shoot down four R-5 light bombers in 45 minutes. Over the next week he reported having destroyed five more bombers plus two transport aircraft, taking his overall total claims to 11. Several other pilots were as successful as Finke and by the end of the month *Hptm*. Reinhard Seiler, the *Kommandeur* of III./JG 54, had himself claimed 16 aircraft. However, the accolade for the most victories in a single night went to *Lt*. Erwin Leykauf, Seiler's Adjutant who, on 22 June, shot down six R-5s in less than an hour and finished the month with a total of eight kills.

Josef Kociok began the war with III./ZG 76 and, after the German invasion of Russia in June 1941, transferred to the IV./Schnellkampfgeschwader (Fast Bomber Wing) 210. When night fighting operations began in Russia, he transferred to 4./(N)ZG 1 and within a relatively short space of time, shot down 21 bombers. He was awarded the Knight's Cross on 31 July 1943 but was killed two months later.

Despite the Soviet losses, which were comparatively small in relation to the number of sorties flown, the bombing raids and the dropping of partisans behind German lines continued. In response to this growing menace, Wolfgang Falck was sent on a fact-finding mission to Russia in August 1942 to find a solution to this particular problem. He began his inspection in southern Russia and travelled northwards, visiting local fighter formations and preparing individual reports on their particular problems and circumstances. At the conclusion of his tour, Falck realised it would not be feasible to transfer existing night fighter *Gruppen* from the West, and that the only viable option would be for local Luftwaffe units to organise their own defences.

During a tour of the Eastern Front in August and September 1942, Falck visited numerous Luftwaffe units to evaluate their ability to protect themselves at night against Soviet bombers. He is seen here visiting the Geschwaderkommodore of JG 54, Hannes Trautloft.

12. Lechner went on to command I./NJG 100 and achieved a total of 45 victories. He was later awarded the Knight's Cross but was killed two weeks later on 23 February 1944 when his aircraft was shot down by anti-aircraft fire.

Coat of Arms of the City of Ansbach

The pilot of III./JG 54 who proved himself most proficient while operating at night in Russia was Oberleutnant Erwin Leykauf. He shot down eight bombers whilst operating from Siverskaya near Leningrad, six of which he claimed in a single night.

Messerschmitt Bf 109 F-4 flown by Oblt. Erwin Leykauf of 8./JG 54, Siverskaya, June 1942

It is thought that Leykauf was flying this aircraft when, between 23.10 and 24.00 hrs on the night of 22 June, he shot down six Soviet R-5 reconnaissance aircraft. At that time Leykauf was relatively inexperienced and had only one previous day victory, but when he landed he had increased his tally to seven. The camouflage on Leykauf's machine consisted of a softly merging 70 and 71 on all uppersurfaces with 76 on the undersurfaces, while the spinner was green 70 with a one-third white segment. The machine carried extensive yellow areas as shown, and the fuselage markings comprised the badge of III. Gruppe forward and below the windscreen, the Geschwader's 'Grünherz' on the side of the cockpit and a white chevron and the wavy bar of III. Gruppe, both edged in black, either side of the fuselage Balkenkreuz. The badge on the engine cowling is the coat of arms of Ansbach, Leykauf's home town, and featured a crown over a shield, upon which were three fish on a diagonal band.

In his subsequent report to the High Command Falck proposed that special training should be given to those pilots who already had some knowledge or experience of flying and fighting at night, and that the most suitable formations to fulfil this role, in his opinion, were those from *Zerstörer* and bomber units. He further suggested that some bomber aircraft, such as the Do 17 and Ju 88, should be withdrawn from their current roles and equipped with machine guns and 20 mm cannon. Where suitable aircraft were not available due to operational requirements, other aircraft such as the slower but highly manoeuvrable Focke-Wulf 58 could be adapted for this role.

Falck was subsequently granted authority by *Generaloberst* Hans Jeschonnek to withdraw a number of bombers from the front line and have them refitted as he had requested. Shortly afterwards, on 6 October 1942, the *Luftwaffe's* High Command ordered night fighting operations to commence in the Poltava area of the Ukraine. In the meantime, selected bomber, *Zerstörer* and reconnaissance pilots were sent to Wiener Neustadt near Vienna, where they received basic night fighter training. By the second week of November the training was complete and the pilots were formed into five supplementary units and transferred back to the Eastern Front. However, within a few weeks of their arrival, the Soviets launched a massive offensive against the German Sixth Army at Stalingrad and within a matter of days the Sixth Army was surrounded. In response to the seriousness of the situation, all available Luftwaffe resources were assigned to the task of supporting the encircled German ground forces. Consequently, before they could be used for the purpose for which they had been trained, the newly qualified night fighter pilots were assigned to ground support operations and low-level attacks against Soviet supply columns. Due to the bitterness of the fighting and the intensity of combat, their numbers declined and their ability to operate effectively was quickly eroded. Even aircraft which were not shot down or destroyed on the ground to prevent them falling into Soviet hands were reassigned to other units, and in a matter of weeks the units had ceased to exist.

In order to bolster the makeshift night fighter units operating in Russia, IV./NJG 5, under the command of Hauptmann Heinrich Prinz zu Sayn-Wittgenstein, was deployed to Insterburg in East Prussia on several occasions during 1943. Wittgenstein accumulated 33 victories against the Soviets.

Units of the *Nachtjagd*, 1 January 1943

Unit	Date Formed	*Kommandeur*
NJG 1		
Geschwaderkommodore *Obstlt.* Wolfgang Falck		
I. *Gruppe*	22 June 1940	*Hptm.* Werner Streib
II. *Gruppe*	22 June 1940	*Hptm.* Walter Ehle
III. *Gruppe*	1 July 1940	*Hptm.* Wolfgang Thimmig
IV. *Gruppe*	1 October 1942	*Major* Helmut Lent
NJG 2		
Geschwaderkommodore *Major* Karl Hülshoff		
I. *Gruppe*	1 September 1940	*Hptm.* Rudolf Jung
II. *Gruppe*	November 1940	*Hptm. Dr.* Horst Patuschka
III. *Gruppe*	March 1942	Unknown
NJG 3		
Geschwaderkommodore *Obst.* Hans Schalk		
I. *Gruppe*	1 October 1940	*Hptm.* Lippe-Weissenfeld
II. *Gruppe*	1 September 1941	*Major* Günther Radusch
III. *Gruppe*	1 November 1941	*Hptm.* Heinz Nacke
IV. *Gruppe*	November 1942	*Major* Eric Simon
NJG 4		
Geschwaderkommodore *Major* Rudolf Stoltenhoff		
I. *Gruppe*	Spring 1941	*Hptm.* Wilhelm Herget
II. *Gruppe*	Spring 1941	*Hptm.* Theodor Rossiwall
III. *Gruppe*	May 1942	*Major* Kurt Holler
IV. *Gruppe*	1 January 1943	*Hptm.* Heinrich Wohlers
NJG 5		
Geschwaderkommodore *Major* Fritz Schaffer		
I. *Gruppe*	September 1942	*Hptm.* Siegfried Wandam
II. *Gruppe*	December 1942	*Hptm.* Rudolf Schoenert
IV. *Gruppe*	December 1942	*Hptm.* Sayn-Wittgenstein

Note: The list shows only the *Gruppen* in existence on 1 January 1943, hence III./NJG 5 is not included as it was not formed until April 1943.

With the surrender of the German Sixth Army at Stalingrad in February 1943 the front stabilised and a limited number of the supplementary night fighter units were reactivated. To bolster their small numbers, 10. and 12./ZG 1 were redeployed to participate in night fighting operations and IV./NJG 5, under the command of *Hptm.* Heinrich *Prinz* zu Sayn-Wittgenstein, was transferred to Döberitz near Berlin, from where it was detached to Insterburg in East Prussia. Wittgenstein – already an established night fighter pilot with 22 victories to his credit – found that, unlike the conflict against Bomber Command in the West, conditions in Russia were considerably better suited to night fighting. With no radio jamming and the Soviet bombers not expecting any fighter opposition, Wittgenstein was in his element and soon added further victories to his tally. On the night of 16 April 1943, he shot down two DB-3 twin-engined bombers and then followed this up with a further 'double' a week later. By the time he and his *Gruppe* were transferred to France at the beginning of May to assist in the defence of U-boat bases, he had shot down a total of five Soviet aircraft.

On 5 July 1943, Hitler launched Operation 'Citadel', his last major offensive in the East. The operation was an attempt to pinch off a salient in the German front line between Orel and Belgorod which had been formed as a result of the Soviet winter offensive of 1942/43. During the build-up for this attack, Soviet bombers caused so much disruption to the German Army's preparations that Josef Kammhuber was ordered to transfer an experienced night fighter *Gruppe* back to the Eastern Front. His choice, because of its previous experiences and successes, was Wittgenstein's IV./NJG 5.

Flying a Ju 88 C-6 fitted with '*Lichtenstein*' and his own version of '*Schräge Musik*' – a single 20mm cannon firing obliquely upwards – Wittgenstein began to take a heavy toll of the Soviet bombers. There were also available by this time nine railway radar stations, five of which were taken over by experienced staff trained in the '*Himmelbett*' procedure. In cooperation with these ground specialists, Wittgenstein shot down a further 29 bombers between 11 July and 9 August 1943, seven of which he claimed in a single night. During this period he operated mainly from Orel, flying with his *Bordfunker*, *Fw*. Herbert Kümmritz, who was destined to remain with Wittgenstein for almost a year and participated in 43 of his kills.

When Hitler finally called off Operation 'Citadel' at the end of July, IV./NJG 5 was retained in Russia where, on 1 August 1943, it was redesignated I./NJG 100. Wittgenstein, however, was transferred back to the West and appointed *Kommandeur* of II./NJG 3 on 15 August 1943. His successor was another experienced night fighter, *Hptm*. Rudolf Schoenert.

Night fighter units were to continue fighting on the Eastern Front for the remainder of the war, but such was the effectiveness of the bombing campaign in the West that the German High Command was never able to release adequate numbers of men or resources to the East. This lack of resources prevented the few German night fighter units fighting the Soviets, often against overwhelming odds, from making their presence more keenly felt. By August 1943, the tide had turned decisively against the Germans, and the Luftwaffe had finally lost its dominance in the night skies over Russia.

At the end of July 1943, IV./NJG 5 was redesignated I./NJG 100 and Hptm. Wittgenstein was transferred back to the West. He was succeeded by Hptm. Rudolf Schoenert, shown here, who finished the war as a holder of the Oak Leaves to the Knight's Cross and with a total of 64 victories.

Below: On 1 May 1942, XII. Fliegerkorps was formed to encompass the growing Nachtjagd and the existing Nachtjagddivision was split into three separate Jagddivisionen. Command of 1. Jagddivision was given to Generalmajor Kurt-Bertram von Döring, who was responsible for night fighter units in Holland, North Belgium and the Ruhr district of Germany. In this photograph von Döring is seen with the rank of Generalleutnant.

'Schräge Musik'

By the end of 1942, the German Night Fighter Force had expanded to a strength of some 400 aircraft distributed between 17 *Gruppen* which in turn comprised five *Geschwader*. The *Nachtjagd's* successes had also increased from 421 in 1941 to 687 at the end of 1942, the latter figure including 435 bombers destroyed between June and September as a result of a combination of good weather and the '*Himmelbett*' system of interception.

Commensurate with the growth of the *Nachtjagd* was an increase in the supporting infrastructure. By the beginning of 1943 there were almost 100 overlapping fighter control areas manned in total by some 40,000 personnel from the *Luftnachrichtendienst* (Air Signals Service) and each equipped with two '*Würzburg*' and an early warning '*Freya*' radar installation. This growth had been so rapid that it had soon become apparent that the *Nachtjagddivision* could not cope effectively with the expansion and, accordingly, in August 1941, XII. *Fliegerkorps* had been formed under the command of *Generalmajor* Kurt-Bertram von Döring to oversee command of a new Night Fighter Division. Overall command of XII. *Fliegerkorps* was given to *General* Kammhuber who was also made General of the Night Fighters, with responsibility for all night fighter units and their ground organisations.

Apart from the improvements in the night fighter system already described, new weapons to combat the bombers were also being developed, the most significant of which would change the very nature of night fighting. The Germans codenamed it '*Schräge Musik*'.

In principle, '*Schräge Musik*' was a vertically firing weapons system that allowed the pilots of the *Nachtjagd* to attack another aircraft from below while they themselves flew straight and level. This not only reduced the chances of being seen and shot down by the gunners aboard a bomber, but also increased the night fighter's chances of shooting down the bomber. It is often wrongly assumed that this type of weapon first evolved during the Second World War, but this is not the case. Towards the end of the 1914-1918 war, a number of German pilots had fitted upward-firing machine guns to their aircraft but the conflict ended before this type of armament could be tested and further developed.

For almost a quarter of a century any thoughts of such a weapon were forgotten until August 1941, when *Oblt.* Rudolf Schoenert submitted a report to *General* Kammhuber in which he outlined his ideas for fitting an upward-firing gun to night fighter aircraft. Although Kammhuber discussed the report with Helmut Lent and Werner Streib, two of his foremost night fighter pilots, they rejected the proposal on several grounds. Undeterred by this initial setback, Schoenert continued experimenting and had some upward-firing 7.9 mm MG 15 machine guns fitted into a Do 17 Z-10 *Kauz* II. Later, on 25 July 1942, Schoenert was awarded the Knight's Cross and when this was presented to him by Kammhuber, Schoenert seized the opportunity to again raise the idea of '*Schräge Musik*'. After a brief discussion, Kammhuber duly authorised Schoenert to modify three Do 217s with the experimental installation.

After five years in the Merchant Navy, Rudolf Schoenert began flight training in 1933 and went on to fly commercial aircraft for Lufthansa. He was commissioned as a Leutnant in the Luftwaffe's Reserve in 1938 and, in June 1941, he joined 4./NJG 1 stationed at Bergen in northern Holland. He gained his first victories as a night fighter on 9 July 1941 and, by 25 July 1942, at which time his total stood at 22, he was awarded the Knight's Cross. He is universally recognised as the driving force behind the introduction of upward-firing armaments in night fighter aircraft, the first prototype of which he introduced into his own Do 17 in 1942. This weapons system, which remained a complete mystery to all but a select few within Bomber Command, was codenamed 'Schräge Musik'.

By the autumn of 1942 the weapons testing centre at Tarnewitz was carrying out extensive trials using vertically firing guns against towed drogues. These, however, showed that aiming a weapon firing at 90 degrees was extremely uncomfortable for the pilot, who had to lean his head backwards. The result was that he lost his sense of balance and orientation and his ability to fly straight and level was badly compromised. This problem was overcome when it was discovered during further testing that the weapon was equally effective when its angle of fire was set at 65 degrees.

On 1 December 1942 Schoenert, who by this time had 23 victories to his credit, was transferred to Parchim and appointed *Kommandeur* of II./NJG 5. Despite the fact that this unit was already equipped with Bf 110s, he brought with him one of the Do 217s that had been fitted with upward-firing machine guns. The prototype installation soon caught the eye of an armourer, *Ofw.* Paul Mahle, who designed and built his own version of '*Schräge Musik*' from two Oerlikon MG FF 20 mm machine guns which he then installed in the cockpit of the fighter so that the barrels protruded through the canopy. Later in the war, when the crew of a night fighter was increased to three and four, the cockpit was no longer large enough to accommodate the weapon system and it was installed in the fuselage.

Mahle's prototype so impressed Schoenert that, without informing the RLM, he ordered his whole *Gruppe* to be equipped with this weapon installation. Word of this new weapons system soon spread to other night fighter units and they brought their own aircraft to Parchim to be fitted out with Mahle's design. The first acknowledged victory using '*Schräge Musik*' was claimed by Schoenert himself during a raid against Berlin and it is believed that this encounter occurred in the early hours of 30 March 1943. If this is correct, Schoenert's victim that night was a Lancaster which he shot down into the Baltic Sea close to the town of Rerik as his 24th victory.

By the middle of 1943 the fitting of '*Schräge Musik*' conversion kits had been officially approved and they were installed into available aircraft, although the machine guns used in the early experimental models were replaced with the more powerful 20 mm MG 151 Mauser cannon. Some pilots, however, such as Hans-Joachim Jabs, did not like the weapon and refused to have it fitted, preferring instead their aircraft's forward-firing armament.

Oberfeldwebel Paul Mahle, an armourer attached to II./NJG 5 at Parchim, worked closely with Rudolf Schoenert and built his own working prototype of 'Schräge Musik', which was soon fitted to all of the Gruppe's aircraft.

Despite these few reservations, '*Schräge Musik*' was eagerly adopted by many night fighter pilots who used it with devastating effect. Moreover, once visual or radar contact with a bomber had been established, it was relatively simple to operate. Having positioned himself directly beneath the bomber, usually at a distance of between 50 and 100 metres, the pilot of the night fighter would aim using an optical sight mounted in the canopy. The vast majority of pilots chose to aim between the engines of a bomber as the main fuel tanks were located in the wings and the crew was offered a chance to escape from their burning aircraft. A short burst of fire, using non-tracer ammunition to conceal the night fighter's position, was usually enough to set the bomber ablaze.

A crash-landed Ju 88 C-6 clearly showing the 'Schräge Musik' installation of two MG 151/20 cannon protruding from the fuselage. This particular aircraft, R4+LS, W.Nr. 750811, was being flown on a daylight mission on 30 January 1944 by Hptm. Friedrich Tober of III./NJG 2 when it was attacked and shot down by a P-47. Tober's machine crashed in a field south-west of Hardenberg, as a result of which it was written off.

A Do 217 of the night fighter training Geschwader NJG 101 showing a battery of four obliquely-mounted upward-firing MG 151 cannon positioned behind the canopy. A similar installation comprising six MG 151 cannon was proposed by Stabs Ingenieur Poppendiek of the E-Stelle Werneuchen but, like the four cannon installation seen here, was not adopted in large numbers as night fighter pilots preferred the usual twin MG 151 installation.

This method of attack became popular amongst the newer pilots joining the *Nachtjagd* who found it easier than the usual *von hinten unten* method which was still preferred by some of the more experienced night fighter crews. Another distinct advantage of using '*Schräge Musik*' was that, once the night fighter was directly beneath the bomber, it was extremely difficult for the bomber's gunners to see it against the darker backdrop of the ground. The night fighter pilot's target, however, was silhouetted against the lighter night sky. Having attacked a bomber and observed that it was on fire, the night fighter would peel off into the darkness, usually away from the wing at which he had fired, in order to reduce the possibility of a collision as his victim plummeted earthwards. Thus if the night fighter had opened fire at the bomber's port wing, it would peel off to port, and vice versa if the attack was against the starboard wing.

'Schräge Musik' in its standard and by far the most preferred form, seen here mounted in the fuselage of a Ju 88.

It is interesting to note that many of the young night fighter pilots, such as Heinz Schnaufer, Paul Zorner and Georg Greiner, who joined the *Nachtjagd* in 1942 and early 1943, became equally proficient in the use of their forward-firing armaments and '*Schräge Musik*' and were able to switch between either weapon as circumstances dictated during an aerial encounter. Those pilots that joined the night fighters later in the war, as post-war interrogations and interviews confirm, preferred to use only '*Schräge Musik*'. However, regardless of the individual pilot's preference, the introduction of '*Schräge Musik*' had a marked effect on the number of victories claimed, and in expert hands it was a deadly and effective weapon. Between April and June 1943 Bomber Command lost a total of 762 bombers, of which 551 were claimed by *Nachtjagd* pilots.

Above and below: First produced in 1940, Rheinmetall Borsig's 30 mm Mk 108 mm belt-fed cannon had a maximum rate of fire of 660 rounds per minute, just three or four of which were sufficient to bring down a bomber. This weapon, seen with incendiary and high explosive rounds, was fitted mainly to Bf 110 and He 219 night fighters.

The 20 mm Mauser MG 151/20 cannon was fitted to almost every type of night fighter aircraft operated by the Nachtjagd. This weapon could fire up to 800 rounds per minute and could also be installed in under-fuselage weapons packs.

The Loss of Three *Ritterkreuzträger*

Despite the successes achieved by the *Nachtjagd* there was, however, a cost. From modest beginnings, the *Nachtjagd* had built up a small core of experienced pilots who had been responsible for introducing, and then perfecting, the techniques which became standard operating procedures. These men led by example and were an inspiration to newer pilots who tried to emulate them, so the deaths of three of the *Nachtjagd's* most experienced and capable pilots within three weeks was a severe blow. The first of these was *Hptm*. Reinhold Knacke, *Staffelkapitän* of 1./NJG 1, who was killed on 3 February 1943 after destroying a Halifax bomber. He was replaced by *Oblt*. Paul Gildner, but three weeks after assuming this post he too was killed when his aircraft suffered an engine failure and he crashed to his death near Gilze-Rijen in Holland on the night of 24/25 April. The last of the three was *Hptm*. Ludwig Becker, who had become a night fighter pilot when the organisation was first formed in June 1940 and had achieved the first victories using the *Dunkel Nachtjagd* method and '*Lichtenstein*' airborne radar. Since August 1942, the American Eighth Air Force had begun daylight attacks against Germany, and on 26 February 1943 during one such mission against Emden, Becker and 11 other night fighter pilots were scrambled from Leeuwarden. By the conclusion of the raid, the Americans had lost seven of their bombers and all but one of the German fighters had returned, the missing aircraft belonging to Ludwig Becker. The exact circumstances under which he was lost are not known, his aircraft having dived into the sea. Becker was never found.

All three of the pilots killed were holders of the Knight's Cross and following their deaths each was posthumously awarded the Oak Leaves. In another strange coincidence, each had 44 victories to his credit and, apart from Helmut Lent, they were the three highest-scoring night fighters in the *Nachtjagd*. Their deaths were an immense loss to the organisation and came at a time when the *Nachtjagd* could least afford to lose such a wealth of experience.

In February 1943 it was decided that 2. Jagddivision would be divided into two separate divisions. While one retained the designation 2. Jagddivision, the other became 4. Jagddivision under the command of Generalmajor Joachim-Friedrich Huth who, as the Kommodore of Zerstörergeschwader 26, had been decorated with the Knight's Cross in September 1940 for his leadership during the battles of France and Britain.

The Knight's Cross was awarded to Hauptmann Wilhelm Herget (second from right) and Hauptmann Hans-Dieter Frank (second from left) at Venlo on 20 June 1943. On the far left is Major Werner Streib and on the far right is Major Helmut Lent. In the centre is General der Flieger Josef Kammhuber.

"With the moon behind me I dived down on my prey like a falcon…"

Oberleutnant Hans Krause, I./NJG 3

TOWARDS the end of January 1943, I had the honour of being tasked by the *Kommandeur* of I./NJG 3, *Major* Knoetsch, to take over command of a detachment of four aircraft at Wunstorf in Westphalia. I foresaw this as a preliminary step towards being promoted to *Staffelkapitän* and was very proud, taking pains to carry out all my duties, which were similar to those of a *Staffelführer*, to complete satisfaction. I was always on the ball. I paid full attention to everything and found my long period as a Technical Officer a great advantage. I was always able to report my aircraft to my superior command post as fit for operations.

The airfield at Wunstorf was admittedly on the small side, but it had been constructed in peacetime and was therefore equipped with all modern facilities. We immediately felt very comfortable there, but because of the small size of the field and the short take-off and landing runway, it was necessary for us to retrain on the Me 110. That, however, was no problem as the aircraft had long been our operational machine. Nevertheless, as is well known, a coin has two sides and the obverse was extremely displeasing: in the two months we spent there we flew just two operations. So that we wouldn't grow rusty we passed our time flying practice interceptions or making short local trips, to the Steinhuder Lake for instance. In truth, it was a lazy sort of an existence, and it had absolutely nothing to do with the war. I formed the impression that our presence there was more psychological and to show the people of Hannover that they were protected by night fighters.

Our movement order to Wittmund-Hafen had already been set for the beginning of April, when I was rewarded with a success on the last of the missions that we flew from Wunstorf. On 29 March, as on every evening, the weather briefing took place in the briefing room at six pm. Judging from the statements of the Met. man, there was unlikely to be any operational flying, not because we wouldn't have been able to fly in the predicted miserable weather – as trained all-weather crews we could always do that – but because the enemy, unable to make out specific targets, would probably cancel any operations planned for that night. As we could see for ourselves, the cloud base was at about 500 metres, the cloud tops were at 7,000 metres, and between was a compact and mostly solid layer of cloud. At first, there was indeed no enemy operational activity, but later enemy targets heading east were reported over the North Sea.

We knew that they would change direction to the south near Stralsund or Greifswald and attack Berlin. Bombs dropped through the cloud usually hit something or other, or the sounding of the air raid alarm led to greater disruption of traffic and manufacturing production than one might like to think. At about 24.00 hrs the first returning bombers were reported, scattered over the entire North German area. One of these returning enemy bombers headed for Hannover, where the alarm sounded, and thus entered our area. Cockpit readiness had already been ordered, and then came the order to scramble. At 02.35 hrs our Bf 110 roared along the runway into the pitch black night. Because of the danger of mid-air collision in the cloud, the other aircraft remained on the ground in reserve for possible action later. I climbed in circles at two to three metres a second, and it seemed an eternity until I broke cloud at 7,000 metres. Then I saw a completely clear, starlit night with a full moon lighting up the far-reaching cloud tops like a white carpet of snow. We felt as if a piece of space had opened up to us.

Knowing that the airfield was beneath us, we flew a short distance to the east. The visibility was so clear that it felt to us like a day mission. Because we were now flying 400 metres higher, we could oversee and observe an area some several kilometres in radius. Then we saw the enemy bomber. It was crawling along like a fat bumblebee over an opaque sheet of glass. For a while we watched from a safe distance above and to the left. It was an Avro Lancaster. It was flying on a westerly course only a few metres above the bright covering of cloud, into which it would certainly have dived if the pilot had suspected danger. Otto Zinn, my wireless operator, passed details to the Ops. room and then requested radio silence. We intended to attack soon. The Lancaster's rear gunner had his four machine guns pointing dead astern, so we assumed that we hadn't yet been seen. With the moon behind me, I dived down on my prey like a falcon and began to fire into its port wing at a range of about 200 metres. The Lancaster immediately caught fire. It was doomed. It dived into the cloud and down into the depths, trailing a ghostly red shimmer behind it. We followed, but in a calculated, controlled descent, losing about five metres a second.

We were unable, however, to observe the moment of the Lancaster's impact, but we did see a bright glow, clearly visible through the clouds that arose from the otherwise dark night. We broke cloud at about 500 metres, and now we could clearly see the burning wreckage. The force of the impact had scattered burning parts over several hundred metres of an area only about 10 kilometres north-west of our airfield.

This photograph shows Hans Krause (centre) with his crew in front of a Do 217. On the left is Ofw. Otto Zinn, the Bordfunker, and on the right Ofw. Fritz Specht, the Bordmechaniker. In the accompanying account, Oblt. Krause was flying a Bf 110 with only Ofw. Zinn aboard.

We landed at 04.35 hrs and climbed into a car to drive to where the Lancaster had come down. The glow, visible from a long distance, indicated the direction in which we had to drive. We were surprised to find so many people near the crash site so early in the morning. Ammunition and signal cartridges were still exploding, so we parked our car a prudent distance away on a side road, and found ourselves near an *Oberst* of the Flak and his adjutant. From their conversation it was clear that a nearby Flak battery were intending to claim the kill for themselves and paint a broad white ring round the barrel of their gun, but during our entire operation we had not seen one single exploding anti-aircraft shell. We discussed it and the *Oberst* was convinced that his arguments were the better ones. We felt sure that the decision would be taken at a higher level. While we were still looking at the burning wreck we heard from our right faint, and then increasingly louder, cries for help coming from an area of bushes and trees. "*Help!*" and then once more, "*Help!*" Otto and I looked at each other in surprise before we made our way along a ditch in the field towards the small wood. Soon we saw the Lancaster's rear fuselage. It was caught in thick branches and undergrowth in the wood and had come to rest about one metre from the ground. Then we saw a member of the British crew, lying on a soft mattress of moss and leaves.

We could see that he had been thrown clean through the sheeting of the fuselage above him and that he was in a pitiful condition. His legs and arms had certainly suffered multiple fractures because they were in strange positions relative to his body. His face and hands were smeared with blood. Another weak "*Help*" passed his lips and he asked for "*Water*". But whenever we touched him, he cried out in pain. We simply didn't know what to do, but we were very strongly of the opinion that our English fellow-flier would have to pay his final account very soon. On the other hand, we realised that he had survived for more than an hour since the time of the crash, and we set about freeing him from his present position. It was obviously very painful for him as we pushed and pulled him along the ditch, taking full cover, to the edge of the field, where he lost consciousness completely.

Now no longer hearing his blood-curdling cries of agony, it was much easier for us to mount a further rescue operation. First of all, several more helping hands lifted the body onto a farm cart that happened to be in the vicinity, and then, as if out of nowhere, our service ambulance appeared, the driver of which had also been attracted by curiosity. Then everything went very quickly and we knew that our patient was in good hands in the care of our Medical Officer, *Doktor* Wesendorf.

As was standard practice, I forwarded our daily and operational reports from the Ops. Room to the *Gruppe* at Vechta for further transmission to the *Kommandeur*. It was already growing light when I was able to lie down for a well-earned rest.

It was just before midday when the telephone rang and the Medical Officer asked me to meet him in the sick quarters. There, he led me into a ward and I feared the worst. But after I had been shown to a bed, I was pleasantly surprised to find the patient very much alive. The Medical Officer had told him who I was, and we smiled at each other as we shook hands, as fellow knights do. The doctor had washed the blood from his patient's body, attended to his grazes and had set the man's broken limbs in splints. He had also removed a bullet from his backside which, in a macabre way, confirmed that the bomber had been shot down by a night fighter and not by Flak.

The airman's backbone and all his organs had escaped serious damage, which had been the reason he had survived. The next day he was taken to a proper hospital, where the German doctor gave him a good chance of survival. After we had exchanged our home addresses, we took leave of each other with good wishes for the future. I lost the address, unfortunately, in the confusion of war. I only know that he was the wireless operator of his crew, came from central England and was 21 years old. I hope that God supported and helped him for the rest of his life, for he surely deserved it.

Note: It is virtually certain that the British crew-member was Sgt. G.A. Jones of No. 49 Squadron, Fiskerton. He was the only survivor of Lancaster ED469, EA-A, flown by Flying Officer G.F. Mabee, RCAF, and subsequently became a prisoner of war.

Summary

By June 1943 both sides were poised to take the offensive to the other. Bomber Command had made considerable advances in target location and marking, and its main force was being increasingly equipped with the Lancaster bomber which benefited from a higher operating ceiling than the Halifax and Stirling and could carry a heavier bomb load. Correspondingly, the *Nachtjagd* had developed an effective system for intercepting the bombers using '*Himmelbett*' and was beginning to introduce '*Schräge Musik*', which made it considerably easier to shoot down the bombers. Each organisation had struggled considerably during the previous three years in a desperate attempt to outwit and outmanoeuvre the other in a type of warfare that was new to both. After three years of fighting, the outcome of the battle was still undecided and victory for either side hung in the balance.

However, Bomber Command was about to introduce a new innovation to the night air war that would virtually blind German ground and air radar. As a result, the German ground defences, including the night fighters, would be rendered ineffective, leaving many of Germany's cities unprotected and at the mercy of the bombers.

The *Nachtjagd* would then find itself once more on the defensive, and as Bomber Command further perfected its techniques, thousands of German civilians were about to become victims of a new phenomenon – the firestorm.

A Schwarm of Bf 110s from NJG 5 taking off from Parchim airfield at the start of a mission. Clearly visible and silhouetted against the darkening night sky are the antennae of their 'Lichtenstein' airborne intercept radars.

On 27 March 1942, Manfred Meurer of 1./NJG 1 shot down a Wellington bomber as the first of his 65 victories. Almost a year later, on 14 March 1943, he was awarded the Ritterkreuz after 23 victories; by 2 August 1943 he had increased this to 50, for which he was awarded the Oak Leaves. This rare colour photograph, taken shortly after the award ceremony, shows Hptm. Meurer already wearing the higher decoration. Note also the Frontflugspange für Nachtjäger in Silver (Night Fighter Clasp) above his left breast pocket, usually awarded after 60 missions. Meurer was killed near the city of Magdeburg on the night of 21/22 January 1944 when his He 219 collided with an RAF bomber.

Heinz Strüning achieved his first victories with the Nachtjagd whilst flying intruder missions to Britain with I./NJG 2. He went on to become Staffelkapitän of 3./NJG 1 and became the 528th recipient of the Oak Leaves on 20 July 1944. He was shot down on 24/25 December 1944 by a British night fighter and was killed when he bailed out of his machine and was struck by the tail unit. He was credited with 56 kills at the time of his death.

Developments in Night Fighter Camouflage

IN 1940, an officer serving on the Royal Navy destroyer HMS *Broke* believed that the dark medium grey scheme which appeared on most RN vessels at that time was probably the least effective form of camouflage. He believed that an improved camouflage effect, especially when ships were operating in areas where the prevailing weather was overcast, would be best achieved by the use of much lighter colours. Despite the views of many who did not understand the rationale behind the scheme and claimed that a very light-painted ship would prove too conspicuous, a camouflage finish of various very light colours and large areas of white was duly applied.

A few months later, an incident occurred which demonstrated the effectiveness of the new scheme. While operating in low visibility and overcast weather conditions, HMS *Broke* was accidentally rammed by another destroyer. At the subsequent court martial of the other destroyer captain, part of his defence rested on the claim that HMS *Broke's* camouflage was so effective that the ship had not been seen until it was too late to take avoiding action.

The overall black night fighter scheme, as seen on this Bf 110 of 3./NJG 3, was the least effective for night operations.

Interestingly, in late 1941, some Luftwaffe night fighter crews also began to realise that the standard overall black finish which had been applied since the *Nachtjagd* was first created in 1940 was in fact the least effective form of camouflage. Even on the darkest night the sky is rarely black as there is usually some light, so when aircraft were seen they generally appeared as dark shapes against the lighter background of the sky. Painting an aircraft black therefore only served to increase the contrast between it and its background, thus making it more conspicuous. What was required to make an aircraft less visible during the hours of darkness was a very pale tone, the exact colour being immaterial as colours cannot be distinguished at night.

On dark nights, on overcast, moonlit nights, and even on clear, starlit nights, very pale paints will reflect indirect light to the same intensity as the sky background. Thus, sufficient blending with the background is achieved for the majority of conditions by favouring a pale camouflage scheme. In direct light, however, such as the moon, searchlights, or the light of dawn or dusk, a pale paint will reflect light which may be brighter than the sky behind it. Although, in these conditions, an aircraft camouflaged in light tones might therefore show up lighter than the background, it was thought that the pale scheme might still give a slight psychological advantage as aircrews on the lookout would have expected to see an aircraft as a dark mass.

By early 1942, therefore – although examples of the all-black finish would still be in use in early 1943 – most night fighters were operating in the standard day fighter colours of 74, 75 and 76. This was applied in a high demarcation scheme with the 74 and 75 on the uppersurfaces and 76 on the undersurfaces. Fuselage sides were mottled with 74 and 75. In a simplified version of this scheme, which at that time seems to have appeared largely on Do 217 night fighters, the 74 was deleted and all upper surfaces which would be seen in plan form were 75 only.

Evidently, Dornier realised that this finish was still too dark and by 1943 had begun finishing its Do 217 night fighters in 76 overall. This certainly met the approval of *Major* Günther Radusch, but other pilots were still not convinced that in the majority of light conditions encountered at night, the lighter finish provided the most favourable camouflage. Radusch therefore arranged for a trial to be carried out under operational conditions in which he would fly a light-painted Do 217 while one of the greatest sceptics of the pale scheme, *Hptm.* Hans-Joachim Jabs, would fly a black-painted Ju 88. It is doubtful if one pilot had any advantage over the other as both were very experienced and either had or were about to receive the *Ritterkreuz*.

A Do 217 night fighter finished in a high demarcation scheme of 76 undersurfaces with 75 over all uppersurfaces. Although a significant improvement on the earlier overall black scheme, the uppersurfaces were sometimes considered too dark to be effective.

Unfortunately, the exact date of the trial is not known, but Radusch was in fact completely vindicated. When he acted as the attacker and closed on Jabs' aircraft, he was able to approach unseen to within firing range; but when the roles were reversed and Jabs became the attacker, it was found that, as Jabs himself later confessed, he was unable to observe Radusch's aircraft until he almost collided with it.

Whether the results of this experiment were ever reported through official channels is not known, but the use of colours 74, 75 and 76 (see opposite) continued in various styles of application until about August 1944, when 74 was officially withdrawn. Rather bizarrely, it also seems as if Dornier began to have doubts about its overall light scheme as other photographs (see opposite) taken later than those showing the overall 76 scheme indicate a return to darker colours.

While photographs of late war Luftwaffe night fighters would certainly suggest that more than the two schemes of 75/76 and 74/75/76 existed before 74 was withdrawn, they show in fact variations which resulted from modifications, either at the factory or at unit level, to the two basic schemes. The most widely observed modification seems to have resulted in almost all the 75 areas being partially oversprayed but in such a way that the areas remaining appear to have been applied *over* the 76. That the reverse was in fact the case is supported by photographs which show aircraft obviously assembled from components produced at different factories. In some such cases, the fuselage had a reverse mottle but the wing uppersurfaces were 75 overall. In other instances, although the wings and fuselage were each oversprayed, the style of reverse mottle on the fuselage was completely different from that on the wings. Yet again the required camouflage effect was sometimes obtained by softly spraying an uneven cross-hatch of irregularly spaced straight lines in 76, this resulting in lozenge-shaped mottles of 75.

This process, however, was wasteful in terms of the paint consumed for it resulted, in effect, in the uppersurfaces sometimes being painted twice. To eliminate such wastage, a second basic scheme was later introduced in which night fighter aircraft were completely finished in 76 only. Thus there was, in effect, a return to the overall light scheme first pioneered by Dornier and tested by *Major* Radusch. However, by this stage of the war, Luftwaffe airfields had become a prime target for roaming Allied fighters and, while the light 76 was ideal for aircraft operating in the hours of darkness, there was an obvious, if conflicting, requirement to camouflage aircraft while parked on the ground in daylight. The result was a compromise in which the 76 uppersurfaces were partly oversprayed with a variety of mottles or meandering lines, the latter applied in the so-called '*Wellenmuster*' or 'wave pattern'. Since, from the end of 1944, the colours available to modify the uppersurface camouflage included 75, 81, 82 and 83, the colours used over the 76 varied as widely as the patterns, depending on the availability of paint stocks and the different painters involved. The basic 76 scheme, with uppersurfaces toned down with various mottled or '*Wellenmuster*' oversprays, remained in use until the end of the war.

Left: The only known photograph of the Do 217 which Major Günther Radusch used in his trial. With the exception of the undersurface wingtips, which appear to be yellow, and the masking of the glazed areas of the canopy and gondola, the aircraft was completely resprayed overall in a very light tone, possibly RLM 76 or a specially mixed very pale grey. As may be seen, all markings, the propeller spinners and propeller blades, the front engine detail and even the radar aerials and gun barrels were included.

Below left and below: Bf 110 F-4 s of 9./NJG 5 at Königsberg-Neumark in 1943. These aircraft have been camouflaged in the standard 74/75/76 day fighter scheme.

Above and right: Two further examples of the continued use of darker night fighter colours may be seen on these Do 217s where the uppersurfaces and fuselage sides have been darkened, one with mottling (left) and the other with a solid application of a single colour, presumably 75.

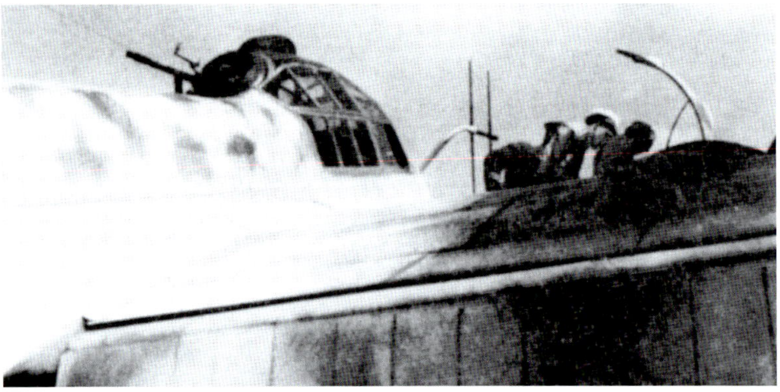

Above: The reverse mottle finish on this Ju 88 G-6a has been achieved by overspraying the 75 uppersurfaces with 76 in such a way that patches of the original 75 remain. Note, however, that the pattern on the wings is quite different from that on the fuselage, a result perhaps of these components being produced in different factories. This particular aircraft, photographed in 1944, was flown by Hptm. Gerhard Friedrich, the Staffelkapitän of 1./NJG 6, who was awarded the Ritterkreuz on 15 March 1945 but was killed the next night when his 33rd victim exploded and his own aircraft was caught in the blast.

Another example of a Bf 110 finished in the 74/75/76 colours.

Note again how the mottles on the fuselage of this Ju 88 differ from those on the uppersurface of the wings. In each case, however, the effect has been achieved by spraying 76 over a base of 75.

A Ju 88 G of 2./NJG 4 at Mainz-Finthen in January 1945. Note the camouflage on the engine cowling where again the original overall 75 uppersurface has been oversprayed but here with irregularly spaced, soft-edged straight lines of 76.

Nachtjäger

PART TWO

Reaping the Whirlwind 1943–1945

"What has happened in Hamburg has never happened before, not even during our attacks against Britain. These attacks on Hamburg strike deep at our nation's morale. If we do not succeed in smashing these terror attacks by day and by night very soon, then we must expect a very difficult situation to arise for Germany."

GENERALFELDMARSCHALL ERHARD MILCH
COMMENTING ON THE HAMBURG RAIDS OF JULY 1943

The Formation of the '*Wilde Sau*'

Hajo Herrmann began his flying career in August 1935 and, after qualifying as a pilot, he was posted to the bomber unit 9./KG 4. He flew during the Spanish Civil War and later during the Polish, Norwegian and French campaigns. Towards the end of the 'Battle of Britain' he received the Knight's Cross and was then transferred to the Mediterranean where he took part in the bombing of Malta with III./KG 30. It was after he had been posted to Berlin in July 1942 that he devised his theory of employing single-engined fighters as night fighters. This method was soon christened 'Wilde Sau' and incorporated into the existing night defence system. Herrmann himself shot down nine bombers using this method and finished the war, as seen in this photograph, as an Oberst with the Knight's Cross, Oak Leaves and Swords.

BY July 1943, the outcome of the night air war over occupied Europe still hung very much in the balance as each of the protagonists evaluated and tested new tactics, technology and weaponry which they hoped would tip the scales in their favour. On the German side, a new system of night fighting was being developed that involved employing single-engined fighters to attack the bombers over the target area itself. The idea for this procedure was first considered in 1942 and came from a most unexpected quarter.

In July 1942, Hajo Herrmann, an experienced bomber pilot, a holder of the Knight's Cross, and *Gruppenkommandeur* of III./KG 30, was transferred to an administrative staff posting in Berlin. There, he was attached to a department known as *Gruppe T* of the Command Staff of the Luftwaffe, and Herrmann, together with five other officers who made up *Gruppe T*, were responsible for evaluating the Luftwaffe's technical and tactical requirements. Each of the officers was given his own field of operational responsibility which, unsurprisingly in Herrmann's case, was that of the bomber force.

Within a few months Herrmann discovered, much to his concern, that the Western Allies were producing three times as many bombers as the German war industry could produce fighters. The seriousness of this situation prompted him to investigate ways in which the Luftwaffe's numerical inferiority could be overcome, even though he realised that Germany could never hope to match the number of aircraft produced by Great Britain and the United States. His solution to the problem was to utilise the available aircraft more effectively, and he submitted a report suggesting that with suitable technical, organisational and training support, single-engined fighters could operate at night, as well as during the day.

When the proposal fell on deaf ears, Herrmann decided to take matters into his own hands and, procuring a fighter and an He 111 to be used as a target, he began conducting a series of test flights from the airfield at Berlin-Staaken. With the assistance of a local searchlight unit to illuminate the bomber, he was able to carry out flying and target practice over Berlin.

After a number of practice flights, Herrmann felt confident enough to take part in a live defensive action and, in order that he could operate safely above the Flak without being shot down, formally requested that its fire be restricted to 6,000 metres. Although Herrmann received the appropriate authority to participate in operations, his request for the height of the Flak to be limited was turned down as Hitler himself had decreed that the anti-aircraft guns should be allowed to operate freely and not be restricted in any way.

Herrmann's first opportunity to put his theory and practical training to the test occurred in April 1943 when German radar picked up an aircraft heading towards the German capital. He immediately scrambled from Staaken and flew to a holding area on the edge of the searchlight zone near Potsdam. While circling at a height of 11,000 metres, he saw a number of searchlights lock on to a target and he immediately made his way towards it at high speed. Flying closer, he saw that the searchlights had coned a Mosquito flying through a heavy barrage of Flak some 2,000 metres below him. Having descended to the same height as his target, he gradually reduced the range and opened fire. His first burst went wide of its mark and, temporarily blinded by the muzzle flash, Herrmann immediately realised he had forgotten to have his weapons loaded with the correct type of ammunition. After quickly regaining his night vision, he made a second unsuccessful attack against the Mosquito, which soon cleared the searchlight zone and disappeared into the darkness.

Despite being disappointed by his performance, the incident provided Herrmann with some valuable experience and emphasised the importance of close cooperation with other organisations within the defence network. The searchlight units were particularly important, as these had also coned his aircraft during the encounter, as a result of which he had been fired upon by Flak. Indeed, upon returning to Staaken and examining his machine, he and his mechanic found that a shell splinter had torn a large hole in the fuselage one metre from where he had been sitting.

The next day, having sworn the ground crew to secrecy about the near miss, Herrmann related his experiences and thoughts during a meeting in Berlin chaired by *Generalfeldmarschall* Milch. Although Milch himself was sceptical of the whole incident and had been advised by Kammhuber that any collaboration between the fighters and the searchlights was impractical, Herrmann found support for his idea in the *General der Jagdflieger*, *Generalmajor* Adolf Galland, who promised to make further fighter aircraft available to him.

Following the briefing, Herrmann set about finding pilots willing to fly such missions and who possessed the necessary night-flying experience. Initially, he recruited instructors from the *Flugzeugführerschule* at Brandenburg-Briest who continued to instruct by day and flew practice interceptions at night. During May and June 1943, Herrmann and his men, known collectively as '*Kommando Herrmann*', waited for the RAF to raid Berlin, but no such attack materialised. Impatient for action and a chance to put what had been learned into practice, Herrmann requested that the unit be transferred to the Ruhr where, during the shorter summer nights it was more likely they would encounter the bombers.

Herrmann's latest proposal was discussed at a conference held in Berlin-Dahlem between the Flak and Night Fighter Staff, and once again the question was discussed of limiting the height at which the Flak operated. *Generaloberst* Hubert Weise, who was in overall charge of air defence and chaired the meeting, refused to restrict the operational ceiling of the 700 heavy guns under his command for the sake of a few fighters. During the discussion, which became quite heated, one of the attending officers, *Oberstleutnant* Boehm-Tettlebach, referred to Herrmann's idea as '*Wilde Sau*', which translated into English means 'Wild Boar', but in German means wild in the sense of being unheeding and reckless. Although the remark was meant in a disparaging way, the term '*Wilde Sau*' stuck, and from that moment on this type of night fighting procedure was referred to by this name.

By the end of the meeting, however, Herrmann had been able to secure from Weise an agreement that his unit could operate in the west on the proviso that he could obtain the cooperation of a local Flak commander willing to work with him. After some swift and effective negotiations with the commanding officer of the 4. *Flakdivision*, *Generalmajor* Johannes Hintz, it was agreed that all anti-aircraft fire that fell under his command within the Ruhr would be confined to a maximum height of 5,500 metres. With no further obstacles to his plan, Herrmann and Hintz's Operations Officer quickly began formulating guidelines on operational procedures and how the fighters and Flak could best work together during a major raid.

Friedrich-Karl Müller, known to his flying colleagues as 'Nose' Müller, flew pre-war as a Lufthansa pilot. Later, Müller shot down his first bomber, a Halifax near Cologne, on the night of 3/4 July 1943, and joined JG 300 later that summer. He was eventually credited with the destruction of 30 bombers and was awarded the Knight's Cross on 27 July 1944.

An opportunity to put these procedures into practice soon presented itself during the evening of 3 July 1943. After being informed of an approaching raid, Herrmann immediately sought, and was granted, overnight leave for his men, who flew to Mönchengladbach as planned. By the time Herrmann himself arrived an hour later, most of the nine pilots from the unit had already taken off and flown to a predetermined patrol area over Essen and Duisburg. There they waited at an altitude of around 6,000 to 7,000 metres.

As the bombers approached the Ruhr from the west, they were intercepted by conventional night fighters which shot down several of them. Soon afterwards, however, the bomber stream changed direction and, instead of heading north towards Essen as had been expected, it turned south and headed towards Cologne. This unexpected change in course presented Herrmann with a dilemma since Cologne fell under the jurisdiction of the 7. *Flakdivision*, with which he had made no prior agreement. However, on seeing the first coloured marker flares descend towards the city and the explosions of the first bombs, he decided to attack despite the threat of unrestricted Flak activity over the target area.

During the mêlée that followed, Herrmann and his fighters flew over the burning city, successfully avoiding the millions of shell splinters that filled the night sky, and shot down 12 of the raiders. The first of these, a Halifax, was claimed by *Oblt.* Friedrich-Karl Müller and, two minutes later, Herrmann himself shot down a Lancaster as his first aerial victory. Unfortunately, when he and his unit landed at Bonn-Hangelar, Herrmann's elation turned to surprise and consternation when he discovered that the Flak units in Cologne were claiming the same 12 aircraft. Following some lengthy negotiations, it was finally decided that the claims would be equally divided between the Flak gunners and the '*Wilde Sau*' pilots.

Exhausted by the experience, but satisfied with his unit's performance, Herrmann retired to bed, only to be woken up several hours later to take a telephone call from Göring. The *Reichsmarschall* explained that he had just been informed about the unit's success against the bombers and ordered Herrmann immediately to fly to Berchtesgaden, where the operation was discussed in detail. Obviously impressed with what he heard, Göring authorised the formation of a new night fighter *Geschwader* equipped with single-engined fighters. The new unit was designated JG 300 and Herrmann was made its first *Kommodore*.

Gerhard Stamp joined the Luftwaffe just prior to the outbreak of the war and, on completing his pilot training, was posted to I./LG1. After 300 missions as a bomber pilot, primarily in the Mediterranean, he was awarded the Knight's Cross on 24 March 1943. In August 1943, Stamp became Kommandeur of I./JG 300 and, until wounded on 29 June 1944, he flew approximately 100 'Wilde Sau' missions, during which he shot down four bombers. In late 1944 he formed an air-to-air bombing unit employing the Me 262 and this unit, known as Kommando Stamp, subsequently became the Stabsstaffel of JG 7. After the war, Gerhard Stamp joined the Bundesluftwaffe as a Major and retired on 30 September 1978 with the rank of Oberst.

Using his existing men and machines, Herrmann formed I./JG 300 to operate from Bonn-Hangelar under the command of *Major* Gerhard Stamp. Further suitably trained pilots were recruited from other operational units and training schools to form the basis of two further *Gruppen*, II./JG 300 and III./JG 300, which were transferred to Rheine[13] and Oldenburg[14] and commanded by *Major* Kurt Kettner and *Major* Hans-Joachim von Buchwald respectively. These two airfields had been specifically chosen for their strategic locations and because they were also home to day fighters which, lying idle at night, could now be utilised by the '*Wilde Sau'*.

In addition to all the usual logistical problems associated with setting up a new *Geschwader*, Herrmann was acutely aware of the many technical difficulties that also had to be overcome, but he immediately set about addressing these with his more usual zeal. Nevertheless, he estimated that he would need at least until the end of September to bring all his units to operational readiness.

Although JG 300's aircraft were all standard fighters and therefore lacked the airborne radar employed by their twin-engined counterparts in the *Nachtjagd*, this was of no concern to Herrmann. On the contrary, he realised that the key to his unit's success was the fact that they were mobile, and the last thing he wanted was to have their operational potential restricted by '*Himmelbett'* and adherence to the existing night fighting procedures.

One of the first things that Herrmann introduced was a simple but effective navigational system which he hoped would enable him to concentrate his forces where they were most needed in the shortest possible time. While attending a military conference in Berlin, he had discovered that the *Kriegsmarine* was using a special type of flare that could be fired through cloud formations to illuminate enemy aircraft flying below it. He was able to procure several hundred of these flares which were distributed to a number of widely dispersed cities. The local Flak units were then instructed to fire, at regular intervals during a raid, two or three of the flares which had been pre-set to explode at an altitude of between 7,000 and 8,000 metres. These could be seen from great distances and would enable the '*Wilde Sau*' units rapidly to make their way to the town or city which was under attack. Furthermore, by being able to quickly identify the target, the fighters' chances of intercepting the bombers while they were still in that area were greatly improved.

In another attempt to improve the chances of success, the fighters were fitted with drop tanks which increased the aircraft's flight time to between two and three hours. With further training and closer cooperation with the searchlight and Flak units, Herrmann remained confident that by the end of September his pilots would be able to match the number of bombers shot down by the existing night fighter force. Unfortunately, due to events and circumstances beyond his control, his training schedule was interrupted as a result of Operation 'Gomorrah', a devastating and sustained RAF attack against Hamburg on 24 July 1943, the effects of which resounded throughout Germany and the Nazi hierarchy. During this raid, jamming rendered the existing '*Himmelbett*' system totally ineffective and only a few bombers were shot down. Desperate to save face and to be seen to be doing something, Göring ordered Herrmann to make all his units immediately operational. With no recourse or room for argument, Herrmann prepared his '*Wilde Sau*' pilots of JG 300 for their first action.

Hamburg and 'Operation Gomorrah'

Since taking command of the newly formed *Nachtjagddivision* on 17 July 1940, *General der Flieger* Josef Kammhuber had succeeded in forming the German night defences into a formidable force, but as Bomber Command mounted effective spoof attacks and developed tactics to confuse and frustrate the German defences, the inflexibility of '*Himmelbett'* and the '*Kammhuber Line*' was exposed. The main criticism expressed by the night fighter pilots themselves was that operating in individual *Räum* not only limited their operational range, but also prevented them from flying into other *Räume* if the bombers bypassed the one in which they were patrolling. On a more personal level, many of the younger and newer pilots were resentful that the best and most productive *Räume* were usually allocated to the most senior crews, thus depriving them of any chance to gain experience and denying them the opportunity to achieve their first victories.

Nevertheless, as the *Nachtjagd* continued to account for the greater share of the bombers shot down by the German defences its operational strength was increased, either by creating new

13. II./JG 300 operated with the Fw 190-As of II./JG 1.
14. III./JG 300 operated with the Bf 109 G-6s of III./JG 11.

units or by adding new *Gruppen* to already established *Nachtjagdgeschwader*. Thus by June, a sixth operational *Geschwader* had been created with the raising of IV./*Nachtjagdgeschwader* 6 under the command of *Hauptmann* Herbert Lütje, followed later in the month by the creation of V./NJG 6 under the command of *Hauptmann* Paul Semrau, although this latter *Gruppe* was redesignated III./NJG 2 the following month. By the end of August, the continued expansion of the existing *Geschwader* had resulted in the creation of III./NJG 5, V./NJG 5, III./NJG 6, IV./NJG 6, a new V./NJG 6, I./NJG 7 and I./NJG 100, so increasing the *Nachtjagd* from 15 to 22 *Gruppen*. On this basis, the organisation therefore possessed approximately 500 aircraft, although not all of these were available for operations.

Looking somewhat bemused by the fuss, Oberleutnant Reinhold Knacke of 1./NJG 1 is wearing his recently awarded Knight's Cross, presented to him on 1 July 1942 for shooting down 23 bombers. On 28/29 July 1942, Knacke became the first German night fighter pilot to shoot down an RAF Mosquito. He continued to score steadily throughout the rest of 1942 but was killed on the night of 3/4 February 1943 when his total number of victories stood at 44. Knacke was posthumously awarded the Oak Leaves three days later. On his right in this photograph is Wilhelm Johnen.

Kammhuber's defences were further bolstered by technological advances that had resulted in the production of several different types of improved ground radar. The first of these, known as '*Mammut*', was basically a larger version of the existing '*Freya*' type with an increased effective range of 200 miles, although as with its predecessor, it could not measure a target's altitude. This, however, was overcome with the introduction of a second type of ground radar codenamed '*Wassermann*', a long-range, early-warning radar which was able to give the height, range and bearing of an aircraft up to 150 miles away. Once in service, both types of radar were positioned along the west coast of occupied Europe where they were able to detect the approach of any bomber flying from the British Isles.

Above left and right: Hptm. Paul Semrau was appointed Kommandeur of V./NJG 6 when it was created in June 1943, but when this Gruppe was redesignated III./NJG 2, he spent virtually all of his career with NJG 2, becoming its Kommodore in November 1944. Here, Semrau is seen taking the salute from the men of I./NJG 2 following the award of the Knight's Cross from Generalmajor Kammhuber in October 1942. Semrau was killed on 8 February 1945 when he was shot down by a Spitfire while trying to land at Twente in Holland. He was buried with his crew at Twente and posthumously awarded the Oak Leaves in April 1945.

Pilots from 5./NJG 5 enjoying a social gathering during a lull in the fighting. This photograph was taken circa April/May 1943 when the unit was stationed at Parchim. Soon afterwards, the unit was transferred to the West where it helped to bolster the night defences against an increasing number of raids mounted against the Ruhr. Seated third from the left in this photograph is the Staffelkapitän of 2./NJG 5, Leopold Fellerer.

This tail unit with 29 victory bars is reported to have belonged to the Ju 88 C-6 flown by Hptm. Heinrich Prinz zu Sayn-Wittgenstein, the Kommandeur of IV./NJG 5, probably when based at Insterburg in East Prussia in May or June 1943. There are many inconstancies between the victory bars shown and Sayn-Wittgenstein's known confirmed victories. For example, although the bars in the bottom row – including the linked bars which represent multiple kills – correspond precisely with Sayn-Wittgenstein's kills in July 1942, the rest cannot be reconciled with his subsequent claims. Moreover, on the night of 24/25 June 1943, he claimed four kills which raised his total from 28 to 32, but why only one of those victories should be shown, bringing the total to 29 bars, is again not known. The grey camouflage on this aircraft, a Ju 88 C-6 code C9+AE, would appear to consist of 74 mottles over 75.

In the air, the *Nachtjagd* was operating with the '*Lichtenstein*' BC airborne interception radar, first used with success on 9 August 1941. Despite early difficulties in acquiring operational sets and some scepticism expressed by many of the more experienced pilots, by June 1943 this radar was used in increasing numbers of night fighter aircraft.

These three types of radar were all very effective in their individual roles, but their one inherent weakness was that they all operated on virtually the same frequency. As long as the British remained unaware of what that frequency was, the radars were safe from interference but during a raid on Frankfurt on the night of 3 December 1942, the bombers had been accompanied by an RAF Wellington from No. 1474 Wireless Investigation Flight. This aircraft was equipped with electronic measuring equipment and, as the RAF had intended, it was stalked and attacked by a number of night fighters. During these attacks, a special radio operator aboard the Wellington was able to measure the frequency of one of the attacking fighters' '*Lichtenstein*' airborne interception radar. Although damaged in the attacks, the Wellington returned to its base with its valuable information.

The RAF's knowledge of the latest German radar technology was further increased on 9 May 1943 when the defecting crew of a Ju 88 R-1 landed their aircraft at Dyce airfield, Aberdeen. This proved to be an incredible stroke of luck for Bomber Command as, once examined by British technicians, the aircraft was found to be fitted with a '*Lichtenstein*' set complete with all electronic equipment. Less than three months later, the capture of this Ju 88 would cost the residents of Hamburg dearly.

Meanwhile, by July 1943, Bomber Command had already expanded to an establishment of 53 squadrons with almost 900 bombers, approximately 650 of which were four-engined types. Since being appointed Commander-in-Chief of Bomber Command on 22 February 1942, in little more than a year Air Chief Marshal Sir Arthur Harris had sufficient aircraft available to carry out his theories on area bombing and could mount raids on the German cities almost on a nightly basis. Many of Harris's machines were being equipped with the most up-to-date electronic aids, one of which, codenamed 'H2S', had first been used operationally on the night of 30/31 January 1943 during an attack on Hamburg. At the heart of this device, housed in a blister beneath the bomber's rear fuselage, was a powerful magnetron valve which sent out high-frequency impulses through a continuously rotating aerial. Any impulses that struck built-up areas, trees or hills, produced strong returns, whereas very few returns were received when they struck fields or lakes or other similar flat areas. Any radio energy reflected from the ground was detected by the same aerial equipment and the impulses were displayed as varying shades of light on a cathode-ray tube, the intensity with which objects appeared on the display being dictated by the strength of the reflected radio energy. As the aerial was constantly sending and receiving signals, a visual representation of the countryside beneath the bomber was produced which enabled the bomber's navigator to identify landmarks. This improved the accuracy of the route flown and assisted the bomber in locating its target.

Both sides had also been working on countermeasures to jam the other's ground and air radar. Potentially, the most effective countermeasure was based upon an idea that had originated in the late 1930s. This involved dropping vast quantities of paper strips, coated on one side with aluminium which, when dispersed in the air, would form vast clouds that produced false echoes on the radar displays. Although the Germans had already produced and experimented with the strips which they codenamed '*Düppel*', when the results were documented and forwarded to Göring, he immediately prohibited further testing. Göring's great fear was that the British would discover their findings and attempt to duplicate them, but the British had in fact already developed their own version of '*Düppel*'. Measuring 27 cm long[15] and 2 cm wide, the strips were supplied in bundles which were to be released at intervals into the slipstream by a member of the bomber's crew. When the bundles burst open, the individual strips obliterated and masked the real echoes produced by the bombers. The British code name for this countermeasure was 'Window', and for the first time it was about to be employed operationally.

As Bomber Command's offensive against the Ruhr neared its conclusion in July 1943, Harris had already turned his attention to planning an all-out attack against a major German city. The selection of Hamburg in north-west Germany as the target was not a difficult decision for Harris, as he had intended to carry out a large-scale raid against the city for some time. In fact, had the weather

15. 27cm was half the wavelength of the radar that controlled the German anti-aircraft guns, searchlights and fighter control radars.

not intervened, then Hamburg, and not Cologne, would have been the target for the RAF's first thousand bomber raid on the night of 30/31 May 1942. Although Hamburg had been bombed on 137 previous occasions since the outbreak of the war, Harris now planned to completely destroy the city in a series of successive raids in which, for the first time, the American Eighth Air Force would carry out follow-up daylight attacks. The operation was codenamed 'Gomorrah' and, in order to thwart the German defences, Harris was given authority to employ 'Window'. On the evening of 24 July 1943, a total of 791 bombers took off and headed out across the North Sea and towards the north German coast.

Having correctly assumed that Bomber Command would not conduct deep operations into Germany during the short summer nights, XII. *Fliegerkorps* had already transferred night fighter units from other theatres of operations to bolster defences in the north of the country. Once the approaching raid was detected, it was tracked and the German defences and the night fighters of the four *Gruppen* of NJG 3 stationed in northern Germany and Denmark were scrambled to meet them. However, when the bombers were approximately 100 kilometres from the German coastline, they began to drop their bundles of 'Window'. The effect upon the German ground defences was almost immediate. Operators at coastal batteries, fighter controllers and '*Lichtenstein*' operators in the night fighters all found their screens swamped with a deluge of echoes and false reports. These gave the impression that the sky was full of many thousands of bombers and made it almost impossible for the radar operators in the fighters to distinguish what was a real target and what was not.

Masked by this huge cloud of tin foil, the first of the bombers reached Hamburg at 01.02 hrs. During the following 53 minutes, 728 bombers released their bombs on the centre of the city and its northern suburbs, killing approximately 1,500 people. Over Hamburg itself, the bombers went almost unmolested since the '*Würzburg*'-controlled searchlights were rendered virtually useless, and only three bombers were shot down by the city's Flak defences. Another nine bombers were also lost, but some of these had inadvertently strayed well outside of the protective 'Window' shield where they were shot down, predominantly by the night fighter crews of NJG 3.

The use of 'Window' during this raid had not only rendered Germany's defences completely useless, but it had also highlighted the inherent weaknesses of the rigid '*Himmelbett*' system of night fighting. After having spent so much time, effort and money in creating it, Josef Kammhuber was naturally unwilling to replace the existing system with another, but other individuals within the organisation were less reluctant. They could see that drastic changes were required if other German towns and cities were to be spared a similar fate. Unfortunately, however, on the afternoon of 25 July, and before any action could be taken, the city was bombed by 100 Eighth Air Force B-17s, and then again the following morning by a smaller force of 60 B-17s.

Bomber Command resumed its own offensive against Hamburg on the night of 27/28 July 1943, by which time the German ground stations had taken to broadcasting running commentaries to the night fighters and local defence units on the progress of the bomber stream, with constant updates regarding its location, height and projected heading. This was only possible because, unlike '*Wurzburg*' and '*Mammut*' etc, '*Freya*' operated on a different wavelength and remained unaffected by 'Window'. At the same time, although the *Nachtjagd* was in complete disarray, while some of its commanders insisted on operating strictly within the '*Himmelbett*' system, others permitted their night fighter pilots to operate freelance within the bomber stream.

Nevertheless, a combination of factors – chiefly the accuracy of the bombing and the weather, which had made the city very dry – resulted in a great many fires which converged into one large conflagration. Soon, with the city's water supplies disrupted and the civil defences overwhelmed by the ferocity of the attack, the fire was raging out of control. The resultant firestorm consumed everything in its path and killed an estimated 40,000 people.

Of particular significance on this night was the involvement of the newly created '*Wilde Sau*' units which, although then far from being completely prepared, had been ordered by Göring to immediate readiness after the first raid on Hamburg. On being scrambled from their respective airfields, the three *Gruppen* of JG 300 converged on Hamburg and began searching for the bombers attacking the city. Thus, while the residents of Hamburg were dying in their homes and shelters, Hajo Herrmann's '*Wilde Sau*' units doggedly pursued the bombers over the burning city, through the heavy Flak and columns of thick smoke, to claim the destruction of four bombers. Bomber Command lost a total of 17 aircraft that night to the German defences, a slight increase over the first raid and an indication that the Germans had begun to overcome the initial problems created by the introduction of 'Window'.

It is thought that even during the first two raids on Hamburg, a small number of the more experienced '*Lichtenstein*' and '*Würzburg*' radar operators were able to differentiate between the false returns created by 'Window' and those created by the bombers. This was certainly the case on the night of 29/30 July when the city was subjected to its third major raid in six nights, this time by a force of 777 RAF aircraft. Although there was no repetition of the devastation caused by the firestorm, further widespread damage was caused and approximately 800 of the city's inhabitants were killed. On this occasion, the ability of some operators to differentiate between bombers and false echoes was clearly apparent as the Flak and fighters accounted for 28 bombers, almost twice the number they had achieved during each of the previous two attacks.

With more twin-engined fighters authorised to fly freelance, eight bombers were shot down before they ever reached the target, while a further four were destroyed on the return leg. Once again, pilots from NJG 3 submitted most of the claims, with *Oblt.* Gerhard Raht of 4./NJG 3 claiming four. Various *Gruppen* from NJG 1 were also involved that night with such established night fighter pilots as Helmut Lent, Egmont Lippe-Weissenfeld and Werner Streib each destroying a bomber. The '*Wilde Sau*' again played a part during the attack, harrying the bombers as they made their bomb runs over the burning city and, according to the *Oberkommando der Luftwaffe* claims files, claiming 17 bombers. Thus a total of 36 bombers were claimed by night fighters on this night, although according to RAF records 28 were lost during the raid to the German defences with a further three written off in take-off and landing accidents. Despite this discrepancy in the respective claims and recorded losses, the *Nachtjagd* still had been able to inflict losses heavier than expected. To be sure, while Harris and his team had anticipated that the German defences would eventually overcome the effects of 'Window', the speed at which this recovery actually occurred was surprising and had resulted in Bomber Command's loss rate increasing from 1.5 per cent to 3.6 per cent in just three attacks.

One of the most respected pilots in the Nachtjagd was Hans-Joachim Jabs who became Kommodore of NJG 1 on 1 March 1944. He began the war as a Zerstörer pilot with II./ZG 76 and shot down 19 enemy aircraft, 12 of which were British fighters over England. This was a remarkable record considering the terrible losses inflicted on the Zerstörer units during the 'Battle of Britain' and for this feat he was decorated with the Knight's Cross on 1 October 1940.

The fourth and final raid against Hamburg took place on 2/3 August 1943, and was by far the least effective. Due to a large electrical storm covering the approaches to the target, only 423 of the 737 aircraft which took off from England actually claimed to have bombed in the Hamburg area. Aircraft that failed to reach the city either jettisoned their bomb loads and headed back to England, or attacked secondary targets. Where aircraft did reach Hamburg, bombing results were poor and caused few casualties and very little damage. The poor weather also caused the bomber stream to become spread out and many bombers found themselves outside the protective umbrella of 'Window'. In addition, those bombers that chose to bomb secondary targets such as Bremen, Wilhelmshaven and Heligoland came within range of night fighter units based in northern Holland. As the returning bombers crossed the Dutch coast and headed back out over the North Sea, they were intercepted by fighters from III. and IV./NJG 1. The *Kommandeur* of IV./NJG 1, *Hptm.* Hans-Joachim Jabs, shot down a Halifax and two Stirlings while two other members of his *Gruppe*, *Ofw.* Karl-Heinz Scherfling and *Oblt.* Georg Greiner, each claimed one and two respectively.

Total Bomber Command losses that night due to the combined action of fighters, Flak and bad weather, were 33 aircraft, taking total losses for the 'Battle of Hamburg' to 87 aircraft, of which 55 were claimed by the *Nachtjagd*. Although Harris had lost in the region of 620 personnel killed, taken prisoner or interned, overall the series of raids was considered to have been successful. For the Germans, the raids finally marked the end of Kammhuber's '*Himmelbett*' system, for they emphasised to all levels of the *Nachtjagd* that, if it was not to be overwhelmed by superior numbers, then tactical and technological changes were urgently required. It is much to the credit of the organisation, therefore, that it was able to rally so quickly after the initial shock of the first raid and the neutralisation by 'Window' of many of its radar-controlled defences.

Thus July 1943, and particularly the Hamburg raids, was a significant period and represented a turning point in the air war over Germany. The lessons learned through trial and error during this very short period forced the *Nachtjagd* to re-evaluate its tactics and implement a series of wide-sweeping operational changes. This in turn subsequently resulted in new tactics employed to great effect by the night fighter crews, ground controllers and technicians for much of the remainder of the war.

The necessary changes, however, had yet to be fully implemented. After the Hamburg raids, the *Nachtjagd* was given little respite by Bomber Command which was preparing for a series of attacks on Berlin.

On 5 August 1943, Hptm. Rudolf Schönert bade farewell to II./NJG 5 at Parchim before taking command of I./NJG 100. He had led the Gruppe since 1 December 1942 and was respected by all who knew him. Behind the guard of honour is a Bf 110 with its 'Lichtenstein' BC aerials clearly visible. Schönert was replaced by another respected and experienced pilot, Hptm. Manfred Meurer.

From the spring of 1943, German night fighters were employed against American aircraft in daylight operations. It was thought that the long endurance of the night fighter aircraft, the navigational skill of the crews and the ability of their aircraft to carry heavy armaments would prove useful in augmenting the German day fighters, but in fact the night fighter crews found themselves thrust into a role in which they lacked the specialised training and experience. In particular, their inability to launch concentrated attacks while in close formation led to unduly heavy losses which continued even when the night fighters were ordered only to attack single bombers separated from their formations. The night units themselves were much against their daylight employment and, taking matters into their own hands, prohibited their most experienced crews from flying daylight operations. Nevertheless, the losses considerably weakened the Nachtjagd's effort against RAF night raids for this period of 1943 and eventually forced the termination of daylight operations. These photographs show a FuG 212 'Lichtenstein'-equipped Bf 110 G-4 of 3./NJG 6 from Mainz-Finthen, probably in the late summer of 1943. The aircraft was camouflaged in 76 but with grey 75 reverse mottles over the uppersurfaces of its wings and fuselage. From the photographs, the mottling appears darker around the cockpit area than elsewhere and all national markings appear in the same grey used for the tactical code 2Z+LL. To improve the aircraft's performance, the flame-dampers, redundant during daylight sorties, have been deleted, leaving a clean area over the exhausts where these have been removed. Note that this machine has the early pattern vertical tail surfaces.

New Tactics and 'The Battle of Berlin'

The most pressing matters facing the German High Command in the summer of 1943, then, were the British jamming of '*Würzburg*' and '*Lichtenstein*', the introduction of new types of radar impervious to all forms of interference, and – if Bomber Command was to be prevented from destroying other German cities at will – new tactics. The solutions to these problems were in fact already under development, but following the devastation of Hamburg there were demands from the very highest levels to introduce them at the earliest possible opportunity.

The new method of night fighting was again conceived by a former bomber pilot, *Oberst* Viktor von Lossberg, who proposed guiding a single night fighter aircraft towards the bombers and then infiltrating it into the bomber stream. This aircraft would navigate by means of an existing position-finding method known to the Germans as '*Ypsilon-Verfahren*', or 'Y' System which, although used to great effect by the bomber and day fighter force, was rarely utilised by the *Nachtjagd*, which favoured the use of '*Würzburg*'. A large number of these '*Ypsilon*' sites, each of which could control up to five aircraft at any one time and had a range of between 250 and 300 kilometres, were spread across Germany and occupied Western Europe. Through radio communication with the aircraft, and by means of a direction-finding aerial, technicians at the 'Y' site could work out the aircraft's range and bearings. From this information the position of the aircraft could be calculated and plotted on a *Seeburgtisch* so that ground controllers could inform the pilot of his position and any changes in course necessary to guide him to the bomber stream.

Major Viktor von Lossberg.

Once this first fighter, known as the *Fühlungshalter,*[16] was in position at the head of the bomber stream, it would transmit a continuous homing signal, enabling other night fighters to join it. However, this continuous transmission proved unpopular with the majority of night fighter pilots, already wary of British intruders, who thought that it might further attract their attention. The *Fühlungshalter* procedure did not therefore become standard practice and the night fighters were subsequently guided into the bomber stream verbally by means of R/T. In time, as more of the fighters were fitted with '*Ypsilon*', even this method was superseded, allowing them to operate independently of each other.

Viktor von Lossberg also advocated equipping all available twin-engined night fighters with '*Lichtenstein*' SN-2, a new type of airborne interception radar developed by the electronics firm, Telefunken. SN-2 operated on a lower frequency than the existing '*Lichtenstein*' BC, was not affected by 'Window', and had a maximum range of four miles. *Generalfeldmarschall* Erhard Milch, the Director-General of Air Equipment, requested Telefunken to speed up development and production so that it could be rushed into service as quickly as possible.

Milch also shared von Lossberg's ideas concerning the role of freelance night fighters and, on 29 July 1943, took him to a high-level meeting where he was given an opportunity to outline his ideas to *Generaloberst* Hubert Weise. Von Lossberg's proposals were soon accepted and his new method of bringing large numbers of night fighters into contact with the enemy bomber stream became known as '*Zahme Sau*', or 'Tame Boar'. It was to evolve into an effective method of night fighting which became standard throughout the *Nachtjagd* and remained in use for the rest of the war.

While the *Nachtjagd* was frantically reorganising itself, Bomber Command's offensive against the Third Reich continued, with its next heavy raid being a precision attack on the weapons research facility at Peenemünde on the Baltic coast. The destruction of the site was so imperative that for the first time Harris employed a 'Master Bomber' to oversee the raid and ensure the bombing was as accurate as possible. To further ensure the accuracy of the bombing, the raid was carried out during the full moon period on the night of 17/18 August 1943. A total of 596 four-engined bombers set out on the raid, while at the same time a small force of eight Mosquitoes took part in a diversionary raid against Berlin. At first, this feint proved very effective and drew the majority of the night fighters to the German capital and away from Bomber Command's intended target but when the deception was discovered, some 30 night fighter pilots flew north to Peenemünde and operated freelance '*Wilde Sau*' operations over the facility.

Single-engined night fighters also took part in the action, and amongst the successful pilots that night were *Hptm*. Friedrich-Karl 'Nasen' Müller from I./JG 300, who claimed two Lancasters, and *Oblt*. Paul Zorner of 7./NJG 3, who also made a similar claim. A combination of good visibility over

16. Literally, 'Contact-keeper'.

"Like corpses' fingers"

Leutnant Peter Spoden, 6./NJG 5

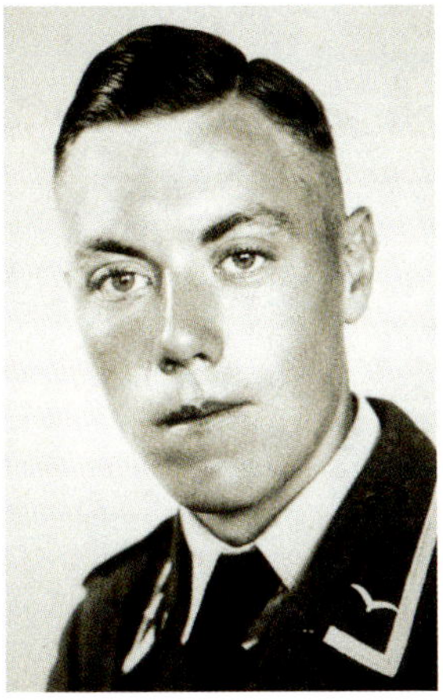

I was still at high school in early 1940 when RAF bombers began bombing the industrial Ruhr district as well as my home town of Essen. So far as I remember, no German bombs had fallen on England in those days because the German bombing of England only occurred later in August 1940 as a result of the RAF's bombing of Berlin.[1] It was then that I decided to become a pilot – a night fighter pilot – so that I could defend my home town and other areas where bombs were falling.

My application to join the Luftwaffe was accepted in October 1940 and the subsequent training to become a night fighter pilot lasted a total of 27 months. Firstly, I underwent three months of infantry training with a *Fliegerausbildungsregiment* and then, from March to December 1941, I attended the *A/B Schule* at Munich where I qualified for my pilot's badge and amassed 180 hours of flying time. I then went on to *C-Schule* No. 17 at Pütnitz-Pommern where I flew Ju 52s, He 111s and Do 17s before transferring to a *Blindflugschule* at Copenhagen in Denmark.

I then went to a *Nachtjagdschule* at Kitzingen before finally transferring to a front line unit, II./NJG 5, which was based at Parchim in Mecklenburg for the protection of Berlin. My *Gruppenkommandeur* was *Hauptmann* Rudolf Schönert, who was one of those fine officers that you find in every air force. He told us young night fighter pilots to, *"Shoot the bombers between the engines where the fuel tanks are, as they burn easily and the boys have a chance to parachute!"*

One of my first missions was on 25 July 1943 when 791 RAF bombers attacked Hamburg. This was a complete disaster for the *Nachtjagd* as the RAF dropped 'Window' for the first time and rendered our radar, anti-aircraft guns and ground organisation useless. We night fighters were kept at our radio beacons instead of being allowed to fly to the burning city where we would have been able to see the bombers silhouetted like moths. Only 12 of them were shot down and more than 45,000 German civilians were killed.

And what did we think about the RAF crews? The mental and physical burdens they experienced during a flight of eight hours or more must have been enormous, and on many occasions they impressed us very much.

On the night of 23 August 1943 there was turmoil over Berlin as Bomber Command lost a total of 56 bombers. It was one of those nights you remember for the rest of your life! First of all, high explosives were dropped, followed by phosphorous incendiaries which were released into the shattered ruins of the buildings so that fierce fires were soon blazing in the great city. It was an inferno without equal. Hundreds of searchlights rose towards us, sweeping the heavens like '*Leichenfinger*',[2] dazzling friend and foe alike. The anti-aircraft guns fired a furious barrage up to ten thousand feet, and above were the single-engined '*Wilde Sau*' and the twin-engined '*Zahme Sau*' night fighters. At times I could see between 30 and 40 aircraft all milling around together. The night sky was criss-crossed with cannon and machine gun tracer and illuminated by cascading flares of every colour, to which were added the recognition flares fired by the night fighters when the Flak opened up on them. There were also huge clouds of garishly illuminated smoke rising into the sky, white condensation trails everywhere and, down below, fearful explosions. A Lancaster attempting to escape from a cone of searchlights did a full loop. I had the impression that everyone was firing at everyone else and I was in the middle of it all. It was hell – Dante's Hell!

1. Author's note: This statement is clearly incorrect as almost 2,000 HE bombs and many more incendiaries were released on mainland targets in the UK in July 1940 alone. It is highly likely that what Peter Spoden means is that no bombs had fallen on London.
2. Literally 'corpses' fingers', a Luftwaffe term for searchlight beams.

Peenemünde and the fact that, despite 'Window', a number of radar operators could identify the bombers on their radar screens, resulted in the night fighters exacting a heavy toll. Although Peenemünde was heavily damaged, 27 of the bombers were shot down over, or close to, the target, and a further 13 were lost on the return leg.

Less than a week later, on the night of 23/24 August 1943, Bomber Command flew the first of 19 major operations against Berlin in a sustained campaign that was destined to last the best part of seven months. Harris was determined to completely destroy the city even though he estimated it would cost him 500 aircraft to do so. This first raid also marked the occasion of the first '*Zahme Sau*' operation, which proved highly successful, but over Berlin itself the vast majority of the fighters still operated by means of '*Wilde Sau*'. Through a combination of both methods, the *Nachtjagd* and the Flak defences destroyed 56 bombers, or 7.9 per cent of the bomber force, which was Bomber Command's highest loss of aircraft in a single operation to date. Following an attack against Nuremberg on the night of 27/28 August and a further raid against Berlin on 31 August/1 September, the German night fighters inflicted further heavy losses on the bombers, and by the end of August the *Nachtjagd* claimed to have destroyed some 250 enemy aircraft. Encouragingly for the defenders, over 200 of these were claimed by freelancing night fighters, whereas '*Himmelbett*' victories had only accounted for 48.

However, just as a spirit of optimism and confidence was developing within the *Nachtjagd*, Bomber Command introduced various changes in tactics to counter its growing losses. These included the implementation of more diversionary raids to confound and confuse the German ground controllers and to conceal the bombers' true targets, and the introduction of new electronic countermeasures[17] which jammed the controllers' broadcasts to the night fighters. In addition, by mounting operations during periods of bad weather over Germany, Bomber Command reduced the effectiveness of '*Wilde Sau*' operations. All of these measures resulted in a significant reduction in night fighter claims and culminated in Göring relieving Kammhuber of his command of XII. *Fliegerkorps* on 15 September 1943. Kammhuber was succeeded by *Generalmajor* Josef Schmid, and for the time being continued as *General der Nachtjagd*.

Above: When Generalmajor Josef Kammhuber was relieved of his position as General der Nachtjagd, production of the He 219 night fighter was delayed. First conceived in 1940 as a high-speed bomber and reconnaissance aircraft, the He 219 was developed in late 1941 to meet a need for a new night fighter. Although Kammhuber was enthusiastic about the He 219, the project suffered setback when he was dismissed and further development and production was delayed due to a combination of short-sightedness within the RLM and opposition on the part of Generalfeldmarschall Milch. When the type did finally enter service, it proved almost universally popular with the crews who found it fast, manoeuvrable and well-armed. This photograph was purportedly taken on 22 January 1942 during a visit by Generalmajor Josef Kammhuber to the Heinkel factory at Rostock/Marienehe. The purpose of the visit was to observe test flights of the He 219, then still under development. Behind Kammhuber is Major Wolfgang Falck and on the far right of the picture is Ernst Heinkel.

Almost two weeks later, on 26 September 1943, disenchanted by the failures of the existing night fighter force, Göring ordered the formation of two further single-engined night fighter *Geschwader*. These two units, each initially comprising just a single *Gruppe*, were designated JG 301 and JG 302 and were stationed in Bavaria and Brandenburg respectively.

Following a further series of failures to protect German cities in October, caused mainly by a breakdown in communications between the air raid reporting services and the Flak, Göring ordered a complete reorganisation of the Reich Air Defence. Once again Kammhuber was a casualty of these changes and he was relieved of his position as *General der Nachtjagd* and transferred to Norway where he took charge of *Luftflotte* 5. The position of *General der Nachtjagd* was then abolished and responsibility for night fighters came under the direct command of the *General der Jagdflieger*, *Generalmajor* Adolf Galland.

In an attempt to improve the command structure, XII. *Fliegerkorps* was reduced to just three *Jagddivisionen* and redesignated I. *Jagdkorps* with overall responsibility for the defence of the Reich. II. *Jagdkorps* was formed to protect occupied France, while 7. *Jagddivision*, with its headquarters in Munich, was set up to defend Germany against Allied bombers operating from the Mediterranean.

The effectiveness of these changes was put to the test on the night of 18/19 November 1943 when, following a two-and-a-half month pause in which Bomber Command tried to improve the accuracy of its target marking, Harris recommenced his offensive against Berlin. The previous attacks against Berlin in August and September had not been deemed successful and it was now hoped that this problem would be overcome by the recent introduction of the new 'H2S' Mk.III.

---

17. The code name for this device was 'Tinsel'. It consisted of a microphone fitted in the engine bays of RAF bombers. Once a wireless operator had tuned into the German ground controller's wavelength, he would switch on the microphone and drown out the broadcasts with engine noise.

As a result of an accident while landing on the night of 17/18 November 1943, Major Walter Ehle, the Gruppenkommandeur of II./NJG 1, and his crew – Ofw. Leidenbach (Bordfunker) and Uffz. Derlitzky (Bordschutze) – were all killed. Here a guard of honour flanks the graves during the funeral ceremony, while three members of the unit present each of the crew's decorations on black cushions. The centre cushion carries the decorations of Major Ehle and is being held by Lt. Otto Fries.

Undefeated by the enemy – the final resting place of Major Walter Ehle.

Above: A Bf 110 G equipped only with aerials for SN-2 radar. As SN-2 had a maximum range of 6.4 km but a minimum of 477 metres, which was still beyond visual range, 'Lichtenstein' radar was later added so that it was possible to continue to track the target down to 238 metres. The installation of aerials for both types of radar, however, as shown (below), had an effect on the aircraft's directional stability. To overcome this the twin fin and rudder assemblies on the Bf 110 were modified to increase the surface area, as shown in the photograph at the bottom of page 129.

A spectacular view of an early Bf 110 G of III./NJG 3 raising clouds of dust as its engines are started. The use of 'Window', first used by the RAF during an attack on Hamburg on the night of 24/25 July 1943, rendered existing ground and airborne radar useless and it was not until October 1943 that this was overcome with the introduction of the new FuG 220 'Lichtenstein' SN-2 radar which operated on a different frequency. In the meantime, 'Zahme Sau' tactics dominated, with the conventional twin-engined fighters using FuG 227 'Flensberg' to home in on the RAF's 'Monica' tail-warning radar or various jamming transmitters. This aircraft is finished in a 74/75/76 scheme and has retained the traditional shark's mouth design of II./ZG 76, from which III./NJG 3 was formed in 1941. The aerials on the nose are for the FuG 220 SN-2 radar and the pitot tube, normally on the starboard wingtip, has been relocated inboard to avoid interfering with the aerial for the FuG 227 'Flensburg' radar homing device.

A Ju 88 G-6 showing the FuG 220 aerials on the nose and fairing on the canopy which housed the FuG 350 'Naxos' radar receiver. This equipment allowed Luftwaffe night fighters to home in on the transmissions from the 'H2S' navigation device in British bomber aircraft and was first introduced at the end of 1943. The fairing itself was offset to port and consisted of a plywood frame covered in canvas. Note the individual aircraft letter 'A' on the nose indicating that this machine was flown by a Staffelkapitän or a Gruppenkommandeur and that some lower parts of the radar antenna have been painted white with a red stripe as a warning to ground crews.

By the time this second phase of the Berlin offensive began, more night fighter aircraft had been equipped with the SN-2 radar. Although SN-2 was at first somewhat restricted by its minimum range of 477 metres, as an interim measure until improvements could be made the night fighters were also equipped with simplified versions of the older '*Lichtenstein*' BC, which had a minimum range of 238 metres. This compromise resulted in two sets of aerials being fitted to the nose of the fighter and, in the case of the Bf 110, eventually resulted in a change of flight characteristics which necessitated larger rudders.

Although a shortage of SN-2 equipment caused a delay of a further six months before there was sufficient to equip the entire force, the sets that were available were put to good use from the early autumn of 1943 and on the eight occasions when Berlin was attacked between November and December 1943, no fewer that 479 bombers[18] were shot down. During a number of these raids, the bomber stream became widely scattered due to poor weather conditions over Germany, and many of the errant aircraft became easy prey for '*Zahme Sau*' freelancing twin-engined night fighters. These bomber losses, combined with those from the earlier three raids, had already surpassed Harris's estimate of 500 for the entire offensive and his loss rate was averaging almost six per cent.

There was, nevertheless, no respite for the residents of Berlin and, as the new year began, the city was again attacked on the night of 1/2 January 1944 by 421 aircraft, all of which were Lancasters. Due to delays caused by the weather, the bombers were forced to fly a more direct route to Berlin which took them over Holland and made them more vulnerable to the night fighter units stationed there. Operating from Deelen in Holland, and flying a Ju 88 C equipped with SN-2 and '*Schräge Musik*', *Major* Heinrich *Prinz* zu Sayn-Wittgenstein, the newly appointed *Kommodore* of NJG 2, managed to infiltrate the bomber stream and shot down six of them. Another successful pilot that night was *Oblt*. Ludwig Meister, the *Staffelkapitän* of 1./NJG 4, who claimed the destruction of four Lancasters. All told, 16 bombers were shot down before they even reached Berlin and total losses for the raid totalled 28.

In a similar raid against Berlin the following night, the bomber stream passed over Holland on the outward and homeward legs of the flight. A further 27 Lancasters were lost as they battled their way towards the target, combating adverse weather conditions as well as approximately 150 to 200 night fighters. Running battles with the night fighters took place over Berlin as the bombers carried out their bomb runs and at least ten bombers were shot down over the target while others fell as they headed away from the city. Once again the *Nachtjagd* accounted for the majority of those lost, with 21 claims being submitted in all. For the next three weeks Berlin was reprieved from further attacks, partly due to a period of full moon, although other cities, such as Stettin on 5/6 January and Brunswick on 14/15 January, were raided.

Harris, frustrated by the poor bombing results of the previous raids, sent his bomber force back to Berlin on the nights of 20/21, 27/28, 28/29 and 30/31 January 1944, in what was a concerted effort to try and finish what he had started five months earlier. Despite attempts to reduce bomber losses by routing them further out over the North Sea, away from German night fighter bases in Holland and Belgium, Bomber Command still lost a total of 147 aircraft as a consequence of these operations.

By now the offensive had become a battle of attrition, and although the German night fighters had enjoyed some increased success, they too had suffered losses and since the attack against Peenemünde in August 1943, the *Nachtjagd* had lost 71 aircraft and some of its foremost night fighter pilots. Amongst those lost was *Major* Hans-Dieter Frank who had destroyed 55 bombers at the time of his death on 27/28 September 1943. Two nights later, *Hptm*. August Geiger, with 54 victories, was shot down and killed by an RAF night fighter over the Zuider-See. But by far the greatest blow to the *Nachtjagd* occurred on 21/22 January 1944, when it lost two of its most prestigious and highest scoring aces. On this particular night, Bomber Command's target was Magdeburg and two of the pilots operating against the bombers were *Major Prinz* zu Sayn-Wittgenstein and *Hptm*. Manfred Meurer, the *Kommandeur* of I./NJG 1. After shooting down five aircraft, and briefly becoming the *Nachtjagd's* highest scoring night fighter pilot with 83 victories, it is believed that Wittgenstein was killed when his Ju 88 was attacked by a

Major Heinrich Prinz zu Sayn-Wittgenstein, the Kommodore of NJG 2, with his crew at Rechlin in January 1944. In the middle of the group is Wittgenstein's Bordmechaniker, Kurt Matzüleit, and to his left is Friedrich Ostheimer, the crew's Bordfunker.

18. Figures taken from 'The Bomber Command War Diaries' by Martin Middlebrook and Chris Everitt.

Continued on page 115

Werner Streib

Following his 43rd night victory, Streib was decorated with the Oak Leaves to the Knight's Cross on 26 February 1943. On the very same day two other prominent night fighter pilots, Paul Gildner and Ludwig Becker, were both killed and posthumously awarded the same decoration.

IN terms of his personal achievement and his contribution to the development of night fighting during the Second World War, one of the most outstanding personalities of the *Nachtjagd* was Werner Streib.

Streib was born in the Black Forest town of Pforzheim on 13 June 1911 and, after leaving school with his *Abitur*, spent a further three years training for a career in commercial finance. However, at the end of his examinations, Streib decided that he was not after all suited to a life in the business world and decided to join the Army. His formal application to join the *Heer* as a soldier was successful and he subsequently joined the 14. *Infanterie Regiment* in 1934. A year later, in March 1935, and shortly after having completed his basic infantry training, he heard about the formation of the Luftwaffe and immediately put in a transfer request to join this new arm of the services.

With his request accepted, Werner Streib entered the Luftwaffe as an officer cadet on 1 October 1935 and began training as an observer in a reconnaissance unit. However, this was a time of rapid expansion for the Luftwaffe and an increased demand for pilots, and in 1936 Streib was selected for fighter pilot training. After qualifying for his pilot's badge, he was promoted to *Leutnant* and posted to II./JG 132 '*Richthofen*', then stationed at Jüterborg-Damm, some 70 km south of Berlin.

This *Gruppe*, like many others in the Luftwaffe, underwent a number of changes as the service continued to expand. For example, with the development of the Bf 110 twin-engined destroyer, II./JG 132 was selected as one of the first units to receive this type and in November 1938 the *Gruppe* was redesignated I./ZG 141. Streib, together with other pilots from the *Gruppe*, received conversion training on the type and when war finally broke out in September 1939, the unit had been redesignated I./ZG 1 and was equipped with the Bf 110 C.

It is believed that this photograph was taken during the early phases of the invasion of France in May 1940. At that time Werner Streib (far left) was the Intelligence Officer for I./ZG 1. On the far right is Oberstleutnant Joachim-Friedrich Huth, the Kommodore of ZG 26 'Horst Wessel' and, to his right, Hptm. Wolfgang Falck, the Kommandeur of I./ZG 1.

During the invasion of Poland, Streib and I./ZG 1 participated mainly in bomber escort and ground support missions and, following the successful conclusion of this brief campaign, the *Gruppe* was transferred back to Neuhausen ob Eck in Southern Germany. Although Germany was now at war with England and France, the winter of 1939/40 proved a relatively quiet period and allowed many of the Luftwaffe's fighter units to rest and re-equip. Streib busied himself with his duties as Communications Officer for I./ZG 1 and, in February 1940, the unit received a new *Gruppenkommandeur* – *Hauptmann* Wolfgang Falck.

Streib had first met Falck at Jüterborg-Damm when they had both served with II./JG 132, and although neither of them realised it at the time, this association would not only cement a lifelong friendship but would also shape their future careers in the Luftwaffe.

The period of quietude known as the 'Phoney War' came to a dramatic end on 9 April 1940 when, under the code name '*Weserüebung*', Hitler launched the invasion of Denmark and Norway. During this operation, I./ZG 1 took off from its airfield at Barth in Northern Germany and helped secure the airfield at Vaerlöse-Copenhagen. Although the Danes capitulated almost immediately in the face of insurmountable German forces, I./ZG 1 was forced to continue flying support missions to Norway as resistance to the *Wehrmacht's* invasion continued to grow. Operating from their recently captured airfield at Aalborg in Northern Denmark, Falck's *Gruppe* came under direct attack in nuisance raids conducted by Bomber Command aircraft returning from night attacks on targets in Germany.

As a consequence of these attacks, Falck, with other selected pilots from his unit, including Streib, attempted to intercept these bombers, and this experience resulted in Falck submitting a report on the possibilities of night fighting to the Luftwaffe's High Command. But on 10 May 1940, and before this report could be properly evaluated, Germany invaded France and the Low Countries, and any thoughts of night fighting were shelved. On the opening day of the offensive, however, Streib found himself operating against aircraft of Bomber Command which were flying day missions and, following a short skirmish, he attacked a Bristol Blenheim which he destroyed as his first and only daylight victory.

Following the bombing of Rotterdam on 13 May 1940, Bomber Command began attacking targets in Germany itself, and to counter these Göring ultimately ordered the formation of the *Nachtjagd*, and when Falck was made *Kommodore* of NJG 1 – the first night fighter *Geschwader* – I./ZG 1 was redesignated I./NJG 1. Operating from Gütersloh as the *Staffelkapitän* of 2./NJG 1, Streib shot down a Whitley bomber from 51 Squadron in the early hours of 20 July 1940, and so achieved the *Nachtjagd's* first success. The following month, Streib shot down a Wellington and a Hampden on the night of 30/31 August, and during raids against Berlin and other targets in Germany on the night of 30 September he was credited with three more victories.

On 6 October 1940, after his seventh night victory, Streib received the Knight's Cross and promotion to *Hauptmann*. Two weeks later, he was appointed *Gruppenkommandeur* of I./NJG 1 and took over command from

Oblt. Heinz-Wolfgang Schnaufer of 12./NJG 1 photographed in February 1944 with the tail of his Bf 110 G, W.Nr. 720260, which was then marked with 47 victory bars. The last of these victories were all claimed on the night of 15/16 February when, between 22.58 and 23.33 hrs, Schnaufer shot down three Lancasters. Schnaufer ended the war with the rank of Major and a total of 121 night victories claimed in only 164 sorties. He was awarded the Ritterkreuz in December 1943, the Oak Leaves in June 1944, the Swords a month later and the Diamonds on 16 October 1944 when he reached 100 victories. Post-war, Schnaufer was seriously injured in a road accident in France on 13 July 1950 and died two days later.

roving British intruder.[19] Some 30 minutes later, Manfred Meurer lost his life when his He 219 A-O collided with the Lancaster he was attacking and both aircraft crashed 22 kilometres east of Magdeburg. This was Meurer's 65th and final victory.

Following the attack on 30/31 January 1944, there was a two week lull in the offensive during which Harris made good his losses. Then, on the evening of 15 February, the German early warning radar detected a large bomber force crossing the North Sea. This was the largest number of aircraft assembled to attack Berlin and consisted of 891 bombers, 561 of which were Lancasters. As the bombers crossed the east coast of Denmark they were attacked by *Gruppen* from NJG 3 and NJG 5 and harried all the way to the target area. By the time the outskirts of Berlin were reached, the German countryside was already littered with at least 20 destroyed bombers. On the return leg, the bombers flew over northern Holland and were attacked by fighters from III. and IV./NJG 1 which claimed the destruction of a further seven aircraft. A total of 43 bombers was lost, and among the most successful night fighter pilots that night was *Hptm*. Erhard Peters from 9./NJG 3, who claimed five, and *Oblt*. Heinz Schnaufer, who claimed three Lancasters and so increased his personal tally to 47.

Four nights later, the *Nachtjagd* enjoyed another notable victory during a raid against Leipzig when everything seemed to go wrong for the bombers almost as soon as they had taken off. Due to incorrectly forecast winds by the meteorological office, the bomber stream became widely dispersed and many of them reached the target too early. This resulted in large numbers of bombers circling the target area waiting for it to be marked by the Pathfinders, and some 20 bombers were shot down by Flak while at least four others were lost in collisions. Furthermore, a diversionary raid to Kiel had failed to draw away many night fighters and, as a consequence of this, the bomber stream found itself under attack all the way to Leipzig. Conditions were ideal for '*Zahme Sau*' and the night fighters reaped the benefit of good weather conditions and a widely dispersed bomber stream. In all, 78 bombers were lost, the equivalent of 9.5 per cent of the force. This was a staggering loss for Bomber Command and an unequivocal success for the German defences.

As a direct result of this raid, Harris turned away from Berlin and began to target industrial cities in the south of Germany which had, up until now, been spared much of the bombing. This was a shrewd decision for the path to these targets would take the bombers over France and thus well away from many of the night fighter bases in Holland and Belgium. For six weeks, such cities as Frankfurt, Augsburg and Stuttgart were attacked with considerably reduced losses. In the meantime, however, Harris was acutely aware that he would be forced to divert his resources to assist in the preparations

19. There is some evidence to suggest that Wittgenstein was attacked by a Mosquito from 141 Sqn. piloted by F/Sgt. D. Snape and F/O L. Fowler.

A Ju 88 C-6 of 5./NJG 2, probably photographed in late 1943, clearly showing the aerials for the FuG 202 'Lichtenstein' BC radar on the nose. The night fighter versions of the Ju 88 C series were originally introduced relatively slowly due to limited availability of the radar and were later replaced by the Ju 88 G which began to appear in mid-1944. Given the period in which this machine was photographed, the full code would almost certainly have been R4+GN, although in 1944 the Geschwader's operational code was reversed to '4R'.

for D-Day and he was determined to have one more go at the German capital before this happened. On 24/25 March 1944, therefore, he committed his force to their 19th and final raid against Berlin.

High winds disrupted this raid from the very start and, once again, the bomber stream became spread out. However, although '*Zahme Sau*' night fighter operations were made easier, very few of the bombers were lost as they made their way to Berlin because of their northerly route over the North Sea. Once they reached Berlin, they were engaged by all three '*Wilde Sau*' *Geschwader* which had been waiting for them over the city and subsequently submitted claims for the destruction of 17 bombers. Meanwhile, almost the entire *Nachtjagd* was airborne with a great many of its fighters circling to the south, waiting for the bombers to emerge from over the city. In the first 60 miles of their homeward journey, 19 bombers were shot down, but more losses were to follow. Having monitored the progress of the bomber stream, the German ground controllers had shrewdly kept NJG 1 on the ground until certain of the bombers' return heading. Once the bomber stream had been detected heading westwards across Northern Germany, the ground controllers, guessing that it would probably fly over Holland, ordered NJG 1 to scramble all available units. Thus the greatest losses occurred as the bombers struggled back over Germany and into Northern Holland. Among the successful night fighter pilots was Heinz Schnaufer, the recently appointed *Kommandeur* of IV./NJG 1, who took off from St. Trond and shot down three Lancasters, while his friend Martin Drewes, *Kommandeur* of III./NJG 1, also claimed three bombers. Total Bomber Command losses amounted to 72 aircraft and, despite Harris's ambition to destroy the city, the raid proved to be the last major attack mounted against Berlin for the remainder of the war.

Much of the success achieved by the *Nachtjagd* during this prolonged Berlin offensive was due to the progressive and continual integration into the overall defensive network of the '*Zahme Sau*' method of night fighting. Encouragingly, as the numbers of pilots who adopted this style of night fighting increased, so did the occurrences of multiple victories by individual crews. Furthermore, with the abandonment of '*Himmelbett*' in favour of '*Zahme Sau*', many more pilots, regardless of their experience or personal success, could actively participate in operations and a greater number of them became aces. The *Nachtjagd* had shown great resilience in overcoming most of the British attempts to jam its ground and air radar systems, and had actually grown stronger and more formidable as a result. At this time, Helmut Lent was its highest scorer with 85 kills, followed by Werner Streib with 65 and Rudolf Schoenert with 60 victories. Buoyed up by its recent victories, the *Nachtjagd* was about to experience its finest hour.

A Ju 88 C-6 night fighter of the 4. Staffel of an unidentified Nachtjagdgeschwader. The camouflage consists of 76 undersurfaces and plain 75 on the uppersurfaces which has been extended well down the fuselage sides. The 75 was then oversprayed with what appears to be 76 but in such a way that small patches of 75 remained. Such a finish, referred to in this work as 'reverse mottling', is often mistaken for 75 mottles applied over 76.

Above: Generally, Luftwaffe night fighters operating on the Eastern Front lacked airborne radar equipment and crews were vectored to intercept enemy aircraft by ground control alone. For increased mobility during such Eastern Front operations, a few Würzburg-Riese radars with their associated equipment and personnel were mounted on a series of railway wagons. The unit shown here belonged to 'Sumatra II', a mobile station which operated in cooperation with NJG 100.

Left: Another example of a camouflage finish probably modified at unit level may be seen on this Ju 88, believed to have belonged to NJG 2. Note that the mottled uppersurface finish, which already comes well down the fuselage sides, has been further extended with sprayed streaks to include the ventral gondola.

Below: For a short time in 1943, NJG 100 was under the command of Major Heinrich Prinz zu Sayn-Wittgenstein. In this photograph, he is seen examining a weapon recovered from the wreckage of a Soviet aircraft.

Above right, below and opposite page: In November 1943, Oberst Walter Grabmann became Kommandeur of 3. Jagddivision and was a frequent visitor to the units under his command. The photograph shows Grabmann at Störmede on 10 April 1944 with Major Heinz Bär (left), the Kommandeur of II./JG 1, and Oberst Walter Oesau (right), the Kommodore of JG 1. Parked in the background is Grabmann's personal Fw 190 A-5. (Below and opposite page) is another Fw 190 A-5, W.Nr. 410054 which Grabmann first flew in July 1943 when he was Jagdfliegerführer Holland, retained after his appointment as Kommandeur of 3. Jagddivision, and continued to fly until at least May 1944. The 3. Jagddivision, which had a link via the 1. Jagddivision to the original Nachtjagddivision, controlled NJG 1, NJG 2, NJG 4 and NJG 5, hence the 'Englandblitz' badge of the Nachtjagd on the aircraft's engine cowling. Grabmann, who was promoted to Generalmajor on 1 August 1944, remained with 3. Jagddivision until 1945.

Focke-Wulf Fw 190 A-5, W.Nr. 410054, flown by Oberst Walter Grabmann, 1943-1944

This aircraft was camouflaged in the standard mid-war 74/75/76 day fighter scheme and the green 70 spinner had a white ring near the tip. Although this aircraft has elsewhere been identified as 'Red X', careful comparison in the accompanying photographs between the tone of the letter and the known yellow areas under the wingtips and under the nose indicate that the aircraft letter was also yellow, edged in white. The badge of the Nachtjägd was applied to the engine cowling and the aerials under the fuselage were non-standard.

An Fw 190 A-6 coded 'Black 8' of 2./JG 300 in the autumn of 1943 showing the FuG 217 'Neptune' aerials mounted on the wings and in front and behind the canopy.

A close-up of another Fw 190 night fighter fitted with FuG 217 aerials. This example was equipped with underwing long-range tanks.

Above and below: Fw 190s of JG 300 preparing for a night sortie.

The Nuremberg Raid

After its successes during the early months of 1944, morale within the *Nachtjagd* was now high. The force had emerged from a difficult period and although it may have seemed that a full recovery was impossible, it had quickly reorganised itself until it was once again a potent and dangerous adversary. Indeed, its effectiveness and the increasing losses inflicted by the defences on Bomber Command during the 'Battle of Berlin', many of which had been due to German night fighter action, had led Harris to end his offensive. But Harris was still convinced that his policy of area bombing was correct and that this was the only way to bring the war to a swift conclusion. He also knew that he was quickly running out of time for, as D-Day approached, his bombers would soon be required to divert to tactical targets in preparation for the invasion.

On 20 February 1944, the USAAF began a series of long-planned attacks against German aircraft factories. This photograph was taken on 22 February, when 289 B-17s of the US 1st Bombardment Division attacked Ochersleben, Aschersleben, Halberstadt and Bernburg, but lost 38 bombers. Although the US attacks continued for a week, it was on this date that Luftwaffe night fighter pilots from NJG 3, NJG 5, NJG 6 and NJG 102 achieved their greatest success and claimed a total of 11 victories. Here, a Bf 110 is seen attacking B-17s of the 91st Bombardment Group.

On 26/27 March 1944, just two days after the last Berlin raid, Harris sent 705 bombers to bomb the industrial city of Essen in the Ruhr. After so many recent attacks against targets deep in Germany, the ground controllers monitoring the course of the bomber stream expected an attack somewhere in central Germany and the shallow intrusion took them completely by surprise. Consequently, a great many of the available night fighters were patrolling in the wrong area and only a small number of them actually came into contact with the bombers. With such little opposition, combined with accurate target marking by the Pathfinders, significant damage was caused to Essen for the loss of only nine bombers. *Hptm*. Paul Zorner, the *Staffelkapitän* of 8./NJG 3 claimed three of these, while *Major* Wilhelm Herget, the *Gruppenkommandeur* of I./NJG 4, claimed two others; but overall it was a very disappointing night for the *Nachtjagd* which also lost 20 of its own aircraft in the process. This was an unacceptably high loss rate and one that, if sustained, it could ill afford.

However, four nights later on 30/31 March 1944, the situation was dramatically reversed in what would be regarded as the *Nachtjagd's* most successful defensive action. Relieved by the low losses incurred during the Essen attack, Harris now planned a maximum-effort raid against Nuremberg, a city of economical and political importance to the Nazi state. A force of 795 aircraft was gathered together from 51 Squadrons, the vast majority of which were Lancasters. RAF planners, in an attempt to divert some of the night fighters away from the main force, sent 49 Halifaxes to the south of Heligoland to lay mines, while Mosquitoes were tasked with attacking night fighter airfields and carrying out spoof attacks against Aachen, Cologne and Kassel.

Monitoring the increased RAF radio and 'H2S' activity, the Germans correctly anticipated that a large-scale attack was being planned for that evening but were unable to deduce which city might be the target. Once the main force had taken off, it was tracked by German radar and fighters were assembled at two radio beacons: '*Ida*' near Bonn, and '*Otto*' in the vicinity of Frankfurt/Main. Although the bombers released bundles of 'Window', which masked the individual aircraft, this tactic was of little avail. German controllers had since learnt to gauge the direction of the bomber stream from its radar returns and more German night fighter aircraft were now equipped with the SN-2 interception radar which was unaffected by 'Window'. On this night, not only were the bombers detected by '*Freya*' and SN-2 radar, but the weather, in which the bombers were clearly visible, played an integral part in the events of the night and was almost wholly responsible for what proved to be a disaster for Bomber Command.

High cloud cover had been predicted during the planning stages of the operation and it was hoped that this would mask the moon, which was almost full at that time of the month. However, a reconnaissance flight on the morning of the attack revealed that the high cloud cover would not materialise to conceal the bombers but that cloud would cover the city itself. In spite of the unfavourable weather reports, Harris unwisely ordered the operation to proceed.

The bombers flew across Belgium on a south-easterly heading before turning east as they neared the town of Charleroi. It was as they approached the Belgian-German border that the first bombers began to encounter night fighters. It is estimated that at this point there were over 200 night fighter aircraft from some 23 *Gruppen* in the air, all of which were heading for the '*Ida*' and '*Otto*' radio

beacons. Unfortunately, the course of the bombers was such that it took them towards these beacons and the bombers flew straight into a trap. The first bomber shot down during the Nuremberg raid was a Lancaster from 467 Sqn. which was intercepted by *Hptm.* Martin Drewes of III./NJG 1, who positioned himself 50 metres below the bomber and opened fire with his '*Schräge Musik*', setting one of the bomber's wings ablaze. The doomed bomber remained airborne for five minutes and crashed to the north-east of Spa, becoming Drewes' 16th victory.

Drewes had encountered the bomber stream while still making his way to '*Ida*', and within minutes of his victory other fighters from bases in Holland, Belgium and France were also making contact with the bomber stream. Conditions for '*Zahme Sau*' were perfect. One of the effects of the change in cloud cover was a change in the forecast wind speed, which caused the bomber stream to become scattered over a very wide area. In addition, because of the cold, clear air, some of the bombers were leaving condensation trails and these, together with the bright moon, indicated the direction in which the bomber stream was heading and assisted the night fighters in locating their targets. Having turned eastwards, the bombers now faced a long straight flight of 265 miles, known as the 'Long Leg' until, reaching the vicinity of Oberstadt, they would turn south towards Nuremberg on a shorter, straight leg of about 79 miles.

A Ju 88 C-6 with the four aerials for FuG 202 'Lichtenstein' BC or FuG 212 'Lichtenstein' C-1 radar and still wearing the early overall black night finish. This particular machine almost certainly served with NJG 2 which retained the type until well into 1944, while other units continued to operate the type until the surrender in May 1945.

Skilfully guided by the controllers, the night fighters had infiltrated the bomber stream at a very early stage and wreaked such havoc that by the time the bomber stream reached the turning point at the end of the 'Long Leg', 41 Lancasters and 18 Halifaxes had been shot down in the previous hour. A good many of the night fighters were fitted with '*Schräge Musik*' and used the weapon to such great effect that many of the bomber crews shot down were unaware that a fighter had been responsible.

Paradoxically, however, the most successful pilot that night, *Oberleutnant* Martin 'Tino' Becker of I./NJG 6, did not have '*Schräge Musik*' fitted to his Bf 110 and accomplished all his victories using only his forward-firing armament. Becker was already an established ace with 19 victories and had shot down six bombers during an attack against Frankfurt on 22/23 March. On the night of the Nuremberg raid he took off from Mainz-Finthen at 23.43 hrs. and set course for '*Ida*'. He too happened across the bomber stream and shot down a Halifax[20] at 00.20 hrs to the south-west of Cologne. Becker's preferred style of attack involved trailing the target to starboard, usually at a distance so that he could not be seen by the rear gunner. Then, at the right moment, he would sweep across and underneath the bomber and, raising the nose of his aircraft, fire a long, accurate burst into its port engine. This is the method he used on this night and three minutes after having shot down his first bomber he proceeded to shoot down a second, followed ten minutes later by a third. During the next 17 minutes, he continued to follow the bomber stream eastwards and dispatched three more aircraft in much the same way. After his sixth victory, he returned to Mainz-Finthen, refuelled and was airborne again 30 minutes later.

In the meantime, the first of the bombers had already reached the last turning point and were heading south towards Nuremberg. By the time the main force had reached the city and carried out their bomb runs, almost 80 had been shot down since the first loss over Spa in Belgium. In view of all their difficulties, that approximately 512 bombers were still able to reach Nuremberg was an amazing achievement. Unfortunately, however, despite their courage and determination, the results of the bombing were disappointing. Thick cloud covered the city and the bombing was spread out over a wide area, causing very little damage and few casualties.

As the bombers, now considerably fewer as a result of the losses, continued on the homeward leg of their journey, many of the German night fighters were obliged to land to refuel and re-arm, but accounted for a further five bombers shot down between the German border and the Channel. One of these was Martin Becker's seventh and final encounter of the night, which occurred over

[20] According to Martin Middlebrook's 'The Nuremberg Raid' this aircraft was a Halifax from 432 Sqn. piloted by P/O C.R. Narum RCAF. Only three of the seven-man crew survived the encounter.

Saarbrücken at 03.15 hrs. As the bomber, which has since been identified as a Halifax of 429 Sqn., cleared the town, it was attacked by Becker and one of its wings was set on fire. The entire crew was able to abandon the doomed aircraft before it crashed at Eichen in Luxembourg. Although this last kill was carried out using '*Himmelbett*', Becker's other victories had all been achieved using '*Zahme Sau*' and demonstrated how effective this type of night fighting could be. Three weeks later, on 20 April 1944, Becker's achievement was recognised when he was awarded the Knight's Cross.

Eckart-Wilhelm von Bonin began his career with the Luftwaffe in November 1937. After the war began, he transferred to the Nachtjagd in October 1940 and achieved his first kill victory with 6./NJG 1 on 10/11 May 1941, when he shot down a Wellington. He went on to claim a total of 37 bombers and was awarded the Knight's Cross on 5 February 1944.

Many other pilots were also successful during the Nuremberg raid, and while it had presented an ideal opportunity for a large number of newer pilots to obtain their first night victories, some of the more experienced also claimed victories, including multiple kills by *Lt.* Wilhelm Seuss of 11./NJG 5, *Lt.* Hans Raum of 9./NJG 3, *Ofw.* Rudolf Frank of 3./NJG 3 and *Oblt.* Helmuth Schulte of 4./NJG 5, each of whom claimed four victories.

The Nuremberg raid resulted in the total loss of 95 bombers and a further nine crash-landed back in England. The *Nachtjagd*, and indeed all facets of the German defensive network, had performed exceptionally well, and as a result of close cooperation had been able to inflict on Bomber Command its heaviest loss of the war. However, one battle does not win a war, and the Nuremberg raid proved to be the last occasion on which the *Nachtjagd* would achieve such an overwhelming victory.

Meanwhile, since early March, Bomber Command had been involved in a small number of bombing operations over France and Belgium, attacking railways, military installations, ammunition depots and munitions factories in preparation for the invasion of the European mainland. In April, following the Nuremberg operation, the number of these raids increased dramatically, resulting in a marked decrease in the number of attacks against Germany, and this allowed the night fighters to temporarily transfer to airfields in France to support night fighter units already operating there.[21] II./NJG 1, under the command of *Hptm.* Eckart-Wilhelm von Bonin, was transferred from St. Trond in Belgium to St.Dizier, south-west of Verdun, along with I./NJG 5, under the command of *Hptm.* Werner Hoffmann. In addition, III./NJG 1 under *Hptm.* Martin Drewes and *Hptm.* Paul Zorner's III./NJG 5 were transferred from their respective airfields to Laon-Athies in Northern France.

These *Gruppen* experienced varying degrees of success during this period depending on the location of Bomber Command's targets, for if the targets were near the coast, the raids were invariably over before the night fighters could react. However, the *Nachtjagd's* most notable success came on the night of 3/4 May 1944, when 346 Lancasters attacked a German military camp near Mailly-Le-Camp, approximately 90 miles west of Paris. The target was well marked and, initially, the raid went well for the bombers but then a communications problem caused a delay in the bombing by the main force, during which night fighters arrived over the target. In a running battle with the bombers, the fighters claimed 47 kills and although RAF records only show the loss of 42 Lancasters, it was nevertheless an admirable total, with *Hptm.* Helmut Bergmann of 8./NJG 4 topping the list of victories with a total of five for the night.

In a concerted effort to reduce the operational efficiency of Luftwaffe units in occupied western Europe, the RAF and USAAF also carried out round the clock strafing and bombing attacks on night fighter airfields. These persistent attacks were effective in many ways and disturbed the day-to-day running of the night fighter units. At night, their nocturnal operations were disrupted by Mosquitoes which bombed and strafed the airfields, as well as seeking night fighters taking off or landing. By day, Allied fighters roamed almost at will, attacking any aircraft seen, whether on the ground or in the air, as a result of which a not inconsequential number of night fighter pilots were wounded or killed while on daylight test flights. However, when on 29 April 1944, six Spitfires of 132 Sqn. led by S/L Geoffrey Page attacked a Bf 110 making its final approach at Deelen airfield, the results were not what the British pilots had expected. The Bf 110 just happened to be flown by the *Kommodore* of NJG 1, *Major* Hans-Joachim Jabs who, on seeing the Spitfires, opened his throttles and attacked the British fighters head-on. In less than a minute, Jabs had shot down two of the Spitfires[22] but the odds were overwhelmingly against him. He was attacked by the remaining Spitfires and forced to crash-land his fighter, walking away from his damaged aircraft uninjured.

21. I./NJG 4 at Florennes; III./NJG 4 at Dijon; and III./NJG 4 at Juvincourt.

22. The pilots of these two aircraft were F/O J.J. Caulton who became a PoW, and P/O R.B Pullin who was killed as a result of the combat.

In November 1943 there was some concern in certain Luftwaffe circles that the speed of the Ju 88 C-6 and Ju 88 R-1 was insufficient to combat the civil BOAC Mosquitoes which were flying between Scotland and Sweden. The Staffelkapitän of 10./NJG 3, Oblt. Hans-Hermann Müller whose Staffel was then based at Aalborg-West in Denmark, decided to employ the Fw 190, but an appeal for the loan of such an aircraft from a neighbouring unit, 10./JG 11 at Aalborg-East, was refused. Müller then appealed to 2. Jagddivision and was provided with one Fw 190 A-5 which was assigned the code D5+XV. In December, 10./JG 11 was ordered to loan Müller two Fw 190 A-4s which were subsequently coded D5+YV and D5+ZV, and while in the charge of 10./NJG 3 the Fw 190 detachment was known as Nachtjagdkommando 190. However, trials with the single-seat Fw 190s did not result in the expected successes and the Fw 190 A-4s were returned to JG 11 in February. The A-5 was also eventually returned to 2. Jagddivision in March.

Focke-Wulf Fw 190 A-5 of 10./NJG 3 coded 'D5+XV', Aalborg-West, early 1944

This machine had large areas of the fuselage and the entire uppersurfaces of the wings and tailplane oversprayed with grey 74, although an area oversprayed with 75 and mottled with 74 is visible on the vertical tail surfaces. The operational markings on the fuselage were entirely in black.

Right: Less easy to explain are these Fw 190s which, to judge from the 'Englandblitz' badge on the machine in the foreground, clearly belonged to a night fighter unit and may have been one of the Fw 190 A-4s from 10./JG 11 assigned to 10./NJG 3. The machine in the background with the tactical marking 'Red 5' and a II. Gruppe bar aft of the fuselage Balkenkreuz, also has a large white gull painted below the cockpit. Such a marking is known to have been applied to the Fw 190 A-5 flown by Hptm. Dietrich Wickop of II./JG 1 in May 1943. As there is a link back to JG 1 via a number of redesignations, it is possible that Wickop's machine may have been the Fw 190 A-5 later assigned to 10./NJG 3 as D5+XV, and is shown here before being repainted in new camouflage and markings.

Above and right: At the beginning of 1944, German night fighters began to appear with one wing painted black, presumably as a feature to identify friendly aircraft to the Flak units. Such a finish is shown here on a Bf 110 (right) and an He 219 A-2, (above) but it is thought that this undersurface colouring existed only for a short time. The He 219 shown here was flown by Hptm. Ernst-Wilhelm Modrow of 1./NJG 1 who was awarded the Ritterkreuz on 19 August 1944 after achieving 25 night victories and went on to increase his tally to 33.

Above and opposite right: This Bf 110 G-4 of 6./NJG 6 landed at Dübendorf in Switzerland shortly before midnight on 15 March 1944. The aircraft was fitted with auxiliary fuel tanks and had 76 undersurfaces with most of the starboard wing, including the drop tank, painted black. Note, however, that an area immediately aft of the spinner was not painted black and that the black under the wing terminated in an irregular line just short of the leading edge. The uppersurface colouring is most interesting, for while the nose area approximately forward of the windscreen retained the original factory 74/75/76 finish, the rest of the aircraft's uppersurfaces had been repainted in a low demarcation splinter scheme of 74 and 75. Note that the tactical code 2Z+OP was repeated on the nose and the Werknummer 5547 was applied to the tail.

"The bomber began to burn brightly and immediately went into a dive"

Hauptmann Paul Zorner, 8./NJG 3

Paul Zorner began his career with the Luftwaffe as an instructor at Zeltweg-Steiermark in Austria. When Rommel began experiencing supply problems in North Africa, Zorner and other instructor pilots from all over Germany were assigned as transport pilots and flew supply flights between Sicily and North Africa. His career as a night fighter began in January 1942 and, with his specialist training completed, he joined II./NJG 2 on 1 July 1942. His first victory came on 17 January 1943 and by the end of the year he had shot down a further 18 aircraft. When he was awarded the Knight's Cross on 9 June 1944, this total had increased to 48. Three months later, Paul Zorner became the 588th member of the Wehrmacht to receive the Oak Leaves and finished the war with 59 confirmed victories, all of which were achieved at night.

IN March 1944, I was the *Staffelkapitän* of 8./NJG 3, stationed at Lüneburg.[1] At that time of the year, however, experienced crews were frequently moved up to airfields further to the west and took off from Vechta and Nordholz in north-west Germany or, as on 22 March 1944, from St. Trond in Belgium. Detachments to St. Trond were always very relaxed. My deputy was responsible for the unit at Lüneburg, and as I was only responsible for my own aircraft and its crew, we sat down and made ourselves comfortable in the readiness room. This did not last long, however, for on this particular night, at only about seven o'clock, reports started to come through of RAF bombers preparing to take off and we had to reckon with early action. This proved correct, for an hour later, cockpit readiness was ordered, and at about 20.15 hrs we were ordered to take off against aircraft approaching at heights of between 5,500 and 6,000 metres.

I took off at 20.19 hrs and climbed to height. My personal papers did not give me any information about the bombers' approach route, but the RAF leadership was clearly able to conceal it from us because for a long time we were unable to receive any positive air situation reports and searched in the area south-west of St. Trond. It was not until 75 minutes after take-off that, to the south of our airfield and at an altitude of 6,000 metres, we found ourselves in the bomber stream. The weather presented us with no problems as it was a cloudless, moonless night with relatively good visibility.

At about 21.35 hrs, my radio operator, Heinrich Wilke, reported a contact on his SN-2 set. He told me to go down a little and directed me towards the bomber. At 21.45 hrs, at a height of 5,900 metres, I saw a Lancaster in front of me heading east, which meant that he was still on his way to the target. Taking into consideration the dark, cloudless background, I was able to position myself about 100 metres below the bomber. At 21.45 hrs I attacked with '*Schräge Musik*'. After a single burst of fire in between its starboard engines, the bomber began to burn brightly and immediately went into a steep dive. We watched it going down and at 21.45 hrs we saw it hit the ground north of the enemy's target, which we were now able to identify as Frankfurt.

As we still had fuel remaining for more than an hour's flying, we continued to search to the west of the target. After 25 minutes Wilke had another contact flying on a westerly heading and which, to judge by the blip on the SN-2 set, was probably another bomber. At 22.15 hrs I saw directly in front of me but slightly above, a Lancaster. I positioned myself at once and attacked with '*Schräge Musik*' from point-blank range, aiming between the two engines on the starboard wing. This bomber, too, began to burn fiercely and went into a dive. The aircraft came to earth at 22.18 hrs on a bearing of 235 degrees from Frankfurt. We continued searching for some while longer until we had ascertained that it had become quiet over the target. As our fuel was getting low I decided to land at Mainz-Finthen.

1. The *Staffel* was equipped with Bf 110 Gs.
Author's note: The two victories described were Paul Zorner's 36th and 37th.

"After a long burst of fire it went down in flames from 5,500 metres with all of its bombs on board"

Unteroffizier Erich Handke, III./NJG 1

Erich Handke was trained as a Bordfunker during 1941/42 and was posted to 12./NJG 1 in October 1942. Handke first flew with Fw. George Kraft and they participated in 14 victories together. On 17/18 August 1943, they were attacked and shot down by an RAF Beaufighter, flown by the British night fighter ace, Wing Commander 'Bob' Braham. Kraft was killed during the attack, but Handke was able to parachute to safety. He then went on to fly briefly with Heinz Schnaufer and Karl-Heinz Scherfling, before being transferred to III./NJG 1 where he crewed with Martin Drewes for the remainder of the war. On 27 July 1944, he and Drewes each received the Knight's Cross, Handke thus becoming one of the very few Bordfunkers to receive this decoration. When hostilities ceased in May 1945, he had participated in 59 victories, three of which were claimed during the day.

DURING the raid on Nuremberg on 30 March 1944, incoming bombers were reported and we took off for the radio beacon '*Ida*' near Aachen. We didn't think we had reached the bomber stream when 'Schorsch' Petz [the gunner] saw a bomber flying above us. As we were turning onto an easterly heading, I switched on the SN-2 and immediately three targets appeared. I gave directions for the nearest one. Then Drewes saw it at 600 metres. The weather was excellent: a starlit sky, a half moon, small clouds and no mist. It was simply ideal, almost too bright.

It was a Lancaster, flying beautifully straight ahead, so that we were easily able to position ourselves beneath it. From about 50 metres Drewes fired with our '*Schräge Musik*' and its port wing immediately caught fire. Five minutes later the Lancaster came down with a huge explosion in the middle of an area where the attack was just beginning, probably Aachen.

We continued our flight on a heading of 100 degrees until, after ten minutes, we picked up another single target far above us on a similar heading. Until then we had been flying at an altitude of 5,500 metres, but now we had to climb a long time until we reached the Lancaster, which was flying at 7,000 metres. Once again we positioned ourselves 50 metres below our target, but our cannon jammed after only two rounds and we were unable to clear it. However, the Lancaster must have been hit, because all at once it lost height. We had not dived away, so it probably saw us, because it then suddenly curved steeply away.

We immediately went down beneath it whilst it was flying very slowly at a height of 5,500 metres. Now we had to climb to attack in the old way, from astern, where one is exposed to the rear gunner's fire. We were now accustomed to the new '*Schräge Musik*' attack method, as it was a far safer technique.

This time we wanted to fire directly into the wing because the fuselage, with its many bombs, was too dangerous. At last, Drewes climbed to the correct height and from 50 metres fired into the starboard wing, which immediately began to burn. Although we did not break away immediately, the Lancaster crew apparently had no time for defensive action because the aircraft went into a dive and exploded into many pieces. Below there lay a field scattered with many incendiary bombs. We were somewhere in the Vogelsberg area.

Around us, there were still bombers going down like flies. After some time we picked up yet another target and followed it. Drewes saw the target, a Lancaster, at a distance of 700 metres. In the meanwhile, we had been able to reload one of the upward-firing cannon, so once more we positioned ourselves 50 metres beneath the Lancaster. After a long burst it went down in flames from 5,500 metres with all of its bombs on board. Two men were able to bale out before it crashed about 20 kilometres to the north of Bamberg. As we had run out of contacts we flew back and landed at Hanau-Langendiebach, where a further 40 crews joined us.

Above and opposite page bottom: When Oblt. Wilhelm Johnen, the Staffelkapitän of 6./NJG 5, landed this Bf 110 G-4 at Dübendorf on the night of 27/28 April 1944, it was at first feared that he had defected and his family was immediately arrested. In fact, however, after destroying an RAF bomber as his 19th victory near Strasbourg in eastern France, the pursuit of the remaining bombers had continued close to the Swiss border. Johnen then experienced trouble with an overheating port engine, shut the engine down and headed for home but was blinded by searchlights and so lost his bearings that, when the searchlights directed him to an airfield, he landed, only to find that he had strayed into Swiss airspace and was in neutral Switzerland. There, the aircraft and the two other members of his crew were interned. As this machine, an almost new Bf 110 G-4 W.Nr. 740055, was equipped with the latest SN-2b airborne intercept radar, 'Lichtenstein' C-1 and oblique armament, its landing intact in neutral territory was of major concern to the Germans who wished details of its equipment to remain secret. In a deal between the German and Swiss authorities, it was arranged that the Bf 110 would be destroyed, in return for which the Swiss would be sold a number of Bf 109 Gs. The Bf 110 was duly destroyed on the night of 19 May 1944 and the crew repatriated, but neither the Swiss nor the Germans had been entirely honest with each other. The Swiss had examined and recorded details of the radar before the aircraft was destroyed, while the Bf 109 Gs sold to the Swiss were in such poor condition that, post-war, both Messerschmitt and Daimler-Benz were obliged to pay compensation. The Bf 110 was camouflaged in a form of Wellenmuster finish on the uppersurfaces comprising 76 over a base of 75, while the lower surfaces were 76 with the underside of the starboard wing overpainted with black but which terminated in a soft, undulating line just short of the leading edge. Note that the oblique armament had been removed by the time this photo had been taken.

The victory markings on Oblt. Johnen's aircraft were slightly out-of-date as the tally on the port fin recorded only 17 of the 18 victories with which Oblt. Johnen was credited up to the night of 27/28 April. After being repatriated, Johnen later became Kommandeur of III./NJG 6 and increased his victories to 33, for which he was awarded the Ritterkreuz on 31 October 1944. He survived the war with a total of 34 confirmed victories.

Above and right: From August 1943 to 7 May 1944, 6./NJG 4 was based at Taveaux, some 60 miles from the Swiss border in eastern France. In the early hours of 2 May, one of the Staffel's aircraft flown by Fw. Günther Konzac landed in error on the Swiss airfield at Basel-Birsfelden, where the aircraft and crew were interned. Fw. Konzac's aircraft was a Do 217 N-2/R22 with four MG 151 cannon and four 7.9 mm MG 17 machine guns mounted in the nose, plus an oblique armament of four 20 mm MG 151 cannon installed in the fuselage. The four barrels of the latter protruded from the upper fuselage and may just be seen above the wing root in the photograph (above).

Dornier Do 217 N-2/R22 flown by Fw. Günther Konzac of 6./NJG 4, Taveaux, France, May 1944

This aircraft, W.Nr. 1570, was finished in a splinter scheme of 74 and 75 on the uppersurfaces and while the undersurfaces were 76, the starboard wing had been overpainted black up to a point just short of the leading edge and terminated in an undulating demarcation line. Although the full operational code was 3C+IP, only the last two letters appeared on the fuselage in black with the individual aircraft letter edged in yellow. The spinners were 76 and the propeller blades green 70. Note the configuration of the tail cone.

Above: Major Heinrich Wohlers was awarded the Ritterkreuz on 1 April 1944 after 28 Nachtabschüssen. At that time he was Kommandeur of I./NJG 6, but had originally flown in 1940 as a reconnaissance pilot. After transferring to the Nachtjagd, he became Staffelkapitän of 8./NJG 1 in 1941 and remained with this unit when it was redesignated 8./NJG 4 in May 1942. In January 1943 he became Kommandeur of IV./NJG 4, redesignated I./NJG 6 in August 1943, and became Kommodore of NJG 6 in February 1944. He was killed in March when his aircraft crashed while landing in fog.

Left: Personal inscriptions and emblems on aircraft of the Nachtjagd appear only rarely, so this Ju 88 with 'Komm' Zurück' and a four-leaf clover painted on the crew entry door is unusual. The photograph was taken in 1944, in which year 'Komm' Zurück' was a popular song in Germany and may have provided the inspiration for the artwork. Unfortunately, the names of the aircrew are not known, but they may have belonged to NJG 5.

Above: Major Helmut Henz, the Kommandeur of the Truppenversuchskommando – or Service Experimental Attachment – at Werneuchen, seen standing in front of a Bf 110 equipped with SN-2. Note the 74/75/76 camouflage and the yellow areas under each engine cowling which were intended to identify the aircraft as friendly to Axis ground forces and were a widely employed recognition aid.

Left: The yellow identification panels are again in evidence in this photograph of a Ju 88 G-6 fitted with an Fl-A-103Z gun pack comprising two 30 mm MK 103 cannon.

Right: Night fighter personalities at St. Trond, probably in the early summer of 1944. On the far left is Obstlt. Helmut Lent, who was awarded the Diamonds on 31 July 1944 after 100 victories. Lent was killed in the following October when, with 102 victories, his aircraft crashed while landing after a routine daylight flight. Standing next to Lent is Heinz-Wolfgang Schnaufer, the Kommodore of NJG 3, who had recently been awarded the Swords. Second from right is Wilhelm Gänsler, then Schnaufer's rear gunner, who was awarded the Knight's Cross on 27 July 1944.

Below: This ghostly image of a Bf 110 G-4 is unusual in that it was reportedly taken at midnight in the mid-summer of 1944. The aircraft is W.Nr. 110054 of NJG 6.

Above: A detailed view of the flame-dampers on a Bf 110 G night fighter. Whereas the starboard inner flame-dampers directed the exhaust gases under the wing, the other three dampers led over the wings and often resulted in heavy black deposits, as shown on G9+CS of 8./NJG 1 (below).

Above: A heavily exhaust-stained Ju 88 G-1 fitted with a ventral gun pack. Just visible behind the trailing edge of the port wing on this otherwise RLM 76-painted aircraft is the 75 reverse mottling. Although the small Geschwader code ahead of the fuselage Balkenkreuz is indistinct, it is believed to be '4R' which, together with the last letter 'X' in the fuselage code, would indicate that this machine belonged to 13./NJG 2. Although it is not known exactly when or why NJG 2 began using the code '4R' in addition to its usual 'R4', this probably began sometime after the beginning of 1944. No lettering appears under the starboard wing although, unusually for the latter period of the war, the letters 'B' and 'X' of the fuselage code are repeated beneath the port wing, although, in letters of different style and size. The 13./NJG 2, part of V. Gruppe, was formed in December 1944 by redesignating the bomber Staffel 7./KG2.

A Ju 88 G-6 of 6./NJG 2 taxiing in daylight. Note the oversprayed swastika and, just visible on the uppersurfaces of the fuselage, the mottled camouflage finish.

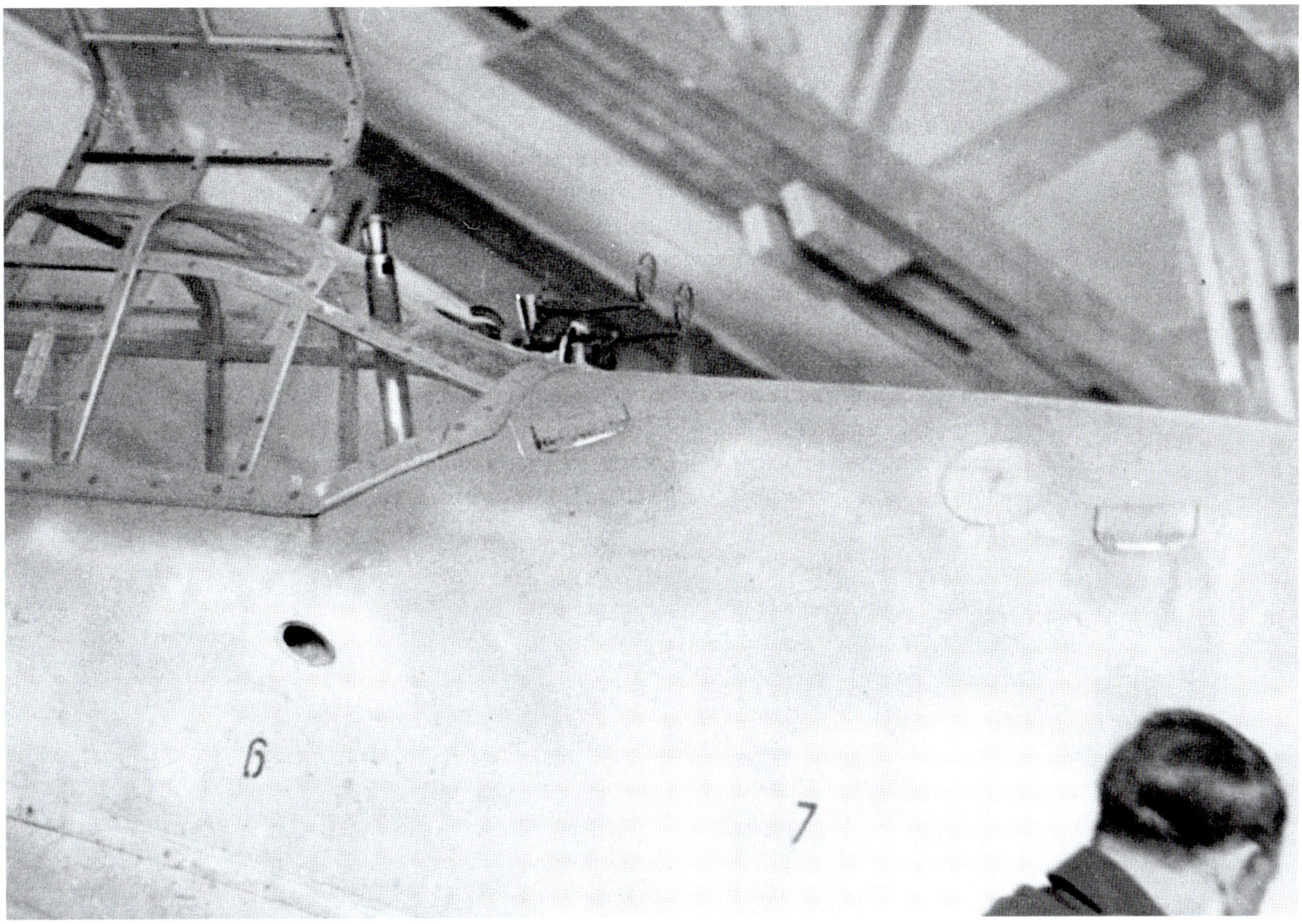

The twin MG/FF weapons of the 'Schräge Musik' installation may be seen protruding from the rear canopy of this Bf 110 G. Also visible in the extreme rear of the canopy are the sights for the 7.9 mm MG 81Z twin machine guns, although the weapons themselves have been temporarily removed. A flare pistol port is situated above station number 6. This close-up view also provides a good indication of the very soft overspray of 76 on the otherwise 75 fuselage.

A Great Coup for RAF Bomber Command

In early July, the British were just beginning to regain the edge over the *Nachtjagd* in electronic warfare when there occurred an event which, more than any other, finally swung the balance in favour of the RAF.

At 04.30 hrs on the morning of 13 July 1944, *Uffz.* Mäckle of 7./NJG 2, flying a Ju 88 G-1, became disorientated after engaging minelaying Stirling bombers over the North Sea and landed at Woodbridge airfield in Suffolk (see following pages). Once the German crew had been taken prisoner, the Ju 88 was thoroughly examined and found to contain the latest SN-2 airborne intercept radar, as well as '*Flensburg*' and '*Naxos*' passive homing devices. Having noted that 'Window' was now apparently almost ineffective against German airborne intercept radar and that the success of their 'Serrate'-equipped Mosquitoes[23] had also fallen sharply as a consequence, the British had for some months suspected that the '*Lichtenstein*' BC sets fitted in German night fighters were being gradually replaced. As a result of examining Mäckle's Ju 88, British scientists were able to ascertain the frequency on which SN-2 operated and reconfigure the 'Serrate' sets to home in on it. In addition, a new, concertina-shaped type of 'Window' was also manufactured and put into service, and this proved highly effective in jamming SN-2.

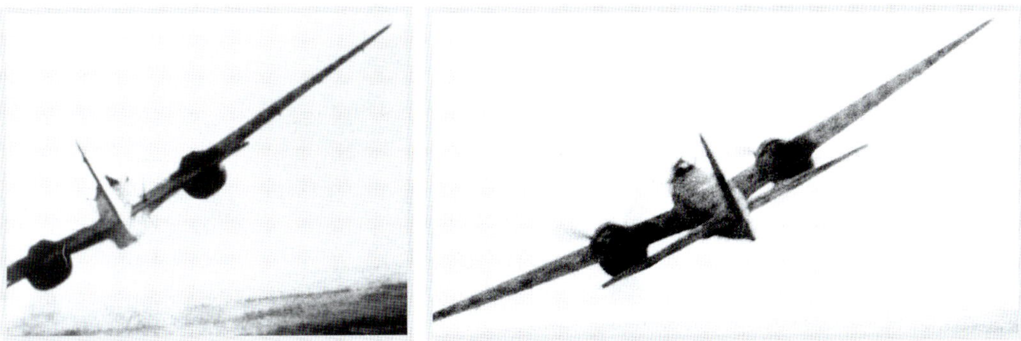

Left: Gun camera stills showing a Ju 88 night fighter under attack in daylight. Photographs such as these provided Allied Intelligence with their first clues regarding the nature of the SN-2 radar. Note the heavy exhaust staining over the rear parts of the engine nacelles. Sometimes this was sufficiently heavy also to stain the horizontal tailplanes.

[23] 'Serrate' was a special receiving device first produced by the British Telecommunications Research Establishment that could detect and home in on the impulses given off by '*Lichtenstein*' BC airborne intercept radar. The device proved to be very effective and was fitted to Mosquito Intruder aircraft which took a heavy toll on German night fighters.

The seizure of a fully working example of '*Naxos*', which had first entered service with the *Nachtjagd* in early 1944, was also a great coup for Bomber Command. The device had been manufactured following capture by the Germans of an 'H2S' set from a 7 Sqn. Stirling that had been shot down on 2 February 1943. After months of intensively studying the remains of the set, the Germans were able to build a device, codenamed '*Naxos*', that could detect the centimetric waves produced by 'H2S'. The discovery of the '*Naxos*' equipment caused such alarm that Harris ordered that 'H2S' sets were not to be switched on until the bombers were within 40 miles of enemy territory, thus reducing their chances of being detected by German ground radars or roving night fighters.

On examining the captured '*Flensburg*', the British soon realised that German night fighters fitted with the device could detect and home directly in on the radio pulses of 'Monica', a tail-warning device first fitted to RAF bombers in the spring of 1943. As of September 1944, 'Monica' was removed from all operational aircraft. Somewhat fortuitously, with the capture of this single Ju 88 night fighter, Bomber Command had been able to overcome the *Nachtjagd's* three principal airborne radar systems in one fell swoop.

Above: On the night of 12/13 July 1944, Uffz. Mäckle, Obgfr. Olze and Obgfr. Möckl of 7./NJG 2 were aboard this Ju 88 G-1 when the pilot became completely lost and, instead of heading for Berlin as intended, apparently flew a reciprocal course which took him to the Suffolk coast of England. By this time, the aircraft was very short of fuel so that when Mäckle sighted the emergency landing strip at Woodbridge, he made a wheels-down landing at 04.25 hrs on the 13th, still believing he was near Berlin. The capture of this machine was of great importance to the British as it was one of the Luftwaffe's latest night fighters and was fully equipped with the most recent radar and radio equipment. The aircraft, W.Nr. 712273, carried the operational code 4R+UR and the camouflage was 75 and 76, being described in RAF AI2(g) Report No. 242 as 'duck egg blue on all surfaces with dark grey mottling on the top surfaces'.

Above: Although the Revi 16 D gunsight had been removed when the photograph was taken, it shows the pilot's instrument panel with standard flight instruments and, in the rectangular housing on the left of the panel, a rounds counter for the four 20 mm forward-firing MG 151 cannon.

Above and below: Just visible in the photograph of Uffz. Mäckle's Ju 88 (above) are the aerials on the nose for the 'Lichtenstein' FuG 220 airborne intercept radar. Note the dorsal gun position with a single MG 131 and the annular flame damper at the rear of the engine cowling. Also visible on the wing and seen again (below), are the aerials for the FuG 227 'Flensburg' which detected and homed onto the emissions of the 'Monica' tail warning radar fitted to RAF bombers. Note that two of the FuG 227 aerials projected from the leading edge of each wing while the third was located above and below the starboard wing.

Above: The four 20 mm forward-firing MG 151 cannon mounted in a large streamlined fairing offset to port under the forward fuselage.

Below: A front view of Uffz. Mäckle's Ju 88 G-1, now under armed guard and being examined by an RAF Technical Intelligence expert. When the machine landed, there was so little petrol and oil remaining in the tanks that it subsequently proved impossible for the RAF to obtain samples for analysis. An interesting feature of this aircraft was that the Werknummer was repeated on all control surfaces and detachable panels.

"...there was the unmistakable thump of cannon fire, and I glimpsed tracers going up vertically on the port side of the bombardier's observation window"

Sgt. Thomas Harvell, 514 Squadron, Bomber Command

A formal photograph of Sgt. Thomas Harvell of 514 Squadron showing the Flight Engineer's brevet on the left breast pocket of his tunic. During an attack on Stuttgart on 28 July 1944, Sgt. Harvell's Lancaster was attacked and shot down by a Ju 88. It is believed that the pilot of this night fighter was Hptm. Heinz Rökker of 2./NJG 2, who claimed two bombers that night.

I was the Flight Engineer of Lancaster LM206 which took off from Waterbeach at 21.40 hrs on the evening of 28 July 1944, destination Stuttgart. I occupied a seat next to the pilot, F/Lt. Robert Jones, carrying out the duties of a co-pilot. This was our twelfth operation, and the second to Stuttgart in three nights. We flew across France at 11,000 feet, skirting to the south of Paris in comforting cloud until we reached the area of Lorraine when we climbed to 14,000 feet into startling, bright moonlight. It was then that some Flak burst close to the aircraft and the skipper, Bob Jones, told me to go into the bombardier's compartment and release some bundles of 'Window'. I wriggled down through the small hatch of the bombardier's compartment and, as I was doing this, the voice of the rear-gunner, Sgt. Alfred Braine, came over the intercom reporting fighter flares being dropped some distance away and from above us.

I had just pushed out two packets of 'Window' when there was the unmistakable thump of cannon fire and I glimpsed tracers going up vertically on the port side of the bombardier's observation window. This was immediately followed by a bright glow of fire that emanated from the area of the port inner engine. Then I heard the rumble of the hydraulic system and I realised that the bomb bay doors were being opened. The aircraft reared up as the 8,000 lb bomb load was released and the skipper's voice came over the intercom saying, "I have let the bombs go, Ken!" This was addressed to our bomb aimer, F/O Kenneth Loader, who was back assisting the navigator, F/Sgt. George Robinson.

I felt frustrated at not being in my usual place in the cockpit and was attempting to get back when the aircraft started to go down. At this moment the skipper informed us, "You had better get out lads!" I re-entered the bombardier's compartment where there was an escape hatch in the floor. As I did so, I had a last look at Bob Jones, who was now out of his pilot's seat and was standing up in the cockpit. I sat on the glycol tank in the compartment and attempted to reach the release toggles of the escape hatch, but the g-forces were now so great that I could not do so. Then came the thump of another burst of cannon fire, followed by a rush of warm air and I was catapulted head first into the domed observation window in the nose of the bomber and blacked out.

When I came to, I realised that I was falling free of the Lancaster and I deployed my parachute. I saw that burning debris from the aircraft was falling towards the canopy of my chute, so I spilt some air out of it from one side so that I went into a sideways glide away from the debris. I landed in a field and badly twisted my right knee, and my scalp was bleeding from lacerations caused when the Lancaster exploded. I was now some distance from the burning wreckage of the aircraft and I later learnt that the only other survivor from the crew was the navigator, George Robinson, who had landed close to the wreckage and was taken prisoner. I evaded capture and, using the alias of Charles Hautier, continued fighting the war with a Maquis group, the guerrilla arm of the French Resistance.

After being extensively tested and evaluated, Uffz. Mäckle's Ju 88 G-1 was allocated the British serial number TP190 and is seen here on display at Farnborough in October 1945.

The Invasion

With the invasion of Normandy on 6 June 1944, the Allies soon gained air superiority during the day, and ground forces began steadily to push inland. As they did so, the Luftwaffe began to lose a growing number of its early warning stations and was, in effect, steadily becoming blind. The result was that *Nachtjagd* units closest to the front line also found that they had increasingly less time to take off and meet the bombers, particularly as the Allies were soon in a position to base tactical bombers on airfields in mainland Europe.

The most significant problem facing the *Nachtjagd*, however, and indeed the entire Luftwaffe, was the increasing shortage of aviation fuel. This began to take hold from August onwards when Soviet advances on the Eastern Front resulted in the loss of the Rumanian oilfields upon which the Germans were dependent for a large amount of their fuel requirements, and was accompanied by USAAF raids on the German synthetic oil refineries. At the same time, the Allied advance through France and into Belgium and Holland forced the *Nachtjagd* to give up its airfields in these countries, and by the end of September 1944 all units had withdrawn to Germany and Denmark. This decrease in the size of the theatre of operations had a detrimental effect upon the night fighters' performance against the bombers, but in spite of the difficulties those crews still able to fly continued to achieve some remarkable personal successes. Most notable of these was Heinz Schnaufer who shot down his 100th victory on 9 October 1944 and, by the end of the year, had increased his total victories to 106. He had surpassed Helmut Lent's total of 102 a month earlier on 6 November, making him the top-scoring night fighter pilot in the *Nachtjagd*, although by this time Lent had died following a landing accident at Paderborn on 5 October 1944.

An interesting event that occurred during the winter of 1944/45 was the formation of a new unit to hunt and destroy RAF Mosquitoes. Raids against German cities by the light and fast Mosquito bombers had featured since January 1943 but such attacks had increased in the summer of 1944 and

Below: After joining I./NJG 3 in the spring of 1941, Rudolf Frank shot down seven bombers in his first six months with the Gruppe, and went on to increase his personal score in 1943 to 26. After shooting down his 42nd opponent he was decorated with the Knight's Cross on 6 June 1944, but was killed on 20 July during an attack against a Lancaster. He was posthumously promoted to Leutnant and awarded the Oak Leaves in recognition of his 45 victories.

Above: Georg Hermann Greiner (centre) qualified as a night fighter pilot in October 1941 and was posted to II./NJG 1 at Stade near Hamburg. He achieved the first of his 51 victories on 26 June 1942 against a Wellington bomber over north-west Holland. By the end of his career, Greiner had been decorated with the Oak Leaves to the Knight's Cross, as well as the Frontflugspange für Nachtjäger in Gold with Pendant, for having flown over 200 missions. He is seen here with his crew shortly after having received the Knight's Cross from Generalmajor Josef Schmid on 27 July 1944. On Greiner's right is his Bordschütze, Uffz. Hans Maurer, and to his left is his Bordfunker, Fw. Rudi Hammerdörfer.

Left: One of the most successful Bordfunkers in the Nachtjagd was Ofw. Johannes Richter, who participated in 67 kills and was decorated with the Knight's Cross on 30 September 1944. Richter joined 4./NJG 1 in the spring of 1941 and was crewed with Rudolf Schönert, with whom he flew for the remainder of the war.

Left: Martin Drewes' military career started in November 1937 when he joined 6. Panzer Regiment at Neuruppin as an officer cadet. On being promoted to Leutnant he transferred to the Luftwaffe and received his pilot's badge in April 1940. After Zerstörer training at Schleissheim, he was posted to II./ZG 76 at Jever on 8 February 1941 and flew a number of operations in Iraq. Returning to Germany, he trained as a night fighter pilot and was posted to III./NJG 3, achieving his first night victory, a Stirling, during a raid on Berlin on 17 January 1943. In June of the same year he was posted to IV./NJG 1 and by 1 March 1944 he was Gruppenkommandeur of III./NJG 1 at Laon-Athies in France. Drewes scored heavily throughout 1944 and was decorated with the Knight's Cross on 27 July after some 48 victories. The Oak Leaves to the Knight's Cross followed on 17 April 1945, by which time Drewes had been promoted to the rank of Major and had claimed the destruction of 50 bombers.

Above and below: Two types of airborne radar are represented by these photographs of aerial arrays. The view above shows the FuG 218 'Neptune' aerial fitted to a Ju 88 G-6, while shown below are the aerials for the FuG 212 'Lichtenstein' C-1 wide-angle airborne intercept radar as fitted to a Bf 110.

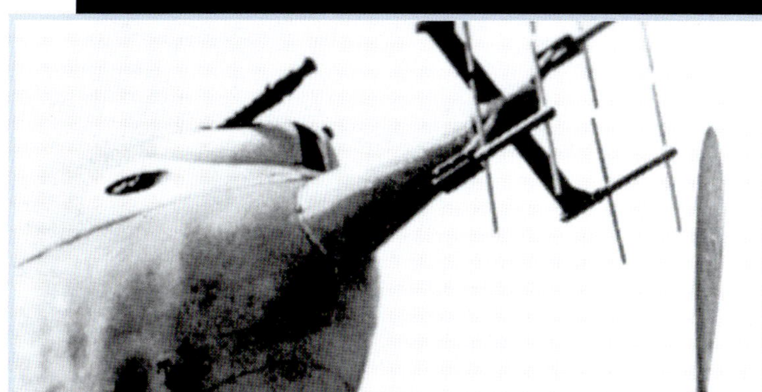

Left: The aerial for a tail warning radar mounted on the tail of a Ju 88 G-6.

"...a bright tail of fire..."

Leutnant Gerhard Wagner, III./NJG 5

Gerhard Wagner joined the Luftwaffe in November 1940 and was promoted to Leutnant on 1 February 1942. After night fighter training at Stuttgart-Echterdingen, he was posted to 8./NJG 5 based at Königsberg-Neumark in East Prussia, and flew his first operational night sortie on 3 October 1943. He achieved the first of his 14 victories on the night of 23/24 December 1943, but his career came to a sudden end on 2 August 1944 when he was shot down by Flak. Captured by the Americans and with serious burns to his face and hands, he underwent a number of operations before finally being released from captivity in February 1946.

FROM 15 May 1944, III./NJG 5, which was wholly equipped with the Bf 110 G at this time, had been flying operationally from Laon/Athies in France and I had been assigned as the Technical Officer of the 8. *Staffel.* At 01.00 hrs on 8 June 1944, we were scrambled against incoming bombers. As success always depended on calculated assumptions, we guessed that the target could be Paris and vectored to an area north of the French capital.

After some time my *Bordfunker*, *Unteroffizier* Gruner, suddenly picked up on his SN-2 set a fast-moving target travelling from right to left at right angles to our own course. I made a steep turn onto a southerly course and, a short time later, Gruner located another target on his radar. We slowly crept up on it until I could see a shadowy form and the exhaust flames of a four-engined bomber. I attacked from astern and saw the burst of fire from the two-centimetre and three-centimetre cannon striking accurately into the port wing and engines. The bomber went down with a bright trail of fire and exploded on contact with the ground.

I saw my next target in the light of the fire from this explosion and flew towards it at full throttle. The second attack was almost a carbon copy of the first, ending with a crash in flames. It was clear that in both attacks the crews had no warning of my presence, because we had not been fired at by the rear gunners of either bomber.

In the light of the fire from the second crash I made out a further bomber, which I headed for at full throttle. In this case, however, streams of defensive tracer from the bomber's rear turret came towards me – poorly aimed, thank God! So I aimed at the rear turret and swept my fire from the left and into the port wing. This four-engined bomber went down with a long trail of flame. The glow of the fires from the third crash provided illumination to find target number four, behind which I positioned myself and attacked immediately. While all of this was going on, the bombing attack had intensified which helped even further to light up the darkness. I had another success in this attack, during which I used all four forward-firing guns, despite the bomber's defensive fire. At the same time I could not help noticing in the course of all of this firing that the 2 cm cannon was firing intermittently and that only one of the 3 cm guns was still functioning, so that I released the firing button on the control column. Nevertheless, the effect on the bomber was sufficient to make it crash in flames.

I had already made out yet another bomber, even though it had already released its bombs and was turning onto a course for home. The brightness of the fires on the ground made it possible for me to remain at a distance and at the same time devote my attention fully to the functioning of my guns. The 2 cm cannon, which should have automatically reloaded after a jam, remained stubbornly silent. The task of reloading the 3 cm cannon (with a pressure button to activate the hydraulic firing) was equally unsuccessful. So, there I was, with a fifth prospective kill right in front of my nose and with none of my guns working!

With gritted teeth we set course for our airfield at Laon. As we did so, our port engine began to falter and the water temperature rose to its maximum limit. Soon afterwards, sparks could be seen spraying from the exhaust and from this I assumed that a coolant pipe had been hit during the final two attacks. The only thing I could do was switch off the engine and attempt to reach the nearest airfield on the remaining one engine. In doing so, however, it soon became clear that we could not maintain our height, despite jettisoning our reserve fuel tanks. I had to maintain strong pressure on the rudder with my right foot but the gradual loss of height was slowly becoming critical. Due to the air raid, airfields close to Paris were not yet illuminated but the hope of finding one was what prevented me from giving the order to bale out. However, we had no luck and eventually it was too late anyway! I could only maintain the pressure on the rudder with my right leg by pressing my right hand on my knee, and as the dark shadows of the hilly ground came ever closer the only remaining option was to risk a blind landing before we collided with the next hill. I throttled back, switching on my landing light as I did so. Suddenly, I saw a church tower pass by me on the port side. I opened the throttle again and looked for the next suitable area. Throttling back, the aircraft stalled – I had by now pulled the control column right back into my stomach. The fuselage made contact with the ground and we skidded on for some considerable distance. These were the most tense seconds as I was sure some obstacle was bound to appear and we would thunder into it. But again, nothing happened! Everything was deathly silent until my crew jumped out of the machine and did a dance of joy. Only then was I able to ease the cramp in my right knee. Once again our guardian angel had flown with us to the very end!

Lt. Kurt Welter was tasked with evaluating the suitability of the Me 262 as a night fighter. Duly impressed by its performance, Welter began to fly experimental night sorties using a standard Me 262 A-1a single-seat version of the jet. As a result of these flights, an experimental night fighter unit, designated '*Kommando Welter*' was formed at Rechlin on 2 November 1944. A small number of suitably qualified pilots were transferred to the unit, which was initially subordinated to II./NJG 11 and then redesignated 10./NJG 11 on 25 January 1945. The *Staffel*, still operating single-seat Me 262s, flew '*Wilde Sau*' operations over Berlin, although towards the end of March 1945 it received a small number of the two-seat Me 262 B-1a/U1 version equipped with '*Lichtenstein*' SN-2 and '*Naxos*'. Although the unit claimed a total of about 42 Mosquito kills[24] with these two variants of the Me 262, there were too few of the night fighter version which, as with the day fighter variant, came into service too late to make any real difference to the final outcome of the air war.

Kurt Welter, who evaluated the Me 262 as a night fighter in the summer of 1944 and later led 10./NJG 11.

Meanwhile, the German aircraft industry had continued to manufacture increasing numbers of aircraft month on month until the end of 1944, by which time the numerical strength of the night fighter force had grown to its highest wartime level. At that time, although it had on paper an establishment of 1,319 aircraft, it actually possessed some 1,355 aircraft, of which 982[25] were available for operations. The fuel situation, however, was now so critical that the increase in aircraft production could have little effect on the outcome of the battle and, eventually, only the most experienced crews, ie. those which stood the best chance of shooting down bombers, were allowed to fly.

The result was that in December, while the night fighter crews fought on against almost insurmountable odds in an effort to stem the escalating bombing campaign against their homeland, in 1,070 operational flights they shot down just 66 bombers but lost 114 of their own aircraft in the process, mainly to Allied night fighters. Similarly, although the successes in January and February 1945 totalled 352 bombers shot down, 94 night fighter aircraft were lost. On various sorties flown on 21 February, Heinz Schnaufer, who had since become the *Kommodore* of NJG 4, shot down nine bombers during attacks against Dortmund and Duisburg, but such individual acts were unable to prevent the destruction of Dresden, Pforzheim and Worms, all of which occurred in the final months of the war.

---

24. Total taken from 'Night Fighter Combat Claims', by Foreman, Matthews and Parry.
25. Figures taken from 'History of the German Night Fighter Force' by Gebhard Aders.

Photographed in Denmark was this Bf 110, believed to be a G-4 although the square intake on the nose for the crew's air conditioning was typical of the 'F' series. It still carries the 'Englandblitz' badge of the Nachtjagd on its nose which was a very important symbol for night fighter aircrew. In some units new personnel were presented with a miniature version in enamel mounted on a long pin. This was worn on the lapel of the uniform jacket, and although an unofficial adornment, was so prestigious that it was considered sufficient punishment to have the badge temporarily confiscated for any misdemeanour.

Combat Reports submitted by *Feldwebel* Karl-Heinz Becker of 10./NJG 11 for 27 and 30 March 1945

Above: Post-war, Karl-Heinz Becker joined the Bundesluftwaffe and is shown in the US during a jet refresher course on the T-33.

Note: In the original Abschussmeldungen relating to the following actions, the type of machine flown is given as 'Ahorn', the code name for the Me 262. Other reports in the same series, however, specifically mention the single-seat Me 262 A-1.

At 20.58 hrs on 27 March 1945, I took off on a night sortie over Berlin. Illuminated conditions were poor and so it was not possible to pick up targets caught in the searchlight beams. After these circumstances forced me to give up acquiring a target, I flew back into the target area.

Above me, and flying on a reciprocal course, I recognised a Mosquito[1] that was trailing a strong contrail and which had released target markers. I carried out a climbing turn and closed slowly on the target. At 21.38 hrs, at a height of 8,500 metres, I clearly saw the target and fired at him while closing to 150 metres. I hit him full in the fuselage. While turning to port, I saw a number of burning fragments go down and scatter on the ground. According to my calculations the destruction of the Mosquito took place near Nauen in *Planquadrate* FF5.

At 21.29 hrs on 30 March 1945, I took off for a night sortie in the Berlin area. Over the target I immediately picked up a contact and attacked directly from astern at a height of 8,000 metres. The enemy aircraft escaped my fire by pulling up to port. I turned and again brought the enemy target into a good position. I then noticed a friendly aircraft alongside me and I pulled away to port. The friendly aircraft had not seen what was happening and he turned away to the left and behind me. I now attacked the enemy which was flying to the right and above, ahead of me. Recovering from my banking manoeuvre and going into a climb, I opened fire ahead of the enemy aircraft which flew into the burst and suffered a number of direct hits in the fuselage and starboard wing. Then the enemy machine turned over onto its back in a port spin and was followed down by the searchlights. I saw the impact with the ground and, according to my calculations, it crashed in *Planquadrate* FG 5/5 at 21.52 hrs, and from a height of 8,500 metres.[2]

1. It is very likely that this aircraft was a Mosquito XVI, serial number MM131 and coded XD-J from 139 Squadron. The pilot, F/Lt. A.A.J. Van Amsterdam DFC was killed, while the navigator, S/Ldr. H.A Forbes DFC, RCAF, was taken prisoner.
2. Note: The destruction of this Mosquito was Fw. Becker's seventh victory.

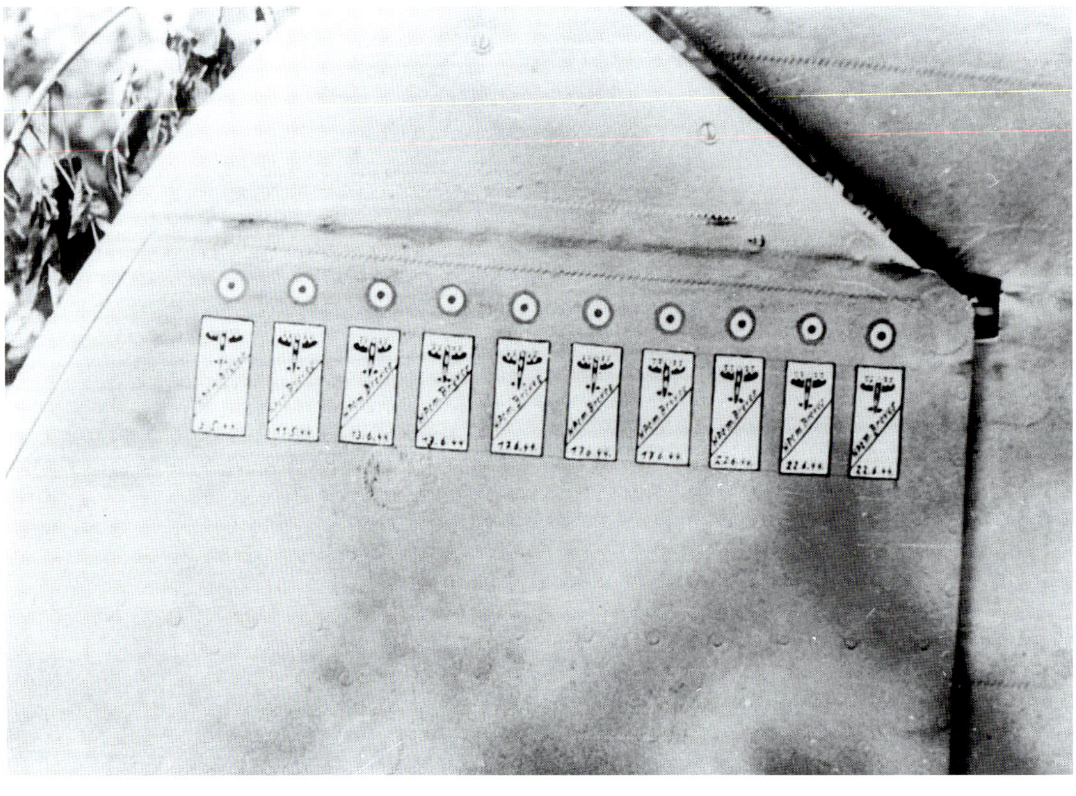

The tail of Hptm. Adolf Breves' Bf 110 G night fighter showing his victory tally in June 1944. This pilot flew with Stab IV./NJG 1 and, on the night of 21/22 June, shot down three RAF Lancaster bombers which raised his tally to ten victories. Note the meticulous bookkeeping, each victory being represented by a white victory bar within which is a silhouette of a four-engined bomber together with a note of the type destroyed and the date of the victory. Hptm. Breves later flew with II./NJG 1, and although records exist showing he was finally credited with 17 victories, it is possible he may have destroyed another in the final months of the war which was not confirmed.

Left and below: A Ju 88 shown in the summer of 1944 with a single experimental obliquely-mounted MG 151 fitted in the nose. It is not known how this armament installation fared in combat, nor how effective the flash suppressor on the barrel of the MG 151 was in preserving the pilot's night vision. This particular aircraft was coded 4R+AK and was flown by Ofhr. Johannes Strassner of 2./NJG 2.

Below: A still from gun camera footage showing a Bf 110 of an unknown unit under fire from an RAF night fighter.

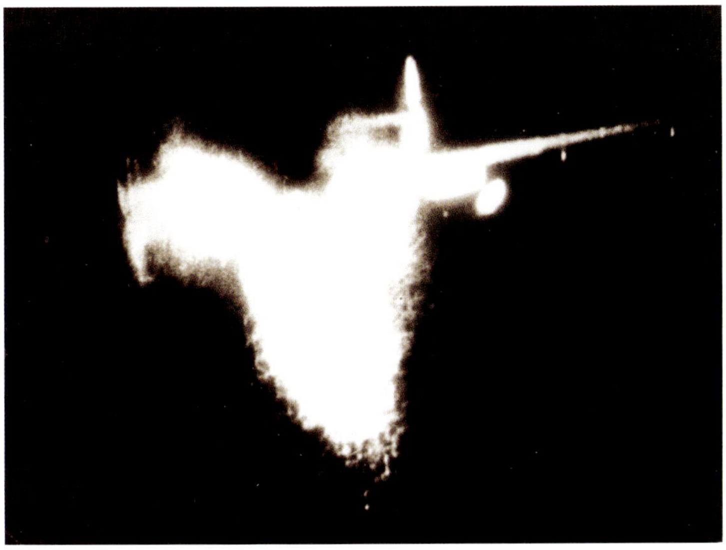

This Ju 88 G-1, W.Nr. 714084, was photographed at St. Dizier in France in September 1944 and had belonged to 1./NJG 5. Note the differences in the finish between the fuselage and tailplane and that the 76 on the wings has been applied over the 75 in broad swathes. The operational code on this machine was 'C9+OH'.

Right: The tail of the Bf 110 G flown by Hptm. Martin Becker while Staffelkapitän of 2./NJG 6. Although not all victory bars are visible in this photograph, the tail was marked with 43 bars, and beneath each was written the type of aircraft destroyed. The last two bars represent two Lancasters destroyed on 12 September 1944. After these victories, Becker was promoted to Hauptmann and on 20 October 1944 he was appointed Kommandeur of IV./NJG 6. At that point, Becker left his machine with I./NJG 6 and this photograph shows a detail of the aircraft as found at Munich at the end of the war. As Becker had received the Ritterkreuz on 20 April 1944 after his 26th victory, it is possible that a representation of the decoration was painted above the top row of victory bars.

An He 219 A-6 of 1./NJG 1 at Venlo in the summer of 1944. Note the small port in the wing root for one of the aircraft's MG 151/20 cannon.

Right: This He 219 A-0 photographed taxiing at Grove in the summer of 1944 belonged to NJG 1. No radar aerials have been fitted to the nose as this aircraft was used for training former Bf 110 and Ju 88 pilots converting to the type.

Ground personnel preparing a Ju 88 G-6 aircraft of NJG 100 for a sortie in the autumn of 1944. This aircraft almost certainly belonged to 5. Staffel which, at the time the photograph is thought to have been taken, was stationed in Hungary. Note the radar aerials angled at 45 degrees and the 76 spinners.

Another Ju 88 G-6, almost certainly coded W7+LN, of 5./NJG 100. Note that as with the machine shown (above), no 'Naxos' equipment was installed as both aircraft were operating on the Eastern Front where 'Naxos', which homed onto the 'H2S' emissions from RAF aircraft, would not normally be required. This aircraft differs from that shown above in having green 70 spinners and propeller blades.

One of the more unusual types provisionally employed in the night fighter role by NJG 100 on the Eastern Front was this Fw 189 A. This machine was fitted with FuG 212 radar and a single, obliquely-mounted MG 151 in the rear of the cockpit and which may be seen protruding from the canopy. Up to six Fw 189s were employed by I./NJG 100 between March and December 1944, while II. Gruppe had a similar number but only used them up to October. Although the operational code cannot be seen on the aircraft shown here, known codes are W7+CB, +DB, +EB, +MB, +NL and W7+WM, most of these being Fw 189 A-4s with a 20 mm MG FF cannon in each wing root in addition to the oblique MG 151. On this aircraft, the standard factory 70/71 uppersurface scheme has been modified with an overspray of 76 mottles.

This Bf 110 G-4 of 6./NJG 1 was photographed at Kaiserswerth-Düsseldorf in October 1944. Pictured with the aircraft is the pilot, Uffz. Gustav Sarzio, and his W/T operator, Heinz Conrands. Their machine was coded G9+JP and was lost in the evening of 4 November 1944 when it was shot down over Mönchengladbach, possibly by an RAF Mosquito. Sarzio, who then had five victories, was wounded, but Conrands was killed.

"The enemy aircraft slowly turned onto its back in a shallow dive from 7,000 ft with both engines burning well"

S/Ldr. Branse Burbridge, DFC, 85 SQUADRON, RAF

Wing Commander Branse Burbridge (right) pictured with his navigator and best man, Squadron Leader 'Bill' Skelton on his wedding day in 1946. In a period of just ten months, this crew accounted for a total of 21 German aircraft shot down at night, more than John 'Cats Eyes' Cunningham and 'Bob' Braham.

The following is the Combat Report submitted by S/Ldr. Burbridge on returning from a high-level Intruder Support Patrol to Brunswick on the night of 14/15 October 1944. The sortie was flown in a Mosquito Mk. XIX.

AFTER an uneventful patrol we decided to follow the bomber route home. We had flown south-west for about seven minutes when we saw the recognition procedure being carried out near a flashing white beacon to the west of us. We lost height to 2,000 ft in this direction and F/Lt. Skelton reported a contact at a range of four miles, 30 degrees to starboard. There followed a ten minute climbing chase, during which the target was taking considerable corkscrew evasive action. A visual was finally obtained on a Ju 88 at a range of 1,000 ft. F/Lt. Skelton confirmed this with the aid of binoculars.

I opened fire with deflection at a range of 600 ft and saw strikes. A second burst produced no visible result before the enemy aircraft dived hard to port and visual was lost. F/Lt. Skelton regained contact at a range of 6,000 ft well off to port and we again closed into visual range. This time a long burst from a range of 500 ft started a large fire in the starboard engine, illuminating the tail unit, so that we could identify it as a Ju 88 G. The enemy aircraft turned onto its back in a shallow dive from 7,000 ft with both engines burning well. It went down to explode on the ground at 03.30 hrs, about five miles north-east of the beacon. One parachute was seen.

Five minutes later, another contact was obtained in the same manner, 90 degrees to port, range two-and-a-half miles. After a similar chase, this was converted to a visual on a Ju 88 at a range of 1,000 ft at 03.45 hrs. I opened fire at a range of 500 ft with deflection, observing strikes and a bright flash. The second burst showed results and then the guns stopped firing. The enemy aircraft was last seen turning steeply to starboard in a southerly direction with sparks and a dull flame coming from the starboard engine. Assuming that we were out of ammunition, we calculated our approximate position and set course for base.

No. 157/T reported an aircraft exploding and burning on the ground approximately ten miles south of Gütersloh at 03.52 hrs. In view of this report it is requested that consideration be given to stepping up the second claim from probably destroyed to destroyed.

Note: Branse Burbridge finished the war as a Wing Commander and the highest scoring British night fighter pilot with 21 victories, two probables and one damaged. After leaving the RAF in December 1945, Burbridge DSO, DFC studied at Oxford, while his navigator, Squadron Leader F.S. 'Bill' Skelton, DSO, DFC studied at Cambridge. Interestingly, both went on to enter the Christian ministry.

This Ju 88 G-6 was one of the few aircraft equipped with FuG 220 SN-2 radar with a 'Morgenstern' aerial. In this instance the aerial has been left uncovered, but it was sometimes faired over within a long, tapered housing. It is thought that this particular machine was photographed in late 1944, at which time the operational code C9+AC on the fuselage side would indicate that it was flown by Major Hans Leickhardt who, from 3 May 1944 to 6 March 1945, was the Kommandeur of II./NJG 5. Note the light area around the 'C' in the fuselage code and what is believed to be the corner of a Kommandeur's double chevron just visible behind the trailing edge of the starboard wing.

Junkers Ju 88 G-6 flown by Major Hans Leickhardt, Kommandeur of II./NJG 5, Stubendorf, late 1944

The camouflage on this machine provides a good example of how the overall grey 75 on the uppersurfaces, which was found unsuitable for night operations, was lightened with an overspray of 76 but in such a manner that irregular patches of the original 75 remained as a result of the method of overspraying.

As the accompanying photograph shows what is thought to be part of a Kommandeur's double chevron just ahead of the letters 'AC' on the fuselage, this profile has been completed accordingly.

Aesthetically less attractive was the modified camouflage on this Ju 88 which consisted of roughly applied patches of medium grey, probably in 75 over an otherwise 76 fuselage. Unfortunately, the bright sunlight renders impossible any further description of the camouflage on this aircraft.

Right: Towards the end of the war, Luftwaffe airfields became a prime target for roaming Allied fighters, and while the light colours of the standard night fighter finish were ideal for aircraft operating in the hours of darkness, such aircraft were clearly visible when parked on the ground in daylight. This is well illustrated by this gun camera still showing a Ju 88 night fighter of an unknown unit under attack.

One partial remedy was to carefully cover the aircraft with foliage, as seen on this Bf 110 night fighter, although removing and replacing the branches when the leaves wilted or the machine had to be moved, became a laborious chore. Note that on this aircraft the grey camouflage finish on the aircraft itself has been applied to the propeller blades, which were normally finished in RLM 70 green.

Right: Fw. Günther Migge, in the dark overalls, claimed his first four victories in the last three months of 1943 while flying the Bf 109 G with 2./JG 300. When NJGr 10 was established in early 1944, he transferred to 1. Staffel and, according to some sources, eventually accumulated a total of eight victories. This cannot be confirmed, however, and the only record of any further victories claimed by this pilot after he left 2./JG 300 is a Lancaster shot down late on 12 September 1944 when he was with 1./NJG 11.

Left, above and below: Migge's Fw 190 A-8 'White 9' of 1./NJG 10 showing the aerials for the FuG 217 radar mounted on the starboard wing and the anti-glare shield over the exhaust. The badge on the cowling originated with JG 300 and symbolised the unit's 'Wilde Sau' tactics. It appeared in various forms and was also used by NJGr 10. The photograph above shows the particular variation of the badge carried on the engine cowling of Migge's 'White 9'.

A late-production Bf 109 G-10 of I./NJG 11 at Bonn-Hangelar. This aircraft, 'White 11', was finished in a late war camouflage scheme of 81 and 82 on the uppersurfaces with 76 on the undersurfaces. Although not visible in the photograph, this aircraft had a long tail wheel and tall rudder.

The Messerschmitt Bf 109 G-10 was also employed by NJGr 10. This example belonged to the Gruppe's 1. Staffel and was painted 76 overall. This unit operated in the anti-Mosquito role and, in order to reduce drag and thereby ensure every speed advantage, the machines are believed to have been highly polished. The spinner on this aircraft would certainly seem to confirm this.

***Above:* An He 219 A-2 of I./NJG 1 at Münster-Handorf in the winter of 1944/45. Note the black undersurface of the starboard wing, the spiral spinners, and the small Roman VI below the canopy which indicated that this aircraft was equipped with 'Lichtenstein' FuG 220d radar.**

Left and opposite: Oblt. Walter Briegleb, the Staffelkapitän of 7./NJG 2, seen here as a Hauptmann seated in a Bf 110, flew Ju 88 G-6, '4R+BR', W.Nr. 622338, (seen opposite). The Junkers had a 'Naxos' housing mounted on the canopy and the SN-2 aerials mounted on the nose were canted at 45 degrees in order to widen the angle of interception. The photograph of the Ju 88 was almost certainly taken just before or just after Operation 'Gisela' when, on the night of 3/4 March 1945, German night fighters mounted a long-range intruder mission over England. Before this operation, Oblt. Briegleb had 24 confirmed victories, as represented by the victory bars on the tail of his machine, but obtained his 25th and 26th during 'Gisela' itself when he destroyed two Lancaster bombers. For the operation, the aircraft involved were fitted with extra fuel tanks and the oblique armament was reduced to a single 20 mm MG 151, as shown here.

Ju 88 G-6 flown by Oblt. Walter Briegleb of 7./NJG 2, March 1945

This aircraft was originally finished in RLM 76 overall with mottles where the base 75 was left exposed. Later, the uppersurfaces and fuselage sides had been oversprayed with a blend of mottles and Wellenmuster type meandering lines in the late war colours 82 and 83. Although 25 victory bars were painted on the fin, Oblt. Briegleb's official tally was 24 victories before 'Gisela' and 26 afterwards.

Operation '*Gisela*'

An unusual operation took place on the night of 3/4 March 1945 when the night fighters mounted a long-range intruder operation. Codenamed '*Gisel*a', the operation involved about 100 night fighters from NJG 2, NJG 3, NJG 4 and NJG 5 which flew to England in three waves in order to make surprise attacks on British bombers landing at their home airfields after an attack against the synthetic oil refinery at Kamen and the Dortmund Ems Canal at Ladbergen. However, the raid did not bring the success that had been hoped for and was indicative of just how desperate the *Nachtjagd* had become in attempting such a mission. Although the German night fighters claimed 22 aircraft destroyed for the loss of 33 of their own, the mission proved a costly failure and, although two more intruder operations were carried out in March, both were on a much reduced scale and met with little or no success.

"My part in Operation '*Gisela*'"

Leutnant Gunther Wolf, 9./NJG 5

Lt. Günther Wolf was transferred to III./NJG 5 in May 1943 as the Gruppe's Technical Officer, and spent the rest of the war with this unit. He flew a total of 64 operations, was credited with four victories, for which he received the Iron Cross First Class and survived being shot down on three occasions. He was captured by the British at Flensburg on 1 May 1945.

ON 3 March 1945, we moved from our airfield at Lüneburg to Wittmundhafen where we landed at 17.49 hrs. We immediately received a thorough meteorological briefing for a very special intruder mission to England and then, at 23.21 hrs, I took off in my Ju 88 G6. My crew comprised my *Bordfunker*, *Feldwebel* 'Hein' Schmitz; my *Bordschütze*, *Unteroffizier* 'Jupp' Horosiewicz; and my *Beobachter*, *Unteroffizier* Unbereit.[1]

After crossing the German coastline, we descended to an altitude of 100 metres to avoid being detected by British radar. As we were approaching the English coast we could see ships to the south of our position that were heading north. This was only possible because the moon had come out and visibility was very good. These ships were of no interest to us, or at least, so we thought at the time!

A short time later we climbed to the cruising altitude of our aircraft and in the distance, along the Wash and the Humber, we saw searchlights probing the night sky. In order to avoid being detected, I looked for an area of sky where the searchlights were not moving and after passing through this area, reduced power and descended to a lower altitude. Shortly afterwards I saw some lights in the distance and flew in that direction. Whilst approaching this location I found an airfield that was fully illuminated. Its approach lights, as well as its runway lights and blue taxiing lights were on high intensity, as if in peacetime.

I began to descend and saw a four-engined bomber in front of me but, being too fast and in order to approach at the correct angle and speed, had to first lower the flaps. Seconds later, as our speed was still too high, I also had to lower the landing gear. At this moment the bomber started to turn and make its final approach. Suddenly, the airfield lights were switched off and from the bomber's blue exhaust flames we could see that the aircraft in front of us was beginning to make another circuit. Retracting the landing gear, we came in closer and the first rounds hit the bomber's right wing, which immediately burst into flames. The bomber began to climb and the tail gunner started to fire like hell. As we passed below him, I fired our '*Schräge Musik*' and a few seconds later the bomber crashed and exploded.

I intended to return to the same airfield but a lot of anti-aircraft guns were firing and we decided to head north. We were surprised to find many lights on in the docks of Hull, and even the cars on the streets were driving with their lights fully on. We intended to cause some damage to the docks but the lights were extinguished and so we turned for home instead. Knowing that there were some anti-aircraft balloons in the area I descended to a very low altitude and flew down the middle of the Humber. Visibility was improved by the presence of the moon.

We passed the lighthouse at Spurn Head so low that its light was above us! We took a deep breath and hoped that the worst was behind us. Wrong! We had climbed to about 5,000 ft when suddenly we were showered with gunfire and the bullets flew around our ears like glow-worms! Remember those ships? It was a convoy heading north and we had just flown through the middle of it. I immediately descended to a lower altitude and successfully passed through this armada unhurt.

We set a course according to the predicted winds and crossed the coastline. I asked Heinz Schmitz for a QDM from Wittmundhafen but he tried on several occasions without success. After seeing a light beacon glowing through a hole in the clouds, we identified its code but did not believe it. This was Leeuwarden in Holland and we had intended to be near Borkum! So, from our present position, we set a course to Wittmundhafen and after a short time Hein made contact with our airfield where we landed safely at 02.56 hrs. This was Operation '*Gisela*' as I remember it.

1. Respectively, Wireless Operator, Gunner and Observer.

The Final Capitulation

One of the pilots taking part in Operation 'Gisela' was Lt. Arnold Döring of 10./NJG 3. On 17 April 1945 he was officially awarded the Knight's Cross, but in the general confusion of the last weeks of the war the decoration itself was not presented. Some 20 years later, a German aviation historian discovered the award documents and Döring finally received his Ritterkreuz in 1965, albeit in the de-Nazified 1957 form which lacked the swastika.

As far as night fighting was concerned, the most remarkable event in March 1945 was the individual performance of one pilot who shot down nine bombers during a raid against the synthetic oil refinery at Lützkendorf on 14/15 March 1945. When he took off that night, Martin Becker had 48 victories and a reputation for being a phenomenal multi-scorer who achieved all of his kills without the use of '*Schräge Musik*'. On this night he infiltrated the bomber stream and shot down six Lancasters in 22 minutes, after which he ran out of ammunition. Determined to carry on, he ordered his *Bordfunker*, *Leutnant* Karl-Ludwig Johanssen, to man the twin, rearward-facing machine guns as they continued to look for other targets. Over the next 37 minutes Johanssen shot down a further three bombers, one of which was a B-17 from 214 Sqn. on 'Jostle' duties.[26] In this action, Becker thus became the only night fighter pilot to achieve such a score in a single mission. On the night of 16/17 March, Becker shot down a Lancaster near Nuremberg as his 58th and final kill of the war, and on the 20th he was duly awarded the Oak Leaves while Johanssen received the Knight's Cross.

Becker's success was almost matched on the night of 16/17 March when *Oblt.* Erich Jung of I./NJG 2 shot down eight Lancasters while defending Nuremberg, but despite these last bold acts of heroism, nothing could now prevent the final collapse of the Third Reich. As the Allied armies pushed deeper into Germany, Bomber Command found that it had virtually run out of targets and strategic bombing operations were wound down accordingly. By the end of April 1945, virtually all night fighter units had surrendered to the western Allies, although a few did fight on into May. The last recorded *Nachtjagd* kill of the war was claimed by *Oblt.* Fritz Brandt of IV./NJG 3, who reported shooting down a Halifax to the north of Hamburg on the night of 2/3 May.

By 8 May 1945, it was all over. Although the terms of the final, unconditional surrender stipulated that aircraft were to be left intact but disabled by removing rudders and propellers, many crews risked punishment and deliberately destroyed their machines rather than allow them to fall into Allied hands. Elsewhere, aircraft which had not already been destroyed in combat or during attacks on their airfields were disabled in accordance with the terms of the surrender. Subsequently, a number of the more interesting aircraft were taken to Britain and the US for examination, while the remainder were scrapped. As for the night fighter personnel, most were held as ordinary PoWs until released, but for the more experienced pilots who had survived there was often detailed interrogation by the RAF.

In the end, the *Nachtjagd* had been beaten by an enemy which had enjoyed an overwhelming superiority in men and materiel. The German crews had fought tenaciously to try and protect the civilian population, but in the end sheer courage and determination were simply not enough. The *Nachtjagd* had suffered, just as the rest of the Luftwaffe had, from inept leadership that went to the very top of the organisation. Internal squabbles within the High Command had also robbed the *Nachtjagd* of suitable numbers of the He 219, which had performed remarkably well against Bomber Command. Since the time of its formation, the night fighter force had sorely needed an all-purpose night fighter but had instead been forced to adopt and adapt aircraft that were not wholly suitable for the role. Had the He 219 been produced in sufficient numbers when first manufactured, this aircraft may have had a greater impact on the battle, but the seeds for the defeat of the *Nachtjagd* had in fact been planted even before the war had begun. When the Luftwaffe was formed in March 1935, no planning or contingency had been made for the type of defensive war which subsequently developed between 1939 and 1945, and in such fields as radar and electronic countermeasures, the Germans were always trying to catch up with developments on the British side.

What the *Nachtjagd* was able to achieve in spite of these problems, however, was indeed most remarkable and earned the healthy respect of Bomber Command. Certainly, if after more than 75 years, the names and the exploits of the men of the *Nachtjagd* still invoke a great deal of interest, then their place in the history of aviation is assured.

26. 'Jostle' was an electronic airborne jammer that could completely blank out the whole spectrum of VHF frequencies used by the German ground controllers. Due to its size, it was fitted into the bomb bays of B-17s that were used by 100 Group, of which 214 Sqn. was a part.

Heinz Schnaufer

Schnaufer was decorated with the Knight's Cross by Generalmajor 'Beppo' Schmid on 31 December 1943. As many night fighters had received the Ritterkreuz after only 25 victories or less, approval of this award was somewhat belated and occurred only after Schnaufer's 42nd victory.

HEINZ WOLFGANG SCHNAUFER was born in Stuttgart on 16 February 1922, the first of Alfred and Martha Schnaufer's four children. Three years earlier, in 1919, Heinz's father and grandfather had together established a wine distribution business in Calw, the success of which ensured the Schnaufer children were brought up in comfortable and secure surroundings.

At the age of six, Heinz attended the local *Volksschule* where it quickly became apparent that he was an academically bright and musically gifted child. From an early age, Schnaufer also showed an interest in all things military, and at the beginning of 1933 he became a member of the local *Jungvolk.*[1] Due to his academic performance, he was selected at the age of 16 to attend a *Nationalpolitische Lehranstalt* or National Political Educational Establishment, which had been formed by the National Socialists in 1933 to educate and train the elite of German youth.

In early 1938, Heinz attended the *Napola*[2] at Backnang in Wurttemberg where, in addition to academic studies, the pupils participated in military exercises and were taught the principles of leadership. The following year, having already submitted a request to join the Luftwaffe as an officer cadet, Schnaufer was transferred to a *Napola* in Potsdam where he began flying gliders from the nearby Güterfelde Hills.

On passing his *Abitur* he joined the Luftwaffe on 15 November 1939 and was sent to *Fliegerausbildungsregiment* Nr. 42 at Salzwedel in northern Germany for basic infantry training. From Salzwedel he was posted to A/B *Schule* Nr. 3 at Guben near the Polish border where, after qualifying for his pilot's badge in August 1940, he was selected to receive further training on multi-engined aircraft at Alt-Lönnewitz. After being promoted to *Leutnant* on 1 April 1941, Schnaufer underwent blind-flying training at Schwäbisch Hall in Bavaria, followed by a further ten weeks of *Zerstörer* training on the Me 110 at Wunstorf, near Hannover.

Heinz Schnaufer in flying gear during training at A/B Schule No. 3 at Guben on the German-Polish border. After almost two years of training, Schnaufer was posted to his first front line night fighter unit, II./NJG 1, based at Stade in northern Germany.

It was at Wunstorf that he first met Fritz Rumpelhardt, the man who was to become his *Bordfunker* for the next four years. Towards the end of the *Zerstörer* training the two men decided to join the *Nachtjagd* and, together with two other crews, they were sent to Schleissheim to complete their night fighter training. The training was rather rudimentary and consisted of cross-country flying, night flights and practice sorties flown in close cooperation with local searchlight batteries. In November 1941, Schnaufer and Rumpelhardt were posted to II./NJG 1, based at Stade in northern Germany.

After taking part in Operation '*Donnerkeil*' in February 1942, the *Gruppe* transferred to the new airfield at St. Trond, in Belgium. In April, Schnaufer was appointed the *Gruppe's* Technical Officer, in which position he was responsible for ensuring that the unit's aircraft were serviced and ready for operations. After many frustrating months of watching the more experienced pilots increase their personal tally of kills, Heinz Schnaufer finally claimed his first victory of the war during Bomber Command's second 'Thousand Bomber Raid' against Essen on 2 June 1942. Following this success, he shot down a further three bombers on 1 August 1942, and eventually finished the year with a total of seven victories.

During the opening months of 1943, Bomber Command made the most of the longer, darker nights by sending their bombers deeper into Germany against such targets as Hamburg and Berlin and, in the south, Nuremberg and Munich. This resulted in the bombers flying predominately over the North Sea and through France, thereby circumnavigating the airfields in Belgium and presenting the night fighter units based there with far fewer opportunities to shoot them down. Schnaufer finally achieved his first victory of the year on 14 May 1943 when he destroyed a Stirling and a Halifax during a raid against Bochum. As the attacks against the Ruhr increased, he scored steadily throughout the remainder of the month, a trend which continued into June and July. He was promoted to *Oberleutnant* on 1 July 1943 and on 20 July, he shot down his twentieth opponent.

The Schnaufer family at their home in Calw in 1940. Heinz Schnaufer's father, Alfred, is standing at the rear while, seated in the foreground are, from left to right, Heinz's mother, Martha, Heinz, his brother Manfred, his youngest brother, Eckart, and his sister, Waltraut.

1. A youth organisation for German boys aged between ten and 14. At age 14 it was then usual for boys to transfer to the *Hitler Jugend*.
2. *Napola*: a colloquialism for *Nationalpolitische Lehranstalt*, the National Political Educational Establishment.

Following his first night fighter victory on 2 June 1942, a Halifax from 76 Squadron, Heinz Schnaufer scored steadily throughout the remainder of that year and, by the end of 1942, his number of victories had risen to seven. He is seen here preparing to alight from the cockpit of his Bf 110 after a test flight.

After shooting down his 89th bomber on 29 July 1944, Schnaufer (second left) was awarded the Swords to his Knight's Cross with Oak Leaves. The decoration was presented a few days later by Hitler himself. On the far left is Erich Hartman, who would end the war with 352 confirmed victories, while on the far right of the line, waiting to be presented with the Oak Leaves, is Lt. Adolf Glunz of 6./JG 26.

Disappointed with the small number of opportunities he had to shoot down bombers with II./NJG 1 at St. Trond, Schnaufer requested a transfer to Leeuwarden, situated in north-west Holland, where he believed he would stand a better chance of increasing his personal score. The request was quickly approved and he joined IV./NJG 1 at Leeuwarden on 13 August 1943, becoming *Staffelkapitän* of 12./NJG 1 in the process.

In the same month, Air Chief Marshal Sir Arthur Harris began his offensive against the German capital, with the first of 19 raids taking place on the night of 23/24 August, during which Schnaufer scored his first kill with IV./NJG 1. To counter the growing threat of being shot down by RAF intruders, a third crew member was added to the German night fighters to help defend the aircraft against any such attack, and in September *Uffz.* Wilhelm Gänsler became the third member of the crew as *Bordmechaniker.* Over the next four months, Heinz Schnaufer shot down a further 20 four-engined bombers to finish 1943 with a total of 42 confirmed kills. On the last day of the year he was awarded a long overdue Knight's Cross, receiving the decoration from the Commanding General of XII. *Fliegerkorps, Generalmajor* Josef Schmid.

By the time the so-called 'Battle of Berlin' came to an end on 24/25 March 1944, Schnaufer had increased his number of victories to 51 and was fast becoming the rising star of the *Nachtjagd.* This was evident from the fact that on 1 March 1944, he was made *Kommandeur* of IV./NJG 1 at the age of just 22. Almost immediately following this appointment, the *Gruppe* was transferred from Leeuwarden back to Schnaufer's former airfield at St. Trond in Belgium.

April 1944 proved to be the most successful month of his career to date and he succeeded in shooting down ten bombers, four of these being achieved on the night of 24/25th. This run of successes continued at an even greater pace into the following month, and during attacks against cities such as Duisburg, Dortmund and Aachen, *Oblt.* Schnaufer claimed the destruction of a further 13 enemy aircraft, including five on 25 May.

By the time he was awarded the Oak Leaves to the Knight's Cross on 24 June 1944, his number of victories stood at 84, second only to Helmut Lent, the leading night fighter pilot in the *Nachtjagd* with 100 kills. It is interesting to note, however, that the Knight's Cross and Oak Leaves were only awarded to Schnaufer after he had attained a very high number of victories. Previously, pilots such as Lent, Meurer and Gildner had received their decorations for approximately half the number of victories achieved by Schnaufer. However, as if to make up for this anomaly, after achieving his 89th victory on 29/30 July, he became the fifth and final night fighter pilot to receive the Swords.

This was a momentous time, not only for Heinz Schnaufer but also for the two crew members who had assisted him so ably during his career. Gänsler, who had flown with Ludwig Becker before joining the Schnaufer crew, was awarded the Knight's Cross on 27 July 1944, whilst Rumpelhardt's Knight's Cross followed 12 days later on 8 August.

Schnaufer in conversation with his Adjutant, Oblt. Georg Fengler, an operational night fighter pilot who finished the war with 16 victories. Post-war, Fengler married Schnaufer's sister, Waltraut, and helped to manage the Schnaufer family's wine business until his death on 8 March 2003.

In comparison to the previous four months, August was quiet by Schnaufer's standards. Although he shot down four of the 20 bombers lost by the RAF during an attack on the Opel factory at Rüsselheim on the night of 12/13 August, these were his only successes of the month. Another five victories in September brought his total to 98 and, during the evening of 9 October 1944, he destroyed two four-engined

Above: The most successful Luftwaffe night fighter crew of the war. It is believed that this publicity picture was taken in late 1944 when Schnaufer was the Kommodore of NJG 4, stationed at Gütersloh. From left to right are Ofw. Wilhelm Gänsler, Major Schnaufer and Lt. Fritz Rumpelhardt.

Above: Heinz Schnaufer and his crew photographed shortly after he was awarded the Diamonds to the Knight's Cross on 16 October 1944. Schnaufer was only the second night fighter pilot to receive this decoration, the first being Oberstleutnant Helmut Lent, killed in a flying accident a few weeks earlier.

Heinz Schnaufer (IV./NJG 1), far left, with the Kommodore and other Kommandeure of NJG 1 at St. Trond in 1944. From the left are: Hptm. Martin Drewes (III./NJG 1); Major Hans-Joachim Jabs, the Kommodore of NJG 1; Hptm. Paul Förster (I./NJG 1); and Hptm. Eckart-Wilhelm von Bonin (II./NJG 1).

bombers to become the second of only two night fighter pilots to achieve 100 victories. A week later, a telegram from Hitler arrived at Schnaufer's airfield at Dortmund-Brakel, informing him that he had become the 21st soldier of the *Wehrmacht* to be awarded the Oak Leaves with Swords and Diamonds.

On 6 November 1944, Schnaufer surpassed Helmut Lent's total of 102 victories[3] when he destroyed three of the 235 Lancasters which took part in a Bomber Command attack against the Dortmund-Ems Canal. In further recognition of his achievements, he was appointed *Geschwaderkommodore* of NJG 4 on 14 November whilst still aged only 22 and two weeks later, on 1 December, he was promoted to *Major*.

The most successful day of Schnaufer's entire operational career occurred on 21 February 1945 when he shot down nine bombers in a single day. His first two victims fell during the early hours of the 21st but then, on the evening of the same day, he took off against a force of 514 Lancasters which had set out to destroy the southern half of Dortmund. In the space of only 19 minutes, *Major* Schnaufer dispatched seven more Lancasters to take his total to 116. His last victories of the war took place on 3 and 7 March 1945, bringing his final tally to 121.

When the final, unconditional surrender of Germany was announced on 8 May 1945 Schnaufer was at Eggebek. After bidding his comrades of NJG 4 farewell, he was interrogated by the RAF and became a prisoner of war. While still a PoW, he contracted diphtheria and scarlet fever and became seriously ill. Although his condition was critical however, he recovered, and when finally released sometime before the end of 1945, returned to his home in Calw to begin a new life as a civilian. He subsequently took over the family business, which had become almost bankrupt as a result of the war, and over the next four years he worked hard to restore the company's prosperity.

Tragically, during a wine buying trip to France on 13 July 1950, Schnaufer was driving towards Biarritz when a lorry loaded with gas cylinders pulled out from a side road and collided with his sports car. It is believed that one of the cylinders was dislodged and struck the 28-year-old German on the back of his head. He was taken to a hospital in Bordeaux with a fractured skull and died there two days later on 15 July 1950. His body was returned to Germany and Heinz Schnaufer, still only 28 years of age, was buried in the family's plot at the local cemetery in Calw.

[3] Helmut Lent had died on 7 October 1944, following a landing accident at Paderborn two days earlier.

Two views of a Ju 88 G-1 of 2./NJG 4 in January 1945. From August 1944, the parent I. Gruppe, to which the 2. Staffel belonged, was subordinate to Jafü Mittelrhein, but in January 1945 was controlled by the 2. Jagddivision. Note the crew entry hatch offset to starboard and the heavy exhaust staining on the rear of the engine nacelles.

Junkers Ju 88 G-1 '3C+FK' of 2./NJG 4, January 1945

The finish on this machine consisted of 76 overall with 75 reverse mottling on the uppersurfaces of the wings, fuselage, engine cowlings and horizontal tail surfaces. The canopy framing was in grey 75 and the spinners and the propeller blades are thought to have been green 70, albeit considerably faded. The Werknummer 714255 appeared in black on the upper tail and a small letter 'D', thought to be an earlier individual aircraft letter, remained on the nose. As no 'Schräge Musik' installation is visible in the photographs, that shown in the profile is speculative and consists of two MG 151/20 cannon mounted side by side.

A Ju 88 G-6 of 11./NJG 3 taxiing at Grove in early 1945. The unit code 'D5' has been applied in smaller characters than the remaining letters, while the individual aircraft letter 'A' indicates that this was probably the aircraft flown by the Staffelkapitän.

Junkers Ju 88 G-6 of 11./NJG 3, Grove, early 1945

In addition to the standard 76 undersurfaces and grey 75 patches on the uppersurface of the wings and the mottled 75/76 on the fuselage, tail surfaces and engine cowlings, the underside of the cowlings on this machine were yellow. The 'D5' of the operational markings on the fuselage sides were black, but the remaining letters were in dark grey and an unreadable Werknummer was carried at the top of the fin in black.

This Ju 88 G-6 with the individual aircraft letter 'A' on the nose is believed to have been photographed at Grove in 1944 and was probably flown by the Kommandeur of II./NJG 3, or perhaps the Kapitän of one of the Staffeln which comprised that Gruppe. The machine was equipped with SN-2 radar and had spiral spinners.

Left: Major Martin Drewes, the Kommandeur of III./NJG 1 (left) with his crew shortly after his 47th victory, a Lancaster, which he shot down in the early hours of 3 March 1945. Drewes flew two Bf 110s, the one in the background here being G9+WD which earlier, in January 1944, when night fighter crews were ordered to attack US bombers in daylight, had been stripped of its radar and 20 mm cannon pack beneath the fuselage in order to increase its speed. In these daylight attacks, Drewes destroyed four US bombers, but for night work he flew his other Bf 110 G-4, G9+MD, which retained its radar but had no victory markings. The G9+MD was eventually destroyed when the bomb load of a bomber that had been attacked with 'Schräge Musik' exploded and debris so severely damaged Drewes' Bf 110 that the crew were forced to bale out. Thereafter, the G9+WD was restored to the night fighter role, although in various post-war correspondence and interviews, Drewes maintains that he had his nose armament changed to machine guns as the 30 mm heavy cannon blew such large pieces off the bombers that he feared his own aircraft would be damaged. Unlike other Bf 110s of the period in which the 'Schräge Musik' was mounted in the rear gunner's position, on G9+WD it was positioned behind the pilot's seat. This machine carried the Nachtjagd badge on the nose and a design on the tail featuring the Knight's Cross and ribbon in natural colours with the number '25' in yellow outlined in black. Major Drewes was awarded the Oak Leaves on 17 April 1945 and finished the war with 52 victories.

This Ju 88 G-6 was flown by Major Berthold Ney, the Kommandeur of IV./NJG 3, who led this Gruppe from November 1944 to 4 March 1945. During this time, the Nachtjagd units began to adopt the same system of staff markings as employed since before the war by the single-engined fighter units. The aircraft shown here therefore carries a Kommandeur's double chevron on the fuselage as well as the operational code D5+AE. This aircraft was equipped with FuG 220d and FuG 350 'Naxos' and, clearly visible protruding from the upper fuselage over the Balkenkreuz, are the twin barrels of the MG 151/20 'Schräge Musik' installation. These were usually mounted at an angle of 70 degrees so that they fired forwards and upwards, allowing the pilot to position his aircraft beneath his target and open fire in a zero-deflection burst. Before becoming Kommandeur of IV./NJG 3 in November 1944, Major Ney had led III./NJG 2 since January of that year but details of his victories and awards are believed to be incomplete. Thus, although surviving records indicate eight victories, he may have had as many as 19 and possibly received the German Cross in Gold.

Junkers Ju 88 G-6b flown by Major Berthold Ney, Kommandeur of IV./NJG 3, early 1945

The undersurfaces on this aircraft were overall 76, and an unusual feature of the uppersurfaces was that, although the uppersurface of the fuselage and tailplane showed where the fuselage grey 75 had been oversprayed with 76 to leave 75 patches, the uppersurface of the wings are believed to have remained overall 75. In addition to the normal operational markings on the fuselage side, the aircraft was marked with the double chevron of a Kommandeur. All national insignia were in the late-war simplified style, with the outline type crosses on the uppersurfaces of the wing in white.

"My last victory had almost sealed our fate"

Hptm. Heinz Rökker, 2./NJG 2

In the cockpit of his Ju 88 night fighter and wearing full flight gear, Heinz Rökker prepares for a night sortie. Rökker flew 161 such sorties and claimed 63 victories at night plus one day victory. During a three year operational career with I./NJG 2, this pilot flew operations in the Mediterranean, Africa and Western Europe. In the following account, Hptm. Rökker and his crew were flying a Ju 88 G night fighter.

AT 18.30 hrs on 15 March 1945, I took off from Twente with my crew, *Funkmess-Funker* Carlos Nugent, *Boden-Bordfunker* Hanns Mattar and *Beobachter* Fritz Wefelmeier, on a night operation against a British bomber attack on Hagen. It was not until the attack was almost over that we knew the target. At 20.50 hrs, after a long period of searching, we found a four-engined aircraft with twin rudders at an altitude of about 4,500 metres. I fired at it from below with my '*Schräge Musik*' and it caught fire, went into a dive and crashed in flames.

Immediately afterwards, at 20.52 hrs, we picked up another four-engined bomber with twin rudders at the same height. He too was dispatched from below with '*Schräge Musik*' in the tried and tested way, and crashed in flames. The bombers were on their way back home from the target, flying in a south-westerly direction, and they attempted to evade the German defenders by diving at high speed. In pursuing the bombers towards the south-west we soon found ourselves over Belgian and French territory, which was already occupied by the Allies. Suddenly, we saw beneath us a brightly illuminated airfield. It could not be a German airfield, because we saw two aircraft flying around it with their navigation lights on.

Towards the end of the war, the British often switched on their navigation lights when taking off, forming up or landing because, during mass attacks by up to a thousand bombers, they were afraid that aircraft might collide. At this time, the risk of being shot down by a German intruder was less than that of a collision. In order to avoid becoming a target for a British intruder, we never switched on our navigation lights during the whole war.

It goes without saying that I immediately positioned myself under this aircraft, which was flying at about 1,000 metres and was probably waiting for permission to land. It was a twin-engined machine with twin rudders. We did not recognise the type. One burst with '*Schräge Musik*' and it caught fire and crashed in flames at 21.26 hrs.[1]

I turned my attention to my second victim, who seemed not to have seen the other aircraft go down and kept on flying straight ahead, still with his navigation lights switched on. The machine was coming into land and when we caught up with him we saw that it was a Mosquito. It had already lowered its undercarriage and was just crossing the airfield boundary. As I could no longer get beneath it to shoot it down with '*Schräge Musik*', I quickly switched on the forward gunsight and shot it down with my four forward-firing cannon. The burning aircraft came down on the airfield at 21.34 hrs and crashed in flames. To our surprise we saw no anti-aircraft fire. We later discovered that this airfield was St. Trond, which the Allies had occupied and were using as an operational base.

As there were no more enemy aircraft to be found, we turned on a heading for home. Suddenly, I saw that the temperature gauge for the starboard engine had risen to its maximum level. When we shot down the Mosquito a piece of debris must have hit the radiator. I switched the starboard engine off straight away so that I would be able to switch it on again for landing. Hanns Mattar established contact with Twente and told our unit that we would be landing in a short time with only one engine. However, our airfield was covered in ground fog and we were told to divert to Vechta. Nevertheless, I flew on to Twente so that I could confirm for myself whether a landing was possible. Old pilots are always drawn to their home base, just as horses are drawn to their stable, but the airfield was indeed covered in a milky soup and a normal landing was out of the question.

We were not wildly enthusiastic about being diverted to Vechta because swanning about in the darkness on one engine is no fun, but at 22.45 hrs we made good visual contact with the airfield. Hanns Mattar informed the field by radio that we were coming in with only one engine and we received immediate landing clearance. Once we were on the circuit, I restarted the starboard engine and came in over the approach lights and towards the runway with my undercarriage down. Just when I had almost reached the airfield boundary I was alarmed to see that, just ahead of me, another aircraft was making a belly landing on the concrete runway. The aircraft slid along the runway spraying sparks like a comet and at the same moment the airfield lighting was switched off. Now what? To try and overshoot with a faulty engine was too risky, but in critical situations such as this, one acts instinctively. I was already so low that I could see the ground by the light of my landing lamp, and with mixed feelings I decided to make a blind landing parallel to the runway.

After a few bounces, our machine came to a halt on the periphery of the airfield, but then small flames appeared from the starboard engine. The fire crews arrived at high speed but there was nothing for them to do, however, because when I switched off the engine, the flames extinguished themselves.

What had happened was that the aircraft that had made the belly landing had been unable to contact Vechta by radio and, of course, the control tower thought that it was we who had made the belly landing. They therefore immediately switched off the airfield lighting as a precaution against English intruders, and thus my last victory had almost sealed our fate!

[1] Heinz Rökker was subsequently credited with destroying a B-25. The Mosquito shot down on the same night was Rökker's 64th victory and proved to be his last of the war.

Above: The rear fuselage of a Ju 88 G-6, W.Nr. 620788, with an unusual SN-2 aerial configuration. The aerials were mounted in this fashion in an experiment to determine whether the SN-2 would be less sensitive to 'Window' jamming, more effective in detecting high-flying bombers, and more efficient in detecting Mosquitoes approaching from behind and below. This particular aircraft, coded C9+AA, was assigned to Eichenlaubträger Major Rudolf Schönert, the Kommodore of NJG 5 at Lubeck-Blankensee, who is thought to have flown the machine with this installation only once. On that occasion, during a sortie east of the Elbe on 27 April 1945, an electrical fault rendered the radar unserviceable and the Ju 88 was shot down by a Mosquito. Schönert survived and was rescued by German troops. He died in Canada in 1985.

Above: An unusual feature of this Ju 88 G-6 of 7./NJG 5 which landed at Dübendorf on 30 April 1945 was the particularly dark uppersurface camouflage and the light colour of the swastika and unit code. It is believed that the original factory finish was 75 on the uppersurfaces and 76 on the undersurfaces, although the uppersurfaces were later modified with what was described in a Swiss report on the aircraft as moss green with dense olive mottles, almost certainly 82 and 81 respectively. Note that all markings are either in white or possibly RLM 77.

A Ju 88 G-6 of Stab I./NJG 2 at Braunschweig in May 1945. This machine carried the operational marking 4R+FB and the 75/76 uppersurfaces have been darkened with a field-applied overspray which appears to be in two colours, possibly in 82 with 81 or 83. The fact that this extends well down the fuselage sides would suggest that this was an attempt to find a compromise scheme suitable for concealment on the ground as well as in the air.

Above and left: A similar finish (as to 4R+FB opposite page bottom) was applied to this Ju 88 G-1, W.Nr. 714607, photographed at Fritzlar at the end of the war. The operational markings were D5+KT in black indicating an aircraft of 9./NJG 3. The meandering sprayed lines on this machine are only one colour, however, and may have been in 81, 83 or 75.

Below: Photographed at Fritzlar in Germany in 1945, this Ju 88 G of 6./NJG 2 with the operational code 4R+EP had a most unusual camouflage. Disregarding the dark patch on the tail, which is merely a piece of camouflage netting, the rest of the machine visible in this view has been camouflaged in a disruptive pattern of what is probably 76 and 75. Very few examples of this scheme have been observed, but it is thought that the uppersurface of the wings and tailplane were finished in a similar manner.

This derelict Bf 110 G-4 belonged to Stab II./NJG 1 and was photographed at Langensalza in April 1945. Just visible ahead of the fuselage Balkenkreuz is the Geschwader code 'G9', while the single chevron suggests this aircraft was assigned to the Gruppe Adjutant.

Messerschmitt Bf 110 G-4 'G9+DC' of Stab II./NJG 1, 1945

The camouflage on this aircraft was the standard day fighter and Zerstörer scheme of 74 and 75 on the uppersurfaces with 76 on all undersurfaces. On the upper fuselage, tailplane and wings, the 74 and 75 had been applied in the form of a splinter pattern but with softer, less angular demarcation lines separating the two colours. The operational markings and the single chevron were in black.

Above and right: This crash-landed Bf 110 was the machine normally flown by Obstlt. Hans-Joachim Jabs, the Kommodore of NJG 1, shown in the centre of the photograph (right) by a crash-landed P-47 with his Bordfunker Oblt. Erich Weissflog on the right and the Kommandeur of IV./NJG 1, Oblt. Heinz Schnaufer, on the left, in early 1944. However, on 1 May 1945, two members of the Geschwader were ordered to fly the Kommodore's Bf 110 from Lüneburg to Schleswig, but with the end of the war clearly in sight, neither the pilot, Uffz. Siegfried König, an Estonian, nor his Bordfunker, Fw. Fritz Hrachowina, who was Czech, wished to become prisoners of the Soviets. They therefore decided to defect to Sweden and the aircraft crashed while landing at Hammerlov where they were interned. Unfortunately for them, it would seem their defection resulted in the very situation they wished to avoid, for it is believed they were later handed over to the Soviets. Ironically, had they flown to Schleswig as ordered, they would almost certainly have become prisoners of the British. The aircraft in which they defected was a Bf 110 G-4, W.Nr. 140655, coded G9+AA, equipped with FuG 218 combined airborne interception and tail-warning radar. The aircraft was armed with two MK 108 cannon in the upper nose position and carried oblique 20 mm weapons firing though the rear canopy.

Another view of Obstlt. Jabs' Bf 110 showing the aircraft's two 30 mm MK 108 cannon and the hole in the nose where the centrally mounted aerial for the FuG 218 'Neptune' radar has been removed.
The small, semicircular plate on the lower nose prevented expended cannon cases falling from the ejector slot from striking the propeller. On each side of the nose, two patches covered the locations where an SN-2 antenna had been removed.

Messerschmitt Bf 110 G-4 'G9+AA' flown by Obstlt. Hans-Joachim Jabs, Kommodore of NJG 1, 1945

Obstlt. Jabs' aircraft was camouflaged in 76 with 75 mottles on the uppersurfaces and carried the triple chevron of a Kommodore and all fuselage code letters in grey. The individual aircraft letter 'A' was repeated on the nose and it is thought unlikely that the machine carried an 'Englandblitz' badge. Note that a single FuG 218 tail-warning radar aerial angled at 45 degrees protruded from the rear fuselage and that the two aerials for the FuG 101 radio altimeter may be seen under the port wing. The exhausts had been modified to accept the later type of flame-dampers which led under the wings.

Right, below and bottom left: Although belonging to 8./NJG 1, this Ju 88 G-6, W.Nr. 710430, carried no radar aerials. The aircraft was photographed at Fritzlar in May 1945 and was finished in the usual camouflage of 76 over 75 resulting in mottled uppersurfaces. The operational code on the fuselage was G9+DS in black. Note, however, the different camouflage colours on the engine cowling, probably a result of field repairs rather than mismatching of components during assembly at the factory.

Right: The tail of a Ju 88 G-6 clearly showing that the contours have been disguised to resemble a Ju 88 C. Several examples of this practice have been observed, but as the disguise was surely invisible to enemy bomber crews at night, the precise purpose of the intended deception is not known. Note that the Werknummer appears at the top and the bottom of the fin.

This Bf 110 G-4, W.Nr. 160791, at Braunschweig, is clearly a new aircraft still lacking any operational code, but the fact that it left the factory in this scheme suggests that the Wellenmuster in 76 normally sprayed over the 75 may have been carried out at unit level. The factory-applied yellow areas under the wingtips and the yellow band around the rear fuselage indicate that this machine was probably destined for the Eastern Front, a fact which may also account for the lack of radar aerials.

Above: Several units received the He 219 but the only one to operate the machine in any strength was I./NJG 1 which, by October 1944, was under the command of Hptm. Werner Baake and based at Münster-Handorf. The unit remained there until 1 April 1945 when it moved to Westerland-Sylt, leaving behind a number of aircraft which could not be flown away. This example, which belonged to 1. Staffel and was still draped in camouflage netting when it was photographed some two weeks later, appears intact but has had the propellers removed.

Below: Other aircraft at Münster-Handorf had been more systematically destroyed, as may be seen by these burned-out aircraft of 3./NJG 1.

Right and below: This He 219, W.Nr. 290004, was found at Paderborn airfield on 10 April 1945 and was the first example of the type to be examined by the Allies. Although the nose, centre section and left wing were burned out, considerable information was obtained from an examination of the remains. Note that all the tactical code, G9+DH, was in black with the aircraft letter 'D' narrowly outlined in white.

Photographed somewhere in Germany in 1945 was this burned-out Ju 88 G-6 of IV./NJG 3. The machine carried the operational code D5+UV or +UW and the Hakenkreuz on the tail does not seem to have a white outline. Most interesting, however, is the extent of the repainting on the fuselage. Although the fuselage mottles are very dark and appear as if they may have been applied by brush, they have in fact been created by spray painting, after which a dark patch has been applied adjacent to the Balkenkreuz and upon which is the Geschwader code 'D5' in black.

It has been noted that three camouflage schemes were applied to the He 219. Having established that the overall black finish applied when the Nachtjagd was first created was unsuitable as a night camouflage, and having developed alternative and more effective schemes, it seems strange that in the last months of the war the use of black was revived for use on the undersurfaces and the outer surfaces of the twin fins and rudders of some He 219s. A possible explanation may be that the RAF's offensive caused such giant conflagrations in German cities that the light from the fires may have illuminated the night fighters' 76 undersurfaces to an unacceptable degree. As seen on this machine, however, where black was applied, uppersurfaces were usually finished in 75 and 76.

This He 219 A-2 found at Hildesheim, almost certainly W.Nr. 290112, shows again the black finish on the undersurfaces. It would be tempting to associate the application of the black with the night strafing of Allied motor transport and other targets of opportunity, a task assigned to the Nachtjagd during the battle for Normandy in the summer of 1944 and which continued through to the battle of the Ardennes. Neither this, however, nor the suggestion put forward (above), explains why such a finish appeared only on the He 219 and, later, the very few two-seat Me 262 night fighters to see operational service. In any event, the black scheme on these aircraft was a permanent, factory-applied finish and it seems improbable that the industry would apply a scheme for use on aircraft where night ground attack was only a temporary role.

The same 75/76/black finish as shown on page 173 may be seen on this He 219 A-2 which was surrendered at Grove in Denmark in May 1945. This particular machine, W.Nr. 290126, had served with 3./NJG 3 and carried the operational code D5+BL on the fuselage. This aircraft was selected for ferrying to the UK and, as shown (above right), all national insignia were painted out and replaced with RAF roundels. When later seen at Farnborough, the legend 'Air Ministry' had been painted on the rear fuselage in white capital letters with the white number '20' painted centrally beneath it.

Heinkel He 219 A-2 W.Nr. 290126 of 3./NJG 1, Grove, May 1945

The uppersurfaces of W.Nr. 290126 were 76 with a reverse mottle of 75, while all undersurfaces and the vertical tail surfaces were matt black. The Werknummer appeared at the base of the fin in white, and the unit code D5+BL was applied to the fuselage sides in grey with the first two characters in reduced size and the 'B' outlined in white. While this profile has been reconstructed from the accompanying two photographs, it may be noted that when seen in its original Luftwaffe markings, the spinners had been removed and certain detail was hidden by the covers over the engines and cockpit. While the photograph of the machine in RAF markings shows most of these details, it is not certain if the aircraft's original spinners were refitted or whether those shown came from another machine. Similarly, all four dipoles for the FuG 220 SN-2 radar were angled at 45 degrees when the aircraft was first captured and painted black, although the two lower ones were later replaced with examples painted white/red/white. The vertical aerials under the fuselage were for the FuG 25 IFF equipment and FuG 16 radio communications equipment, while the long fairing situated between these is believed to be associated with the FuG 12F blind landing system. Note also that there was no tail antenna but the two aerials for the FuG 101 radio altimeter were fitted under the starboard wing and a loop aerial was mounted on the upper rear fuselage.

This He 219 A-2, W.Nr. 290123, was surrendered at Westerland-Sylt and was camouflaged in the same basic scheme as W.Nr. 290126. This aircraft had flown with 1./NJG 1, and although the full operational code was G9+TH, it is not known if the smaller 'G9' was actually applied. Note that on all the aircraft shown on these pages with black undersurfaces, the front engine cowlings were finished completely in 76.

Above and left: On these two He 219s, the undersurfaces are 76 while the uppersurfaces, including the twin fins and rudders, are 75 oversprayed with 76 to produce a reverse mottled effect. Typical of the He 219, the demarcation line between the upper and undersurfaces is high on the fuselage. The aircraft shown (left), W.Nr. 420331, had served with Stab I./NJG 1 and carried the operational code G9+DB on the fuselage.

Below: The remains of an He 219 at Halle in 1945. Although the full operational code cannot be recognised, the unit code '1L' of NJGr 10 is just visible in small characters on the fuselage. The two photographs illustrate the third basic type of camouflage applied to the He 219, this example showing that most of the 76 uppersurfaces and fuselage sides have been oversprayed with 81 or 83, or possibly both of these colours. The undersurfaces were 76 but visible in the photograph (below) is a hard demarcation line on the engine nacelles between the 76 and what is again probably either 81 or 83.

Captured at Aschaffenburg in 1945 was this Ju 88 G-6 of 4./NJG 6 with the port wing clearly showing the 76 sprayed over a solid application of 75.

Junkers Ju 88 G-6 of 4./NJG 6, Aschaffenburg, May 1945

The operational markings 2Z+HM on this machine were in black with the individual aircraft letter 'H' in white outlined in black. The Werknummer 620751 was painted in black above the Hakenkreuz on the fin, and the aircraft was finished in the typical night fighter scheme of 75 and 76.

When Allied troops occupied Wunstorf airfield in May 1945, among the many aircraft examined was this Ju 88 C-6, W.Nr. 640643. This machine carried the operational code 3C+PN with the individual aircraft letter 'P' in red and had flown with 5./NJG 4. Note the red and white markings on the spinner in the foreground of the photograph (above) and that the two-tone appearance on the undersurface of the starboard wing is caused by reflections from the puddle on the hangar floor. In fact, the undersurfaces were 76 with the usual pattern of 75 mottles on the uppersurfaces, those on the fuselage being typically more distinct and hard-edged than on the wings and tailplane. All national insignia were in the late-war economy style in black. Oddly, although appearing fairly complete in these views, AI2(g) Report No. 269 lists this aircraft as being destroyed.

Above and below: A captured Bf 110 G-4 of 2./NJG 5 coded C9+IK, photographed at St. Dizier in France in the early autumn of 1944. This machine was camouflaged in 76 on the undersurfaces with a plain 75 in a high demarcation line over all uppersurfaces with a single patch of 74 on the rear fuselage. Note that the Geschwader code 'C9' – not to be confused with the 'G9' of NJG 1 – is in black, while the aircraft and Staffel letters are in grey. Although the use of black under the starboard wing of Luftwaffe night fighters commenced around March 1944 and was employed only for a few months, this finish still remains on this aircraft, even though the photograph was taken some months later. Similarly, the general camouflage scheme was also phased out in 1944. These features all point, therefore, to this being a relatively old aircraft. The black under the wing terminated in a straight line corresponding to the position of the front spar, and the engine panel above the wing, which also seems black, is unlikely to have been the result of fire damage when the aircraft was destroyed. In the photo above there appears to be an overpainted emblem below the cockpit, perhaps an 'Englandblitz' badge?

Photographed in Denmark at the end of the war, this Ju 88 C night fighter is finished in 76 overall with reverse mottles of 75 on the upper and side surfaces. Note the spinners have been painted with a white spiral in accordance with a general order issued on 20 July 1944 and applicable to twin-engined fighters based in western Europe. The white Balkenkreuz would suggest that the undersurface of the starboard wing was black, and this, together with the 'Englandblitz' badge on the nose, is an unusual feature on a machine photographed in May 1945.

Above and left: This Ju 88 C-6, W.Nr. 751065, was coded 7J+QK and originally belonged to 2./NJG 102. The aircraft was photographed at Copenhagen-Kastrup in May 1945, but as 2./NJG 102 had been disbanded in February, it is thought that this machine had been transferred to another unit but not repainted with its new owner's tactical code. The camouflage is clearly a hybrid scheme resulting from the mating of a replacement rear fuselage, finished in the standard 70/71 mid-war colours, to a nose section and wings finished in the same scheme but with a Wellenmuster overspray in 76. Note the individual aircraft letter 'Q' in the 2. Staffel colour of red.

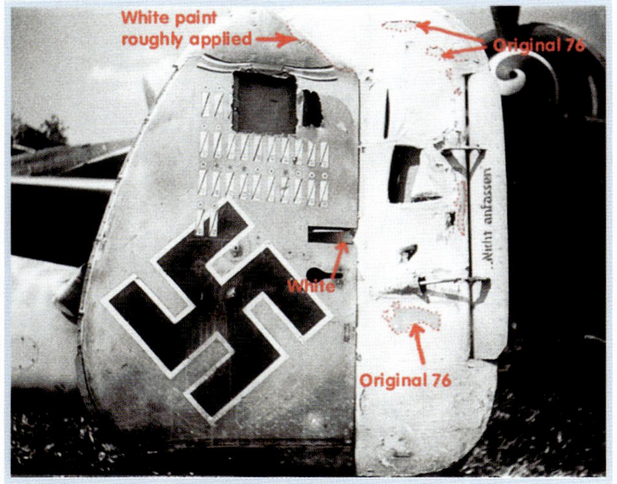

Among the aircraft photographed at Neubiberg in 1945 was this Bf 110 G-4 of 7./NJG 6. Although abandoned at the end of hostilities, that it was once the pride of the crews who flew and maintained it is evident from the port fin which had been painstakingly decorated with a Ritterkreuz, although when this photograph was taken it had been removed as a souvenir. Each of the 32 victory bars is marked with a date and the sequence of RAF and Soviet victories represented by the 21st to 30th bars confirms that this was the aircraft once flown by Oblt. Wilhelm Johnen when Kommandeur of III./NJG 6. Note, however, that the sequence of bars does not exactly match Johnen's known victory tally as his first Soviet victory was his 23rd rather than the 22nd as shown. As on the C9+EN which he flew when with NJG 5 (see page 129), there is therefore one bar missing which results in the aircraft being decorated with 32 bars and a portrayal of the Ritterkreuz, whereas Johnen received this award after 33 victories. The four Soviet victories were all B-25s shot down over Hungary between 11 and 26 August 1944.

Messerschmitt Bf 110 G-4 '2Z+FR' of 7./NJG 6, Neubiberg 1945

This aircraft was equipped with aerials for FuG 220 SN-2d mounted on the nose and with the dipoles angled at 45 degrees. Additional aerials for a FuG 101 altimeter were mounted under the port wing, straight 'Ebersbächer' flame-dampers were fitted, and the 'Schräge Musik' installation was located further to the rear of the canopy than observed on other machines. A 90 mm armoured windscreen was fitted and, although unusual, the white rudder is confirmed by the detail photograph (above right). The uppersurface camouflage on the wings, horizontal tail and fuselage sides was 75 but oversprayed with 76 in such a way that small areas of the 75 remained.

Wilhelm Johnen

A very youthful 'Wim' Johnen poses for the camera.

WILHELM 'WIM' JOHNEN was born on 9 October 1921 in the small town of Homberg, situated on the western bank of the Rhine River and close to the industrial city of Duisburg. He remained in Homberg until the outbreak of the Second World War in September 1939, by which time he had just completed his studies and obtained his *Abitur*. The following month, Johnen turned 18 and he applied to join the Luftwaffe on the basis of qualifications he had already attained as a glider pilot. His formal application to become an officer was accepted and he began his training as an officer cadet with *Fliegerausbildungsregiment* Nr. 32 at Pardubitz (now Pardubice) in Czechoslovakia, where he received basic infantry training. Having endured several months of field exercises, marching and shooting practice, 'Wim' Johnen spent the next eight months learning to fly elementary and advanced single-engined aircraft and qualified for his pilot's badge on 21 September 1940.

Selected to fly multi-engined aircraft, he was then posted to *C-Schule* 11 at Zeltweg-Steiermark in Austria and, during a three month training period, flew such twin-engined aircraft as the He 111 and Do 17 as well as the three-engined Ju 52. On obtaining the 'C' grading to his pilot's licence which allowed him to fly multi-engined aircraft, Johnen attended the *Blindflugschule* at Wien-Aspern before progressing to Schleissheim near Munich where he received *Zerstörer* training and, on 1 April 1941, was commissioned as a *Leutnant*.

It was at about this time, and due mainly to the RAF's intensified air attacks against Germany, that Johnen decided to join the *Nachtjagd*. The war, which he feared would be over by the time his training was complete, had now become more personal. His home town, and particularly the surrounding area of Duisburg, with its Thyssen steel factories and large inland port, had been identified as an important strategic target within the industrial Ruhr valley and had been specifically attacked on a number of occasions by RAF Bomber Command. As his home was in the outskirts of Duisburg, he naturally feared for the safety of his family and it was this concern that led him to apply to join the *Nachtjagd*. Accordingly, on 18 May 1941, he began his night fighter training at Stuttgart-Echterdingen. His regular *Bordfunker* was *Gefreiter* Albrecht Risop, whom he had first met during their training at Schleissheim. After six weeks of intense instruction, Johnen and Risop were transferred to the operational night fighter *Staffel* 3./NJG 1, arriving at this unit's airfield in Schleswig on 25 June 1941.

Johnen with an Fw 44 'Stieglitz', one of the most popular types of aircraft flown by trainee pilots at the A/B Schulen. This radial-engined biplane was first flown in the summer of 1932 and proved to be rugged and agile. It was produced in large numbers and established Kurt Tank and his Focke-Wulf Company as a serious aircraft manufacturer.

Awarded the Knight's Cross on 29 October 1944, by war's end Wilhelm Johnen had been made Kommandeur of III./NJG 6 and finished the conflict with 34 confirmed kills.

On 11 July 1941, after a brief period of familiarisation with the *Staffel*, Johnen flew his first operational mission, during which he encountered a Wellington bomber. However, he failed to shoot it down and thus became aware of the fundamental difficulties involved in fighting at night. Almost another eight months and a further 28 missions passed before, on the evening of 26 March 1942, he took off from Venlo[1] and at 23.30 hrs intercepted a Wellington which he shot down north-west of Wesel as his first victory.[2] A few minutes later, Risop spotted a four-engined bomber which he identified as a Short Stirling. After a brief exchange of fire between the aircraft, the cockpit and fuselage of Johnen's Bf 110 was raked with machine gun fire and the petrol tanks set ablaze. The same burst of gunfire also killed Risop and wounded Johnen, who then fought desperately to extricate himself from the burning cockpit. Nevertheless, the stricken fighter plunged 3,000 metres with Johnen still aboard before it exploded and threw him clear. Although he was then able to parachute safely to the ground, Johnen received second degree burns to his face and a large number of shell splinters in his left leg kept him from operational flying for two-and-a-half months.

A short time after his return to operations, during an RAF raid on Essen on the night of 16/17 June 1942, Johnen shot down a Wellington as his second victory. In recognition of this achievement, he was awarded the Iron Cross Second Class on 26 July 1942.

On 1 December 1942, 3./NJG 1 was redesignated 5./NJG 5 and transferred to Parchim in north-eastern Germany under the command of *Oblt.* Leopold Fellerer. Due to the airfield's location, 5./NJG 5 was less active than units stationed further westwards, and during the first five months of the new year Johnen flew only a small number of sorties.

Johnen with his overall black Bf 110 E at Schleswig in about July 1941, shortly after he joined 3./NJG 1, at that time commanded by Oberleutnant Walter Fenske. Note the Nachtjagd emblem, barely visible behind the port engine.

1. 3./NJG 1 transferred from Schleswig back to Venlo on 1 December 1941.
2. It is highly probable that this aircraft was Wellington X3589 KO-F from 115 Squadron, which crashed at Uedem, approximately 35 km west of Wesel.

Wilhelm Johnen (centre) and his Bordschutze, Ofw. Paul Mahle (right), shown towards the end of the 'Battle of Berlin' in early 1944. The fin of their Bf 110 is marked with 14 victory bars, Johnen's total after destroying a Lancaster on 27 January, one of three he shot down that night.

However, in May 1943, the *Staffel* was posted back to the west to help counter the increasing raids against the Ruhr and in the early hours of 22 June 1943, after more than a year since his last victory, Johnen finally increased his personal tally by shooting down two bombers during a raid on Krefeld. Three nights later, he intercepted and shot down a Halifax as his fifth confirmed victory and, on 1 July 1943, Johnen was promoted to *Oberleutnant*.

In August 1943, when Air Chief Marshal Sir Arthur Harris's prolonged offensive began against the German capital, later known as the 'Battle of Berlin' and which lasted until February 1944, 5./NJG 5 was once again operating from Parchim and found itself in the thick of the battle. On 24 August 1943, Johnen claimed a Stirling and a Halifax to the north-west of Berlin and four days later he was awarded the Iron Cross First Class.

Later, with 18 victories and a growing reputation as a capable night fighter with leadership potential, he was made *Staffelkäpitan* of 6./NJG 5 on 31 March 1944. The following month, II./NJG 5 was transferred to Leipheim in southern Germany, but when the airfield was badly damaged during a daylight raid, the *Gruppe* moved to Hagenau in western France.

At 00.48 hrs on 28 April 1944, Johnen took off from Hagenau with *Oberfeldwebel* Paul Mahle[3] and *Leutnant* 'Brinos' Kamprath, with orders to intercept 322 Lancasters that had been tasked to destroy armament factories in Friedrichshafen, a small town in southern Germany situated on the banks of Lake Constance. After shooting down one Lancaster, Johnen was hit by return fire from another which set fire to his fighter's port engine. Flying on one engine and with no other option, he was forced to land his aircraft at the nearest available airfield, which turned out to be Dübendorf in neutral Switzerland. Surrendering to Swiss soldiers, the three-man crew was interned and lengthy negotiations with the Swiss government followed. Naturally, as Johnen's aircraft was fitted with SN-2, '*Naxos*' and '*Schräge Musik*', the Germans did not want it to fall into Allied hands, and in an agreement finally reached between the German and Swiss Intelligence Services, it was arranged that the machine would be destroyed. In exchange, the Swiss would receive 12 Bf 109 G-6 fighters from the Luftwaffe at a favourable price. The Bf 110 was subsequently blown up on 18 May 1944 and Johnen and his crew were released six days later.

Meanwhile, however, as it was at first believed that the crew had defected, the families of the crew had been arrested and imprisoned by the Gestapo. Later, after it had been established that the crew had carried out an emergency landing due to combat damage, the families were released and the authorities hushed up the whole incident.

On 10 May 1944, II./NJG 5 was redesignated III./NJG 6 and Johnen was given command of 8./NJG 6. From June 1944 the *Gruppe*, under the command of *Major* Herbert Lütje, was transferred to Steinamanger in Hungary, close to the Austrian border. Operating from this airfield, III./NJG 6 was tasked with defending Vienna and Budapest from Allied bombers operating from Italy. Over a period of three months, between 26 June and 21 September 1944, Johnen shot down a further 14 aircraft[4] taking his number of confirmed victories to 33. A month later, on 1 October 1944, he was promoted to *Hauptmann* and, a few weeks later, on 29 October, he was awarded the Knight's Cross. With the Russians advancing through Hungary, III./NJG 6 was forced to withdraw within Germany's own borders to Leipheim, Neubiberg and then to Bad Aibling, south of Munich. On 13 February 1945, Johnen became *Gruppenkommandeur* of III./NJG 6 and, a month later, during a raid against Würzburg on the night of 15/16 March 1945, he shot down a Lancaster for his 34th and final victory of the war.

On the night of 30 April 1945, with the Americans in control of the area around Munich, *Hauptmann* Wilhelm Johnen gave the men of his *Gruppe* orders to destroy their remaining aircraft before they fell into enemy hands. When the war finally ended on 8 May 1945 Johnen was held for a short time in American captivity, and later he studied for several years at Munich University where he obtained an engineering degree in construction. He was then employed by a contractor working for Messerschmitt Pre-Fabricated Buildings, owned by Professor Willi Messerschmitt, and later formed his own construction company which he managed for almost 40 years. Wilhelm Johnen died at his home in Überlingen on Lake Constance, on 7 February 2002.

After shooting down a Wellington bomber on the night of 26 March 1942, Johnen's aircraft was badly damaged by return fire from a Stirling. Johnen himself was able to parachute to safety but his Bordfunker, Obergefreiter Albrecht Risop, was killed by the first burst of gunfire from the Stirling. Risop's body was later recovered from the fighter and buried in Südlohn, close to where his aircraft crashed.

3. Paul Mahle had been a weapons technician at Parchim and, together with Rudolf Schönert, had developed the first operational '*Schräge Musik*' weapons installation. By the time of this particular operation, Mahle had been Johnen's regular *Bordschutze* for several months. Kamprath, the *Gruppe's* Signals Officer, was filling in for Johnen's regular *Bordfunker* who was away on leave.

4. Four of these aircraft were American B-25 Mitchell bombers, supplied to the Soviet Union via the Arctic convoy route.

Although of poor quality, the photograph (left) of a Bf 110 G night fighter is historically interesting as it shows the aircraft flown by Obstlt. Herbert Lütje, a holder of the Oak Leaves and the last Kommodore of NJG 6. The machine was captured at Aschaffenburg in May 1945 and in addition to the operational markings 2Z+AA, carried a variation of the Kommodore's Stab markings consisting of a double chevron and a horizontal bar. Lütje (far left) became a night fighter pilot in 1940, flying first with NJG 1, and after his 27th victory in May he was awarded the Ritterkreuz and became Kommandeur of IV./NJG 6 in June 1943. He became Kommodore of NJG 6 in September or October 1944 and was awarded the Oak Leaves on 17 April 1945, finishing the war with 51 night and two day victories.

Messerschmitt Bf 110 G-4 '2Z+AA' flown by Obstlt. Herbert Lütje, Kommodore of NJG 6, May 1945

The uppersurfaces of this machine were camouflaged in a simple, solid application of 75 over 76 undersurfaces with no additional mottling. The spinners were painted with a spiral design and, as no staining on the uppersurface of the wings is visible in the accompanying photograph, it is evident that the exhausts were the straight underwing type. The aircraft carried FuG 220 SN-2d radar equipment with the aerials on the nose being mounted in the vertical position, and a 90 mm armoured windscreen was fitted. Although the reference photograph shows what may have been some lettering on the starboard fin, this is believed to have been graffiti applied by US troops but, as the profile is intended to represent the aircraft as it would have appeared before capture, it has not been reproduced here.

Above, above right and opposite page top: In an attempt to provide a camouflage finish suitable for aircraft parked on the ground, uppersurface colours were sometimes darkened, as may be seen on this Bf 110 G-4 coded 9W+BO which, despite the 18. Staffel letter 'O', is thought to have belonged to 6./NJG 101. In late 1944, an Einsatzkommando from NJG 101 was operational in Hungary where, in September 1944, Axis aircraft were required to add a yellow band around the rear fuselage and a yellow Vee to the underside of the port wing. In early March 1945 these markings were ordered to be deleted, although on this machine the fuselage band remained. It is thought that either 81or 83 was used to overpaint the Vee (opposite top) and that this was done almost immediately before the unit disbanded at Fritzlar in Germany in mid-March 1945. Although the fin carried victory bars representing victories over nine British and one Soviet aircraft, it is possible that the pilot may have been credited with the RAF victories before being transferred to NJG 101, perhaps as an instructor, where he was credited with destroying the Soviet aircraft.

The port tail fin detail showing the victory bars.

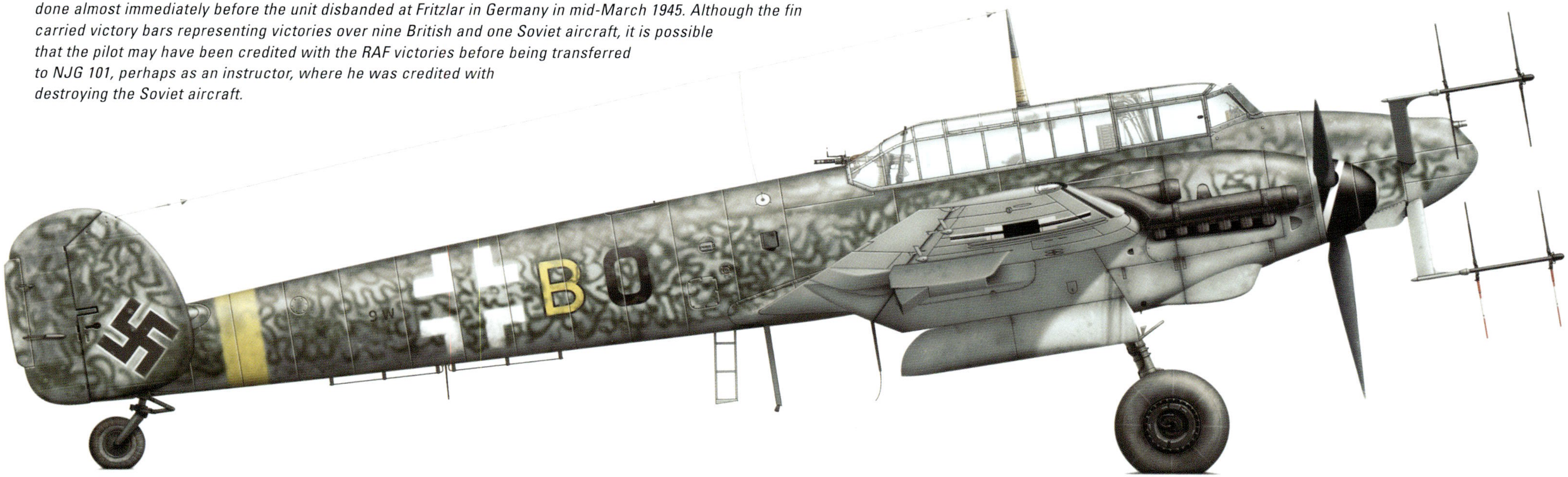

Messerschmitt Bf 110 G-4 '9W+BO' of 6./NJG 101, Fritzlar, 1945

On this aircraft, the original base finish consisted of solid 75 on the uppersurfaces with 76 on the fuselage sides and undersurfaces. The uppersurfaces were then oversprayed with a Wellenmuster pattern in 83, this being more widely spaced on the uppersurface of the wings than on the fuselage. The pilot's victory bars were shown only on the port fin, and the machine had a narrow yellow band around the rear fuselage. As noted above, an earlier yellow Vee under the port wing was overpainted, probably in 81 or 83. The angle between the arms of the Vee was 45 degrees, and the arms, originally some 25 cm wide, extended for approximately 60 cm over the wing leading edge.

Left: Nearest the camera in this line-up of two-seat Me 262s at Schleswig-Jagel in June 1945, are two Me 262 B-1a/U1 night fighters of 10./NJG 11. The aircraft second from the right is W.Nr. 110306 which carried the small tactical number 'Red 9' on its forward fuselage and had the last three digits of the Werknummer repeated in white on the nose.

Below: Another Me 262 B-1a/U1 night fighter found at Schleswig-Jagel was 'Red 8', W.Nr. 110305, shown here with RAF markings applied over the Luftwaffe insignia. Although not visible in the photograph, the demarcation line between the 82 uppersurfaces and the black undersurfaces on the engine nacelles was merged using 83.

Left and opposite page bottom: Me 262 B-1a 'Red 12', formerly of 10./NJG 11, was also surrendered to the RAF at Schleswig-Jagel and is shown still in its original markings being inspected by RAF officers. After being ferried to Gilze-Rijen, this machine overshot the runway and sustained minor damage. It was probably this incident which resulted in the starboard intake being damaged and replaced with the mismatched example shown in the photograph (opposite bottom).

Messerschmitt Me 262 B-1a W.Nr. 111980 of 10./NJG 10, 1945

The camouflage on the fuselage of 'Red 12' was applied in such a way that the occasional meander pattern of 75 was applied over the 76. The uppersurfaces of the engine nacelles, wings and tailplane were almost certainly 83, as shown, and all undersurfaces, including the sides of the engine nacelles, were permanent semi-gloss black. Note that the intake on the starboard nacelle was natural metal but had been roughly oversprayed with 83 on the uppermost surface.

Recollections of a *Nachtjäger* jet pilot

Leutnant Herbert Altner, 10./NJG 11

A few days after my final success with the Ju 88 on 8 February 1945, when I shot down three aircraft over Stettin, *Oberleutnant* Welter landed at Lübeck-Blankensee with his Me 262 A-1a. I engaged him in conversation about jet fighters, in which I had a special interest, and hardly three weeks later *Oblt.* Welter had me transferred to his unit, which had the official designation of 10./NJG 11.

At that time, 10./NJG 11, which had been formed from *Kommando* Welter in January 1945, was equipped with only the single-seat version of the Me 262. With these, the few pilots of this unit flew '*Wilde Sau*' sorties over Berlin against Mosquitoes illuminated in the beam of the searchlights and which, because of their high speed, could not be intercepted by any other fighter.

Oblt. Welter told me that he was waiting for the two-seater Me 262 B-1a/U1, which was supposed to be fitted with the FuG 220 '*Lichtenstein*' SN-2. As I already had plenty of experience in flying *Dunkle Nachtjagd* with the Me 110, as well as having an excellent, experienced radar operator in Reinhard Lommatzsch, Welter selected me to fly the two-seater version.

My familiarisation training on the Me 262 was carried out in a single-seat version and, after a short period of theoretical instruction, with me sitting inside the aircraft and *Oblt.* Welter standing on the wing, I flew a few circuits with this fantastic aircraft. With great admiration I looked at my airspeed indicator and saw that it was registering 800 km/h. I can only repeat the words of Adolf Galland: "It was as if an angel were pushing!"

On 13 March 1945, after I had completed about 15 circuits with the Me 262, my practical training was finished and I obtained permission from *Oblt.* Welter for a cross-country flight to my former unit, NJG 5, at Lübeck-Blankensee. I shot across their airfield at about 800 km/h and, after landing, was greeted by my former *Geschwader* friends with enthusiasm and some respect.

On 22 March 1945, I flew an Me 110 to Staaken to collect the first two-seater Me 262 B-1a/U1, and to flight test it before ferrying it to my new unit. Overall, flying the Me 262 was not a problem, although the night fighter version with its '*Lichtenstein*' SN-2 and second crew member was a lot heavier and demanded a lot more concentration.

During a ferry-flight to Staaken I landed at Lübeck where my Me 262 was pushed into a wooden hangar. During the night the airfield was bombed and the next morning we found that the hangar roof had collapsed on top of the aircraft. As far as I remember, I ferried four two-seaters from Staaken to Burg, near Magdeburg and to Lübeck. These four Me 262 B-1a/U1 were the only ones that were used operationally.

On 27 March 1945 I flew my first night sortie with this type. During the flight, my *Funker* picked up a contact, a Mosquito, on his radar, but due to my high speed I shot past it. I then throttled back too quickly and both engines stopped. As restarting the engines in the air was virtually impossible, our only option was to bale out. We both loosened our straps and, after discarding the canopy, I pulled the aircraft up and then shoved the stick forward so that we were both thrown out. Unfortunately, my *Funker*, Reinhard Lommatzsch, collided with the tail unit and lost consciousness. Thus prevented from opening his parachute, he fell to his death. This occurred near Havelberg.

At the beginning of April, while I was on my way to collect another aircraft from Staaken, the airfield at Burg-Magdeburg was bombed and became unusable. I was therefore obliged to fly this new aircraft to Lübeck from where, on 3 April 1945, I succeeded with my new *Funker*, Hans Fryba, in shooting down a Mosquito.

In order to be safe from bomb attacks during the day, we transferred to the Lübeck-Hamburg autobahn near Reinfeld. At dusk, we moved back to Lübeck for our night missions because the autobahn was not equipped with suitable runway lighting. On 6 May 1945, I flew my 'Red 12' from Reinfeld to Schleswig-Jagel where the last two Me 262 B-1a/U1s were handed over to the RAF. With that the war was finished for me and I had done my duty. I remember with pride that I had flown the first combat jet in the world and was the only Luftwaffe pilot who had been authorised to fly the two-seater version on night operations.

This page: The first production Ta 154 A-1 two-seat day fighter, W.Nr. 320003, was completed in June 1944 and was followed by a further six machines before production was cancelled. However, at least one of the seven machines, W.Nr. 320008, was completed as a two-seat night fighter under the designation Ta 154 A-4. This machine was delivered to NJG 3 at Stade for evaluation, probably in early 1945. Marked with the tactical code D5+HD indicating that it has been assigned to Stab III./NJG 3, it is believed to have crashed in the evening of 30 April 1945. The fate of the crew is not known and the machine was not examined until early May. External differences between the A-4 and the A-1 included the engine cowlings, the blade aerials on the uppersurface of the wings and fuselage, and the slight dihedral to the wingtips. A contemporary RAF report described the camouflage as light blue overall with grey mottled uppersurfaces and was certainly 76 with a light mottle of 75. The mottle is best seen in the view of the tail. (top left)

Left and below: This abandoned Bf 110 G-4 was found by US forces at Bad Langensalza in April or May 1945. This particular machine, W.Nr. 110509, flown by 8./NJG 1, was coded G9+VS and lacked any radar aerials when photographed. On the starboard side, just visible protruding from the underside of the nose in the photograph (left) is the small plate which ensured that spent cartridge cases were deflected away from the propeller.

Left: A Bf 110 G-4 of NJG 6 which surrendered at Munich in May 1945. Parts of NJG 6 and NJG 2 flew night ground attack missions when the practice was revived for night fighters in mid-April 1945. Missions involved road patrols when crews were briefed to strafe any motor transport or signs of enemy movement observed. The results of these sorties, however, went largely unobserved by the crews taking part as only one strafing pass was made. On 15 April 1945, however, four of NJG 6's Bf 110s attacked enemy movements in the Karlsruhe-Rastatt area and claimed 15 vehicles destroyed. Similarly, seven aircraft from NJG 6 attacked transport south of Mannheim on 20 April and destroyed eight vehicles without loss, but such negligible results had no effect on the course of the war. Note that this aircraft is fitted with the new type of flame-dampers, all of which led back under the wings.

Left: This Bf 110 G, G9+AT, had 76 mottling clearly applied over 75 on all uppersurfaces, while G9+HT, W.Nr. 160128, was finished in 76 overall with a mottle of 75 over the uppersurfaces.

Above: A Ju 88 G-1 of the Nachtjagdstaffel Norwegen coded B4+DA. The origins of NJ-Staffel Norwegen can be traced back to November 1943 when a Nachtjagdkommando was attached to 13.(Z)/JG 5. In July 1944, this Kommando became Nachtjagdstaffel Finland, but did not become operational until August. In this photograph, taken in October 1944, the aircraft is shown at Kjevik shortly before a flight to Gardermoen where it remained until the end of the war. Unfortunately, details of the badge on the forward fuselage are not known.

Right: After the war, several aircraft of particular intelligence interest were taken to Britain or the US for evaluation. One such specimen was this Ju 88 G-6 which is believed to be W.Nr. 622311, a machine which had previously served with Stab/NJG 4. If this is correct, then the original operational code was 3C+DA and the aircraft was surrendered at Eggebek and brought to the UK via Schleswig on 15 June 1945 where it became 'Air Min 16'. The most distinctive feature of this machine was that the 'Morgenstern' radar aerial was partially enclosed in a long, streamlined, plywood fairing which had a transparent Plexiglas nose. Although the aerial has clearly been removed from this example, the ends of the antenna would normally have protruded through this fairing. This photograph shows the aircraft at the Royal Navy Air Station at Ford.

Above and right: Found in Czechoslovakia at the end of the war, Ju 88 G-1, probably W.Nr. 714891, was finished in a classic example of the Wellenmuster finish typical of NJG 101.

Above: A post-war view of a Ju 88 G-6, W.Nr. 621197, which landed at Gütersloh on 8 May 1945. Although the aircraft is still marked with the operational code B4+FA of NJ-Staffel Norwegen, this unit had been redesignated 4./NJG 3 in March 1945.

Left: A Ju 88 G-6 with the tactical code D5+KV of 11./NJG 3 at Skrydstrup in Denmark in 1945, possibly with the undersides of the engine cowlings in yellow. The propeller blades and rudder have been removed to comply with the terms of the surrender.

Below: This post-capitulation photograph shows a Ju 88 of NJG 7. The unit badge comprised a yellow shield, upon which was a white eagle with a sword and a flaming torch in its talons. The torch is said to have originated from the unit's tasks in 1944 and 1945 when it was employed as a Beleuchter, or illuminator unit.

Above: The vertical tail unit of this Ju 88 G-1, W.Nr. 713639, shown in Germany in 1945, clearly had its original 76 surfaces toned down with a darker colour, probably 81 or 83, with little thinning. Although appearing hand painted, the additional colour was sprayed on with the spraygun nozzle set to a wide fan.

INDEX

PERSONNEL

German

Allied

Geschwader